CW00484715

Savages

By the same author

A Walk Along the Ganges
Amazon

SAVAGES

The Life and Killing of the Yanomami

Dennison Berwick

HUTCHINSON
London Sydney Auckland Johannesburg

This edition first published in 1992 by
Hutchinson

Random Century Group Ltd
20 Vauxhall Bridge Road, London SW1V 2SA

Random Century Australia (Pty) Ltd
20 Alfred Street, Milsons Point, Sydney; NSW 2061, Australia

Random Century New Zealand Ltd
PO Box 40–086, Glenfield, Auckland 10, New Zealand

Random Century South Africa (Pty) Ltd
PO Box 337, Bergvlei, 2012, South Africa

British Library Cataloguing in Publication Data
Berwick, Dennison
Savages: The life and killing of the Yanomami.
I. Title
306.080987

ISBN 0–09–175322–8

Phototypeset by Raven Typesetters, Ellesmere Port
Printed and bound in Great Britain by
Biddles of Guildford Ltd, Guildford, Surrey

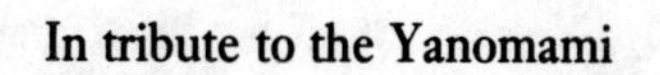

In tribute to the Yanomami

'The only thing necessary for the triumph of evil
is for good men to do nothing.'

Edmund Burke

Contents

Acknowledgements

Some of the people who provided information would prefer not to be named; I thank them and acknowledge their courage in silence.

My public thanks are due to many other people, especially to the people of Ironasiteri and Xamataweteri (these names refer to the communities and not to the places) who were generous and patient hosts to myself and to Chris Steele-Perkins. My special thanks to all the people mentioned in the story and to their wives, who often let their husbands do all the talking but were very much present.

My thanks and admiration to Davi Kopenawa Yanomami. Many, many Brazilians are working to ensure that the rule of law is upheld in Brazil and that the Yanomami land is registered and protected. I would especially like to thank Claudia Andujar, Carlos Zacquini, and Alex Shankland of the Comissão Pela Criação Do Parque Yanomami (Commission for the Creation of the Yanomami Park) for their open-ended cooperation. My thanks also to Father Luis Laudado, Simon LeFevre, Eldizia Martins da Silva, Ernesto Montesinos Filho and to Armando Ribeiro da Costa, owner of the excellent Riomar hotel in Manaus.

Survival International in Britain and KWIA in Belgium are two of the international organizations organising public and financial support to the Yanomami; my thanks to Robin Hanbury-Tennison, Stephen Corry, Charlotte Sankey and Fiona Watson, and to Daniel De Vos of KWIA in Brussels for sharing information and contacts.

At home, my thanks to Njo Kong Kie and to Jane McKenzie, Ann Sutton, Peter Holt, Carol Lee and Chris Steele-Perkins who gave great support throughout and to Diana Bailey, John Chatwin and Diane D'Almeida who gave critical support by reading the type-script.

Special thanks to the Alberta Foundation for the Literary Arts who provided funding to pay my living expenses during the period of initial research and translating and transcribing of interviews.

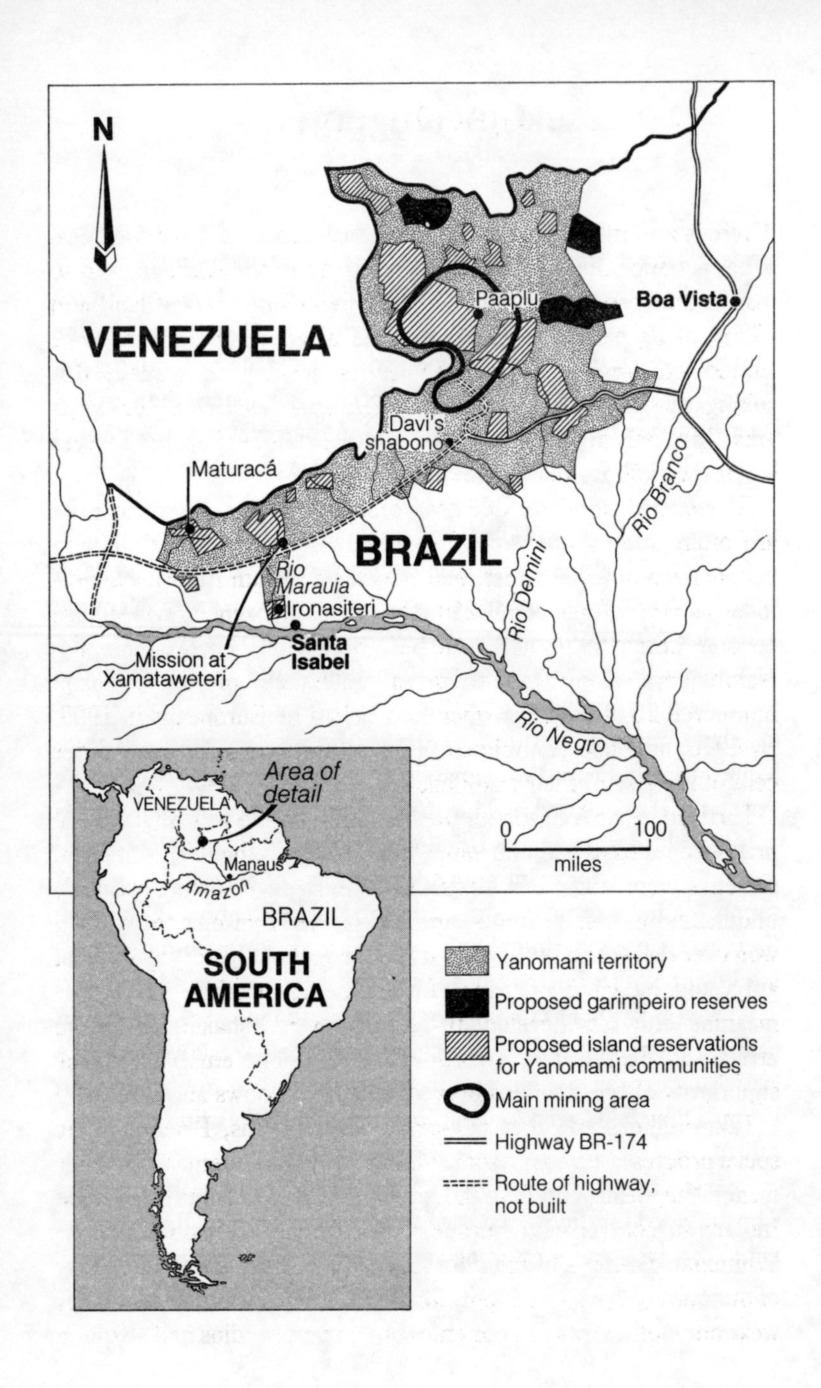
N
VENEZUELA
Paaplu
Boa Vista
Davi's
shabono
Maturacá
BRAZIL
Rio Branco
Rio Demini
Rio
Marauia
Ironasiteri
Santa
Isabel
Mission at
Xamataweteri
Rio Negro
0
100
miles
Area of
detail
VENEZUELA
Manaus
Amazon
BRAZIL
SOUTH
AMERICA
Yanomami territory
Proposed garimpeiro reserves
Proposed island reservations
for Yanomami communities
Main mining area
Highway BR-174
Route of highway,
not built

Introduction

There is nothing inevitable about the destruction of tribal societies. What is happening today to the Yanomami in the Amazon, and to many other peoples worldwide, is the deliberate theft of land and killing of its people, as has happened wherever Europeans have landed on foreign shores. Apologists seeking to explain this subjugation as the unhappy consequence of "evolution" or "progress" are only giving themselves excuses; conquest by these forces is our own killing-machine by another name.

The statistics for mass deaths of indigenous peoples since 1492 are often quoted but worth repeating. An estimated 3.5 million people lived in tribal societies in the area of South America known today as Brazil; only about 250,000 survive. Dozens of tribes have become extinct and others have been devastated. For example, the Nambiquara along the southern watershed of the Amazon numbered 20,000 people when first visited by Europeans in 1909. By 1970, only 600 Nambiquara were left alive in a reserve 0.5 per cent of the size of their traditional land.

I arrived in the Amazon for the first time in 1986 with all the usual preconceptions of a liberal education; I believed the deaths of tribal societies were tragic but inevitable. The stronger (subconsciously understanding this to mean superior) forces from one society had won over the weaker. It has happened throughout history by force of arms and by force of trade. Tribes, being primitive (of course meaning only less developed), fell apart when shaken up by the arrival of Europeans. Armed resistance only emphasized the superiority of our weapons over tomahawks or bows and arrows.

Like millions of other fair-minded Europeans, I believed the social progress that came from contact with the Whiteman inevitably meant the destruction of the tribal Indians of South America. Indians in contact with Europeans are drawn irresistibly into the Whiteman's camp – begging for food or tools proves the superiority of our culture for it can supply items the Indians want; in time, they wear our clothes, pray in our churches, buy our radios and abandon their war paint and feathers. Disease can speed up this implosion, but the process of social evolution continues and, inevitably, the Indian disappears. This is what I believed and it is a lie.

Anthropology has reinforced the unconscious racism because it treats tribal societies as systems and because, frankly, anthropologists have wanted to investigate "authentic" Indians, not those who have "lost" their culture by wearing the Whiteman's trousers. For example, the American Museum of Natural History in New York devotes a large gallery to exhibiting the way of life of Amazon tribes without once showing a metal cooking pot or steel knife, despite their acquisition by some tribes over 400 years ago. Nowhere is any mention made of the realities of the challenges of life after contact with the Whiteman's world. The Indians are kept frozen, like mammoths after the Ice Age.

Change is the only inevitable consequence of the meeting between Europeans and Indians and this can benefit us all. The medicinal value of many plants from the rain forest, for example, is so great that we are bound to want to obtain them. The discrepancy between our technology and the elementary technology of the Yanomami people is too great for them not to want the utility of many of our tools. Just as we regard the fruits of their forests and mountains as bounty for the benefit of everyone – quinine to cure malaria, potatoes to make chips – so do Indians regard our tools. Our desire for forest products and the minerals under the ground does not have to mean mass murder and conquest of land unless that is how we want to make the world. Conquest cannot happen without conquerors with the desire to subjugate. Most tribes want contact with their neighbours and want many of their tools; they want to "progress", but this is far from meaning the people want to give up being themselves or that they forfeit their traditional lands because they use a metal cooking pot or a video camera. Culture is more concerned with expressing the experience of being human than with the quantity of tools we use, though technology displays and may, to some extent, define a culture. Western culture thinks in opposites – the good guys, the bad guys; dominate or be dominated – and produces weapons of mass destruction, not mass education.

Change does not have to mean death and destruction for the Indians or for us unless that is what we want. We too can be profoundly changed, yet not destroyed, by listening to Indians views of life and of the world. At the end of the 20th century, when Industrial Man and Woman falter for lack of good faith in themselves, the Yanomami and many other tribes can teach us – as they have shown me – that we are most fully ourselves when we are related to one another and to everything around us. The psycho-jargon of the city self-help seminars would call this "participating fully" in every moment.

Again and again, contact with the Whiteman has led tribes into a Catch-22 situation. If they remain isolated and ignorant of our world, they are cheated of their land; if they retain their "innocence", they are dismissed or cherished as "savages" who need to be saved for Christ and taught to be workers in the consumer society. But if they learn the languages of the newcomers, if they take some of the tools to use, if they learn to defend themselves according to the laws of the newcomers (which we proclaim for all people), they are declared no longer Indians and their land is forfeited.

I believe that people have a natural right to the land of their ancestors; they are the natural "owners", if we speak of ownership rather than trusteeship. Our own property laws and constitutions seek to confirm and protect this natural right – so why is it so hard to respect the traditional lands of indigenous peoples?

Land is, and always has been, the heart of the conflict between Indians and the Whiteman. The Whiteman wants all the land and all that it contains. This is as true for Canadian tribes still struggling to have their land claims settled after 200 years as for the Yanomami, most of whom only heard rumours of our existence one generation ago. More than anything else, it is relationship to land, and to the visible and invisible forces the land contains, which distinguishes Industrial Society from the societies of Indians.

But which Indians? I had to ask myself when I met people in the Amazon from half a dozen different tribes whose languages, costumes and philosophies were as distinct from each other as the Spanish are from the Danes in Europe. It is for our convenience that we lump them together. Even the word "Indian" is a misnomer; Columbus thought he was meeting the people of India when the Lucayans welcomed him ashore on the isle of Guanahaní in the Caribbean; a place Columbus called San Salvador.

We cling to a double, and contradictory, picture of "the Indian" as being either Noble Savage or Naked Savage that perpetuates images of a bare-breasted young woman grilling fish and a warrior in war-paint and feathers. Is she any less a Yanomami or a Mohawk if today she carries a metal cooking pot?

If we forget our stereotypes and deal with Indians as individual people, then a different history emerges of their contacts with Europeans and of their struggle to survive our arrival. This is the challenge of this book. It is the story of how the Yanomami are being wrenched from centuries of isolation and their efforts to comprehend an alien people (the outsiders, the Whites, the people they call the *nabe*) who invade their land, who bring them miraculous metal tools and who kill with unknown diseases. It is told as much as possible in their own dramatic way of story-telling, based on many hours of conversation recorded with a tape recorder and later translated and transcribed. Edited excerpts are given here. Unfortunately, I do not speak more than a few words of Yanomami, in any of its four dialects, and conversations were restricted to those bilingual Yanomami who speak Portuguese. This was a severe handicap but I persisted for two reasons; firstly, what the Yanomami men and women have to say speaks for itself in any language; secondly, Europeans have much to learn by listening. It is remarkable that, after more than 400 years of contact, only two or three books record what any Amazonian Indians think of the newcomers while there are shelves of books and monographs reciting the European views of the Indians.

Curiosity was the original impetus for me to travel to the Yanomami in early 1988 and it has been my renewable source of energy during all the subsequent months of travelling, interviewing, reading and sickness. My first visit to the Yanomami (described in the book *Amazon*) left me with the simple question, What do the Yanomami think of us? Looking for answers was to grow into a quest both exhausting and compulsive. I have been especially fortunate as a freelance writer to be able to devote the time and money necessary to travel in search of clues to possible answers.

Plain curiosity would be no justification to enter the Yanomami area – risking carrying disease to them and as illegal as the gold miners' invasion. My permission has always come from the Yanomami community of Ironasiteri on the Marauiá river. We first met below one of the waterfalls when I went up the river alone in early 1988 after more than one year's travels in various regions of the

Amazon. "Who are you? Why have you come?" asked the group of eleven people armed with three shotguns. I said that I wanted to learn about the forest and asked them to teach me. At first, they thought I was a gold miner but they found neither equipment for gold panning nor shotgun when they searched my sacks. The group took me up the river as their guest to the community *shabono*. I have returned three times since then, always at their invitation. Each visit has been preceded by a medical check-up. "Do you have permission to go there?" asked Davi Yanomami, the most prominent Yanomami leader, when we first met. "I have the permission of the communities, but not of the Whiteman in an office 2,000 miles away," I replied. Davi was satisfied. Yanomami "ownership" of their land must automatically include their right to control access; to say "yes" as well as "no".

Yanomami friends have given and taught me so much and I have wanted to acknowledge this generosity by doing whatever I could to help them defend themselves. It is my hope that this book might alert more people to the continuing expropriation of land and destruction of indigenous peoples all over the world still being done today in the name of "progress". This would be sufficient justification for my visits to Ironasiteri.

I knew from my first chance visit in 1988 about the illegal invasions by gold miners and the killer epidemics and, having promised at the end of that stay to return one day, I wanted to be of some practical service when I went back in fulfilment of my pledge. I am not a doctor nor a millionaire who could provide air transport but a chance meeting with Davi Yanomami one morning sparked a simple idea which I set about putting into action. My purpose was to spread Davi's warnings to communities in the west about the dangers of the gold miners and the need for scattered communities to link together.

The Yanomami live in the forests and mountain valleys between the mighty Amazon and Orinoco rivers, an area divided by the mountainous frontier between Brazil and Venezuela. In 1986, an estimated 22,000 people were living in approximately 320 isolated communal houses. Built like huge doughnuts open in the middle to the sunshine and rain, each *shabono* (or village) stands in a clearing in the forest several days' journey from its neighbours. Communities are semi-nomadic, moving when game animals become scarce, or when manioc, bananas and other crops no longer flourish in the tired soils of their forest gardens. More than forty-four percent of the land where the Yanomami live was classified as "unsuitable for agriculture or ranching" by the Radam-Brasil survey in the early 1970s. Their method of shifting cultivation is proof of how well the Yanomami understand their forest – communities in Brazil are spread over an area the size of Portugal. This is the ecological living space which they need.

Several communities within the same area of rivers, forest and mountains may regard each other as regional allies. Travel beyond these regions is discouraged by the shorter, denser rain forest that grows on the ancient and leached rock formations north of the Rio Negro. Rocky, fast-flowing streams in the mountains impede travel by canoe. Trade of baskets and tools, and inter-marriage is restricted to neighbours within a week's walk. Yanomami in the west have had no direct contact with their fellow tribesmen in the east. Such isolation has fostered suspicion of people from outside, including Yanomami from other areas, which still sits deep within the psyche of each community; distrust wrestles with hospitality and an eagerness for exchange of news, ornaments and tools. Strangers may be suspected of sending bad spirits to kill people. Such accusations sometimes lead to war-skirmishes between villages in which three or four men might be killed and their women taken to be wives. Semi-isolation has allowed the Yanomami language, religion and customs to diverge into four main groups during the past 5,000 years. The need today is for the Yanomami to draw together again as one people, but countering the pattern of thousands of years is not simple.

Before the arrival of the Whiteman, contact between the Yanomami and other tribes was restricted to immediate neighbours with whom the Yanomami traded or, in one case, worked. But even these contacts stopped in the 17th, 18th and 19th centuries when their neighbours vanished. Portuguese or Spanish raiders captured men and women as slaves for their plantations or to gather rubber, or made war on them if they resisted. For example, the Manau, who traded gold along the Rio Negro and the Amazon, resisted the Portuguese in the 18th century under their chief Ajuricaba. He was eventually captured but jumped into the river in chains rather than be enslaved. The city of Manaus is named after the extinct Manau tribe.

Priests also came up the rivers offering metal tools to people who had hardened wooden or stone axes to chop down trees and cut up meat. Whole tribes descended to the mission stations, there to die soon after baptism of the newcomers' diseases, such as viral infections or smallpox. At least their "converts" did not die heathens, the Christians told themselves.

The Yanomami were protected from this annihilation by their deeper isolation in the forest far up unnavigable rivers. Even the word "*nabe*", meaning a non-Yanomami person, fell out of use when their neighbours disappeared and the Yanomami were able to expand into empty areas of the forest.

This isolation ended for most Yanomami in the mid-1950s when Catholic missionaries ascended to the headwaters of the tributaries of the Orinoco River in Venezuela and the Rio Negro in Brazil to pacify and save the souls of the Yanomami. Contact with these outsiders brought killer diseases, including influenza, chickenpox and whooping cough. Contact also brought miraculous steel tools and new foods. Many, many people died but communities were able to re-establish their populations and to adjust to the small numbers of newcomers who were useful to provide tools, medicines (for the new diseases) and who spoke of places and spirits the Yanomami had not yet encountered.

In 1974, during the military dictatorship in Brazil, the Army began to construct the Perimetral Norte road cutting through the middle of the Yanomami area in order to integrate this remote region near Venezuela into Brazil. "Integration" was the cry of the decade; to open up, to dominate, to penetrate, to occupy all parts of the Amazon with Brazilians. Indians could not be trusted to safeguard the country's northern border – they were only recently elevated from the status of "legal minors", ineligible for citizenship and of equal legal status to the insane.

The arrival of road construction crews driving bulldozers among people who had never even seen a Whiteman, much less a machine that moved and gave out smoke, was calamitous. No warning was given of what was coming, no prevention was made to control the spread of diseases. Death was commonplace. Whole communities vanished. At least thirteen villages, with about 1,300 people, were reduced within three years to eight small family groups camped by the road. Half the people in one *shabono* were killed by two epidemics of measles. Many Yanomami blamed their neighbours for sending evil spirits against them. No-one had any notion of the National Security Council's decision in Brasília to "integrate" them into Brazil.

The road stopped after 225 kilometres because the earth was too soft and construction too expensive, but the events were a red light to post-Vatican II missionaries, anthropologists and others who now wanted to help the Yanomami against this aggression. The first studies to define their traditional area were undertaken by a coalition of Brazilian supporters in 1968. The government officially closed, or interdicted, the area in 1982 but did not create a Yanomami park with legal protection. The government continued to issue mining permits for mining companies to explore within the area.

In 1985, the year Brazil's military dictatorship ended, the military chiefs began the Calha Norte project; a secret scheme to colonize the country's northern border with Brazilians. To this end, the military built airstrips deep in the Yanomami area and conducted an aerial geological survey. An illegal invasion of the eastern half of the Yanomami area by 45,000 *garimpeiros* (gold or mineral prospectors) took place in 1987. The authorities did nothing to hinder this. At least 2,000 Yanomami, out of 9,000 in Brazil, died during the invasion. Even in late 1991, the Yanomami area was still without clear legal protection from the mining and logging companies eager to "develop" the region.

Contact with the Whiteman is bringing profound challenges to all communities, even in areas where gold or other minerals have not yet been found. Metal knives and cooking pots have reached all *shabonos* through trade, but the pace of further confrontation – with firearms, money and the social hierarchy of the Whiteman – varies greatly. For example, one community on the River Marauiá has gone in one generation from ignorance of metals to tape recording themselves singing. Another community, farther up the same river, met a Whiteman for the first time only in 1990. This book tells two stories that are intertwined yet distinct. One is of the arrival of the *nabe* and people's responses to the challenges of contact with him. The second story is the fight to defend the traditional land of the Yanomami against the illegal invasion of miners and those sections of the Brazilian government and military determined on a policy of genocide. Is there any other word to describe more than twenty years of continued failure to demarcate the Yanomami homeland while simultaneously making the region accessible to miners and selling exploratory rights to mining companies?

Contact between the Yanomami and the outside world is inevitable. Change through this contact is also inevitable. However, genocide by invasion is not inevitable but planned as the evidence and interviews in this book show clearly. The endurance of tribal cultures and their strength to adapt to change is proved by their survival despite conquest and genocide throughout the past 500 years. The Yanomami are well able to adapt to the changes brought by their contact with us. Their extinction is only inevitable if we and our agencies, such as our governments, banks and multinational corporations, choose to make it so.

The fundamental question, which all those working to "develop" the land of the Yanomami (and of all other tribal peoples) ignore, is whether people have the right to the land they have traditionally lived on. When this first right of "ownership" is respected, all the problems of conflict, cultural change due to contact and even mining interests can be accommodated. But respect between people – different and equal – is rare despite the political rhetoric.

Time spent with the Yanomami, and perhaps with people of any sharply contrasting culture, creates a sense of journey and exploration involving far more than miles covered by canoe or on foot. The greatest distances, and the greatest obstacles, lie in the traveller's mind. To learn anything about another way of being, it's necessary to unlearn the reality we already know, to allow ourselves to be led by our guides, to listen more than to talk. It's necessary to trust. This is especially true when listening to the *shamans*, or trained healers, who move between two realities with a facility that leaves the unaccustomed traveller out of breath. One of these realities is what we see around us every day. The second lies behind what, perhaps rather ornately, I have called the *shaman's* labyrinth. This second reality is reached by the *shamans* with the aid of hallucinogenic drugs. The Yanomami inhabit this additional reality as much as they live in the ordinary reality; day-to-day living – and much of their reaction to the arrival of the Whiteman – comes from their experience of travel in the *shaman's* labyrinth.

The Yanomami, like other Indians, use collective nouns to describe us. Outsiders are called *nabe*, (pronounced na-bay) meaning non-Yanomami; or in Portuguese *branco*, meaning white i.e. non-Yanomami and non-Indian. "*Homen branco*" is the verbal shorthand throughout Latin America to describe European culture, descent or affiliation. It refers to a state of mind not to the colour of a person's skin. I have used the word Whiteman (capitalized like Indian) as the equivalent generic term to cover male and female.

None of the Yanomami are called by their real names in this story, because this would break their taboo against alerting bad spirits to a person's whereabouts. Traditionally, people avoided the danger by referring to their neighbours as, for example, "mother of so-and-so". Today, Yanomami who have contact with the Whiteman find it convenient to call each other by "Christian" names, because these are non-names which the spirits cannot recognize. The use of these "non-names" should not be construed as a conversion to Christianity, but rather as the adaptation of the *nabe's* custom for their own convenience. The Yanomami in this story are called by their non-names.

Yanomami words are spelt in English as nearly as our letters can reproduce the sounds. The system of accented transliterations used by anthropologists has not been followed because it would require an additional book to understand.

1

"My eyes are open! My eyes are open!" the Yanomami chief cried every day of our five-day journey down the Rio Negro to the city of a million people. He had been to Manaus before but never with a *garimpeiro* carrying a sack filled with what he claimed were fifty kilos of topazes. Inevitably, our visit was a disaster; the stones were worthless pebbles, the *garimpeiro* ran away, and the Yanomami men hated the city.

Seventeen months later, I was fulfilling my promise to return and steering my canoe up the Marauiá river, a tributary of the Rio Negro, 440 miles northwest of Manaus. Eight Yanomami men were also hitching a ride with me, with their seven canoes lashed to mine.

The men were from the *shabono* beside the Salesian mission, beyond the community I was visiting. We had met by chance on a bend in the river and I had offered them all a tow. They were as keen for an easy journey, instead of paddling upstream, as I was relieved to gain companions to ascend the five waterfalls. I did not want to repeat on my own the effort at each waterfall of unloading, carrying and reloading the sacks of foods, trade gifts, the motor and the containers of gasoline, nor to drag the hardwood canoe across steep inclines of rough granite.

The five waterfalls are dangerous though they are not high; no more than thirty feet when the river is low. The Yanomami have names, such as "Big Beast" and "Little Beast", for each fall and tell me spirits wait under the rocks to drag down the unwary traveller. I believe them. The river rushes over the rocks with a colossal force that catches and carries away anything weaker than itself. Water plunges onto boulders and thrashes with white foam to escape in a stream of criss-cross currents. My respect for the spirits of the waterfalls is sincere; I would have drowned on my first descent if companions had not formed a human chain to pull me from the water.

Hour after hour, our flotilla advanced round the bends in the river between the silent forest. We climbed easily the first waterfall, then relaxed on the long stretch of river up to the second. The narrow blue sky and sunlight on the silent brown water lulled our minds to sleep or to day-dreams. The Yanomami dozed or watched with their guns ready for monkeys, cormorants or *capybary* along the river banks. My arms and back ached from gripping the rudder attached to the five horsepower motor and long propeller shaft that was vibrating against the current.

My mind's eye summoned again a scene from my previous trip, the two chiefs, Renato and Domingos (to call them by their "non-names"), standing wondering how to cross the main avenue in Manaus. We had grasped arms and run together, with laughter hiding their fears. Who had been duped the most, or lost the most? I wondered again, thinking of the Yanomami and of the two Brazilian men who had put their families into debt to pay to join the topaz prospector in his dream of sudden riches.

Renato and his kinsmen sat round the fire in his house the night before going downriver with the Brazilians, calling out their dream list of machetes, knives, fish hooks, hammocks, axes and shotgun cartridges which Renato and Domingos intended to buy with their share from the sale of the fifty kilos of topazes.

They took the sack of small stones, collected by the Brazilians from beaches and pools on the Marauiá, down the waterfalls and down to Manaus, the stinking city of electronics factories and slum housing in the middle of a thousand miles of rain forest.

Renato and Domingos stayed in the ramshackle home of one of the Brazilians, amid blaring radios and televisions and drunken brawls in the streets. "It's so violent here," is all Domingos said after ten days. He wanted to go home.

The truth about the value of the stones shocked everyone; the Yanomami with their dream list of trade goods and the two Brazilian men who had financed the *garimpeiro*'s expedition. I nicknamed the *garimpeiro* Brazilian Uncle for his sham concern for the Indians. I knew his promises of trade goods and a school for the Yanomami, in exchange for prospecting up the river, were lies because I'd seen the disdain in his eyes when he'd first met them. This wiry man, with a repellent smile, fast words and faster fingers on the guitar he carried, vanished as soon as we knew the sack of stones was worthless. His enraged companions would have lynched him if he hadn't fled.

"They're only stones. The *garimpeiro* lied to us. All lies. He knows nothing," Renato said slowly, as if someone had broken his dream, which they had. The stones were not topaz nor agate, but only little coloured rocks not worth anything. "Our hearts are dying," he said. "We are completely unoccupied here." In Yanomami, he might well have said that his liver was dying, because it's in the liver, not the heart, that a person's emotional being resides. Domingos and Renato were without money in the Whiteman's city and as intimidated by the traffic and tall buildings as I had been by the noises and pageant inside the forest. Renato reacted to their situation by chattering. Domingos was silent. I wanted to protect them in the city (as they had cossetted me in their world) and perhaps I was patronizing when I showed them around. "I know! I know!" Renato shouted when I explained how to get on a bus at the back and go through the turnstile.

The afternoon to say farewell came. Renato's eyes filled with tears. I paid their passage on a boat up the Rio Negro, though they would have to hitch rides the last 300 miles and to walk home for two days through the forest. We hugged and he pressed his head to my shoulder to kiss me. Tears trickled down his cheeks. Domingos and I embraced and shook hands. "When will you come again?" he asked softly. My promise was to return within two years.

Will they still be in their village? Will they remember me at all? Will the area already have been invaded by illegal *garimpeiros* prospecting for gold or tin ore? Will it be feasible to make the 250-mile journey through the forest to the Yanomami in the east? I wondered, coming up the narrow Marauiá river with the eight Yanomami, seventeen months later.

Cold shadows of thunderclouds broke my reverie. Forest and river were coloured opaque grey by a wall of torrential rain sweeping towards us. Bushes and branches of the trees on the bank fluttered in the gusts of the advancing storm. Our canoes pitched and rolled with the choppy waves hitting our sides.

The Yanomami straightened the broad banana leaves in their canoes to keep their hammocks and few possessions dry. A lucky few crouched under the plastic sheeting covering the sacks in my own canoe. The rest of us sat perfectly still with our heads bent into the rain to let the water run off our hair and not get into our eyes. Our second storm that afternoon hit with the loud sizzling of billions of raindrops striking the surface of the river. No-one suggested stopping, as I would have done on my own, to take shelter by the river bank. Perhaps they thought the risk of the bank and trees collapsing greater than the danger of hitting a half-sunken branch, obscured by the spray on the water, and capsizing in mid-stream. Cold rain lashed our bare backs and legs. Water poured into the canoes as fast as the men could bail out, swilling round our feet like a tide-mark of doom. The roar of the storm lasted twenty minutes, until we were all goose-pimpled and shivering. Then the storm passed and the sun shone hotly again. Steam rose from the river and our bodies dried off once more.

A thrill ran through my body when we reached the second waterfall and found men from Ironasiteri, the community of Renato and Domingos, reloading three canoes below the falls with bundles of *to-o*, a forest vine stripped of bark and used for making baskets.

"Dennison!" they called. We had hardly embraced, and so verified by touching that we were reunited, before they were asking what I was bringing in the sacks and warning me not to trust the eight Yanomami.

"They're curious about all you have," said Martins, one of the Ironasiteri community betraying his own desire to know. The eight Yanomami had yet to ask any question about who I was, where I was from or what I was carrying in the two big white sacks. "Come with us down to Santa Isabel," enthused Martins. "Renato and Gabriel have walked there through the forest."

"Don't worry. I brought the things for you, not for them. If they take everything we'll go down to Santa Isabel and buy again," I said. Towing seven canoes was using a lot of extra fuel so I gave money to Martins and asked him to buy more gasoline in the town after exchanging their *to-o* for the trade goods they wanted.

"Can I spend the change?" he asked.

"Buy the gasoline first. We need to go hunting and fishing." I asked another man to make sure Martins bought the fuel.

"We've moved. "We're not at Apuí any more. We have come to Coatá, near the Tucuman waterfall," said the other man, hastening to join his companions already embarked in their canoes.

The eight men and myself heading upriver made camp after sunset at the top of the fourth waterfall. They had wanted to keep going after dark but agreed to stop when I said it was too dangerous to travel with the motor only by the light of the stars. I was exhausted after eight hours supporting the weight and vibration of the motor shaking through the propeller shaft. My back and my bottom ached from sitting on a hard bench.

"Go to sleep and we'll wake you when the food is ready," said one of the men. Three men were already fishing above the waterfall in the fading daylight while others gathered firewood and hung up hammocks among the trees overhanging the dry rock at the side of the falls. Boiled fish, *farinha* and a bag of rice (my contribution) made an excellent supper under the stars.

A third thunderstorm woke us in the middle of the night. "Brother-in-law, rain!" came a voice in my dreams. "Roll your hammock and come with me."

Two men swung flaming logs in front of them to scare off alligators or any other creatures that might be on the rocks in the dark. Everyone tucked their hammocks and blankets under cover in the canoes, then we stood in underpants or nude waiting amid lightning and thunder for the rain to hit us. Someone started a small fire under a sagging thatch shelter, about the size of a dog kennel, just inside the forest. Four of us huddled here together, surrounded by flashes of lightning and cracks of thunder rending the sky. Wind and rain struck our bare backs for hours while the welcome fire toasted our faces. We stayed crouching until the storm had passed, returned and finally departed. Then nine dark shadows emerged from their varied hiding places under a plastic sheet in one of the canoes or crouching under giant palm leaves in the forest. We retied our dry hammocks to the trees and went back to sleep.

We reached Coatá, where the community of Renato and Domingos was living, a few hours after sunrise and waited beside the canoes until an adult came from the *shabono* to greet us. Children crowded the sandy river bank, smiling and chattering to each other while they looked over the canoes to see what we had brought.

"Dennison! Dennison!" exclaimed Domingos as he came quickly down the path to squeeze me with a hug and shake my hand. The Yanomami are a short, stocky people and Domingos' head reached only to my chest when we embraced. "So you've returned," he said and put his arm up round my shoulder and held me firmly all the way through the shaded garden of tall manioc plants to his own home at the far side of the *shabono*. Each family built and lived in one section of this doughnut-shaped communal village. Designs of the *shabonos* vary from region to region; in the east, the roof rises like a dome allowing only a small opening in the middle to the sky. The *shabono* at Coatá was completely open, built like stalls round a sunlit plaza.

"Good day, Dennison," said Piarina, Domingos' wife, getting out of her hammock to greet me. I was still unsure of etiquette with the women but smiled gladly; Piarina had spoken to me with a tongue sharper than a machete the year before. Now she was laughing and offering me a plate of *cara* potatoes (slightly sweetish and with a purplish skin). This enthusiastic welcome relieved my apprehensions like a hot bath relaxes an aching body.

Domingos heated coffee on the fire beside his hammock for the visitors squatting at the edge of the house like a line of weary sparrows. Their journey paddling down to the Rio Negro had been a failure, they reported, because the *ebene* seeds, for which they had gone, would not be ripe for at least another month. They smiled at their misfortune but paddling home would seem much farther without the raw material to prepare the hallucinogenic snuff used to encounter the *hekura*, the humanoid spirits of Yanomami that can be either good or bad. They invited me to take them to their *shabono* but there was not enough fuel to tow several canoes for another two days up the river. I took them, with Mateus, Domingos' youngest son, up as far as Apuí, and gave them some fishing line, hooks, strong cord and tobacco. One of the men asked to take my machete. Several men had handled and admired it on our short journey.

"No charge for the tobacco, fish hooks and line," I said, "but the machete costs a lot of money and I want to sell it." The man had already asked how the people of Ironasiteri paid for the trade goods I brought them. "Feathers, baskets, bows and arrows," I had replied.

"I'll give you feathers," he said. We agreed on two macaw tail feathers and two armbands made of black scalp feathers of the forest turkey. "When you come up the river, they'll be ready for you," he said.

Three of the men made a fire to boil a pot of *custirim* gathered from a tree that morning. This hard black palm fruit makes a chocolatey drink and we sat on the granite boulder beside the river to enjoy this filling "wine", as Domingos always called it, before parting with handshakes. The eight men paddled off upstream, almost touching the branches overhanging from the river bank. Mateus and I returned to Coatá before dark.

Domingos put up my hammock in his home and put my sacks of trade goods on the raised platform where he kept his own possessions out of reach of the children and dogs. I was too tired to put a sheet over the motor to keep off the rain and fell asleep immediately. Domingos roused me after dark for supper of boiled fish and *farinha* with the family. Someone else took the trouble to cover the motor.

Next morning, Valdira, Domingos' eldest son, was out of his hammock at dawn taking down the family shotgun hanging from a rafter. He was hoping to repeat his success of yesterday when he'd shot a small red deer. He gathered a plastic bag of shotgun cartridges, his fishing line, hooks and machete and left without a word, with paddle in one arm and shotgun and tackle over his shoulder.

Aoria, his wife, hung a blackened pot over the flaming fire to boil water for coffee (from my sack) and moved her husband's hammock to the front of the home away from her own at the back. The fire had burned all night to warm the air and to discourage mosquitoes with its lingering smoke. No-one else yet stirred from their hammock. I lay enjoying the peaceful interval between dawn and sunrise when the air is cool and the black *pium* fly, with its itching bites, has not yet appeared. I had woken several times during the night, sometimes chilled, sometimes sweating. My neck ached. My throat was sore.

We were all out of our hammocks by the time the water was boiling. Piarina took coffee and sugar from me while I went to the river to wash and shave. Half a dozen women were already bathing their babies. Early mist was rising from the river. One woman, her wrinkled breasts attesting to the number of her grandchildren, was crawling up to her neck in the sandy shallows, drawing a fine-meshed net through the water. She lifted out the green net after each pass to let a grandson scoop dozens of tiny fish, like whitebait, into a bowl on the shore.

Mateus and I returned with a bowl of clear drinking water from the river as Piarina was peeling *cara* potatoes still steaming from a cooking pot. I took coffee and sugar to Francesca, Renato's wife, on the other side of the *shabono*. She was sitting in her hammock near the fire making a large basket.

"You're going to have a baby," I said, having been told by Piarina.

"Yes, yes. Very soon," replied Francesca, looking up with a smile from the basket in her lap. "Renato was speaking of you before he went by the forest to Santa Isabel: 'When will he come again? When will he come to see us?' he was asking," said Francesca with delight.

"Now I'm back. I said I would come back and here I am," I said.

Domingos put a pot of sweet black coffee and a plate of *cara* potatoes on the ground in a circle of low stools as soon as I returned. Other families were having tapioca porridge or boiled meat or fish from yesterday before going to the gardens to gather manioc roots or plant more banana trees. Relatives arrived in Domingos' house for a taste of the coffee, then left to do their work. Domingos settled to stripping bark from the slender *to-o* vines. Piarina sat in her hammock making a basket on her knees. I hung up the gill net I had been making on the journey from my home and counted out the floats and weights to be tied on, before giving it to Valdira as a gift. I felt dizzy and lay down from time to time.

"Where's the *xama*?" I asked Valdira when he returned, referring to a pig-like animal with a short snout. They are the largest animal in the forest, standing waist-high to a Yanomami, and the most prized game for a hunter.

"It went away," he replied, hanging up the shotgun and helping himself to warm coffee and *cara* potatoes before resting in his hammock. He left again soon to cut down and fetch poles and wire-like vines from the forest to make a workbench for the small motor Domingos now possessed.

"Daddy brought it from Manaus," Valdira replied when I asked her where it had come from.

Domingos continued the story: "I and my wife went to Manaus last year with Mateus (their younger son). Mateus had blood in his mouth. It was tuberculosis. While he was being treated, I went to the Funai (the National Indian Foundation) and I talked with the chief. I told him, 'We are needing a motor here to grind the manioc. We are needing many things on the Marauiá.' He said he knew this and he gave me the motor."

The motor was old, and had needed several repairs, but it spluttered into life after Valdira mounted it on his new workbench and pulled the cord half a dozen times. Piarina's kinswomen arrived with high baskets loaded with peeled manioc to put through the grinder driven by the gasoline motor. Growing manioc and making the starchy root edible are two of the main tasks shared by everyone in the community. Gardens of pencil-stemmed manioc surrounded the *shabono* at Coatá with foliage half as tall again as the Yanomami. These had been planted only two months earlier, when the community moved from their larger *shabono* up river to gather the abundant *to-o* vines from the surrounding forest.

Manioc grows well in the rain forest soil partly because the bitter variety is poisonous, which discourages the abundant hungry insects. Sweet manioc can be eaten after boiling and tastes like white, starchy potato. Bitter manioc needs peeling, grinding and washing to rinse out its prussic acid. Old canoes are used as baths to wash the gratings. Then women scoop the manioc in sacks of fine-netting and wring these out on the edge of the baths. More liquid is forced out of the manioc in an ingenious basket suspended from a rafter. The woven tube, the length and width of a slender pole (called a *tipiti*) is packed with wet manioc. A strong wooden pole goes through a loop at the bottom. Pushing down on the pole extends and thus constricts the basket, squeezing more liquid from the manioc inside. The manioc is dried to a coarse sawdust, called *farinha*, by toasting in wide flat pans heated over fires.

Two more foods come from bitter manioc. Fine white flour settles in the liquid in the old canoes and this is toasted into tiny crunchy balls which is tapioca. Yanomami communities adopted manioc cultivation either from neighbouring tribes or from missionaries. The word *tapioca* comes from the Tupi and Guarani Indian languages; "*tipi*" meaning dregs and "*ok*" squeezed.

The prussic acid rinsed from the manioc decays after a few hours and the yellowish liquid in the canoes can be used for soup (amazing for curing hang-overs!) or to coagulate the white latex from rubber trees.

The roar of the motor ended and broad metal bowls filled with manioc were dragged to the *tipitis* by the men assisting the women. Domingos returned to stripping the *to-o* bark, and I continued tying floats and weights to the gill net. Jacinto, the oldest man in the community, watched me for a few minutes before asking the question that had brought him to the house.

"Have you brought me tobacco?" he asked. Jacinto was the most senior *shaman* and the uncle of both Renato and Domingos.

Physically, he was an ugly man. A fuzzy grey beard, dirty with stains of tobacco juice, was stuck awkwardly to the bottom of his bony face. His black and grey hair was a mop. But his thin, wrinkled limbs still moved with the grace of a young dancer when each day he took blasts of the hallucinogenic *ebene* snuff up both nostrils and danced and chanted to the spirits. His big brown eyes were bright with kindness.

"Thank you," he said, when I fetched him a packet of tobacco from the supplies I was keeping separate from the sacks of trade goods for the community. Almost everyone sucked tobacco rolled like sausages in the front of their mouths, between lips and their bottom teeth. Even children of four or five years shared these wads and asked me for tobacco. The Yanomami word for poverty translates as "being without tobacco". I took the offered rolls of tobacco from time to time, to people's delight, but was never able to dispel my own foolish fancy that the rolls looked like dogs' turds.

Jacinto came back later in the morning, still sweaty from dancing and chanting to the spirits, as I lay in my hammock chatting and swaying with Alberto, one of his sons. Jacinto bent down and hugged me tightly with both arms round my neck and pressed his musty beard, still mucous-laden with *ebene*, into my face with a smile. I embraced him likewise. Jacinto spoke almost no Portuguese, I spoke no Yanomami, yet every day he smiled with muttered greeting when we met on the path through the garden to the river or when he came to share food in Domingos' house. At the end of my first visit, he'd presented me with a pair of scapulars of iridescent turquoise tipped with purple from the wings of a small bird. I thought of having my ears pierced just to be able to wear them.

Piarina and her daughter-in-law Aoria served boiled smoked deer meat for lunch, with rice (from my supply) and *farinha*. Valdira's kill of yesterday had been grilled over the open fire since last night then boiled to make a strongly flavoured consommé with chunks of meat at the bottom. A plate of plantain bananas, chubby-fingered and deliciously sweet, was passed round as we lay in our hammocks to snooze after the meal.

Rain came in the afternoon, cooling the air and keeping away the *pium* flies. Domingos, Piarina, Aoria and I settled on low stools to strip *to-o*. Domingos giggled as he remembered our visit to Manaus with Renato and the topaz *garimpeiro*. "Renato was furious," he said with mirth. Whatever disappointment Domingos felt at the lies and loss of the promised trade goods, he could release from his mind with the same deep sigh and giggles with which he would regret a big *piraíba* escaping from his fishing line.

"We got a ride on a boat to Santa Isabel and we came home walking through the forest," said Domingos.

"You had an adventure!" I said.

"We did!" he agreed, giggling like a schoolboy caught doing something naughty.

"Have any more *garimpeiros* gone up river?" I asked.

"One man passed here. Renato and I went too. He was invited to teach the Yanomami there [upriver] to look for gold. The priest at the mission found out and he ordered the *garimpeiro* to leave. The blame's with the chief there because the priest found out. The priest told them they were mad to think no other *garimpeiros* will come if they found gold. 'They will. It's like this!' the padre told us," said Domingos.

Domingos told of a more serious visit of *garimpeiros* earlier in the year. Several versions of what happened surfaced from other people during the next months but all said a large party of *garimpeiros* had come looking for gold on the Marauiá river but left without finding any. It does not greatly matter if the details of their accounts conflict or if the events did not occur as they are related. Even rumour can have a deep influence on the way people view what is happening to them and how they respond. Yanomami story-tellers actually enter their stories, playing all the parts and giving a dialogue they may not have actually heard. The technique enthralls listeners and tells a truth, *their* truth, as they are moved by the experience. A party of prospectors certainly did ascend the Marauiá looking for gold.

Domingos said thirteen *garimpeiros* arrived at the mission station farther up the river, in an aeroplane provided by Funai (the National Indian Foundation responsible for keeping gold miners out). "So the padre had to let them pass because they had the documents from Funai. I complained to the chief of Funai when we went to Manaus with Mateus but the chief denied he had sent the *garimpeiros*," said Domingos. "They didn't find gold."

"Do you know what will happen if they find gold here?" I asked. "Thousands of men will come with guns to kill the Yanomami and take the gold."

"They CANNOT!" replied Domingos.

"In Brasília, the capital of Brazil, I met a Yanomami *shaman* from the forest where the sun rises, over there!," I told Domingos. "Thousands and thousands of men have come to take the gold. They are bringing sicknesses – malaria, influenza, illnesses you do not have here – and the women and children are dying," I said, still shocked by what Davi Kopenawa Yanomami, from the Demini River, had told me in the city less than a fortnight earlier.

"And there's a plan," I continued, "to divide the Yanomami land into small areas, one small area for each community, and to take away the rest. This is what Davi, the *shaman* I met in Brasília, is fighting. He sent a message to the community here, to tell you what is happening to his relatives, to his forest."

Domingos stripped bark from two or three lengths of *to-o* before looking at me. "I'll tell a story," he said. "Once, long ago, a man came and told us that we had to leave here and go to the island of Venezuela beyond the head water of this river. But we're of the island of Brazil, all this is an island, all the forest," said Domingos. "How can we leave? This is our land. I was born here."

"Why do you think the man said this?" I asked.

"To take our land for himself. All the land."

"Why?"

"I suppose to take the gold or just to have it all," he replied.

Piarina sat in her hammock beside us making a fine basket decorated with strands of *to-o* stained red with *urucú*, an oily seed collected in the forest. Her daughter-in-law was busy cooking food.

"Why don't you come to live with us?" Piarina asked, just after hearing that my land had fields with cattle and vegetables instead of forests with monkeys and vines for basket-making.

"There's a place over there for your house," said Domingos, pointing to a gap in the circle of the *shabono*.

I chuckled but continued stripping bark from the *to-o*. "If I live here, how could I marry?" I said after a few minutes. "I have no woman to exchange with the bride's family here. My sister's already married!"

"It's all right to bring a cousin," replied Piarina quickly.

We stripped another bundle of *to-o* while the rain continued falling. I was miserable by then, my body sweaty and shivering, my sore throat grating like an iron rasp with each swallow. I asked Domingos to boil a pan of water to make tea. Fifty Earl Grey teabags were my single luxury and pleasure to be enjoyed sparingly to lift my spirits when I was feeling low.

Domingos peered at the small square teabag. "What is it?" he asked. A small crowd gathered. "Is it like *ebene*?" someone inquired.

"It's a drink and it makes you feel strong," I said, tearing one of the bags and pouring its dusty contents onto Domingos' hand.

"Is it to sniff?" he asked.

The ritual of tea-making with powdered milk was attended by a great crowd. Everyone watched and waited when Domingos took one sip of the tea from a spoon. He swallowed and exclaimed a phrase in Yanomami making everyone laugh. "It needs sugar," he said to me in Portuguese.

I smiled. "That's not what you said. You said, 'Oh God, it tastes like monkey piss!'" Everyone laughed with renewed amusement. Domingos burst into a fit of giggles and had to sit down. Someone added sugar to the several mugs of tea we had made and passed them to Jacinto and the other men. Piarina took one for the women. I shared mine without sugar with the children clambering into my hammock.

The river rose several inches during the night, making safer our ascent early in the morning through the scattered rocks and submerged jagged cataracts safer. Samuel, one of Renato's kinsmen, hitched a ride with us, with his short canoe. We left him half an hour up the river to fish and hunt alone. Valdira and I continued for several miles until he pointed to a small stream, or *igarapé* (meaning canoe path) on the right bank where black water merged into the muddy brown of the Marauiá. We tied my gill net behind us across the mouth of the *igarapé* with the laughter of people who never expect to catch anything. Then we set off up the cool, shaded gorge of black water between trees and bushes. Valdira sat in the bow paddling with long steady strokes, steering the canoe between bushes and sunken obstacles and occasionally using his machete to sever branches blocking our passage. We went probably only a mile, though it seemed much farther, until he pulled into the right bank where a faint trail led from the water into the forest.

"We came here to get *sorva* last year," he said. (*Sorva* is another latex some Yanomami have learned to collect to exchange in the town for trade goods. It is used to make chewing gum.) We ate a couple of plantains each, though I was feeling giddy and my throat was horribly sore. Valdira gathered his shotgun and plastic bag of four cartridges and set off along the trail. I followed him as closely as his own shadow through the dappled sunlight between thin-stemmed trees, hardly able to see any trail between the short bushes and plants and litter of leaves on the ground. I was afraid of being lost.

Valdira halted abruptly many times. He slowly turned his body from side to side listening for the crunching of wild pigs eating fallen fruits or the rustle of dry leaves of a *shama* or deer walking nearby. The forest seemed empty. Even the Screaming Pihas, also called the Captains of the Forest, had suppressed their shrill call.

"Do you want?" he asked once when he spotted a small tortoise beside his bare feet.

I shook my head.

"It's good baked," he said, taking the tortoise to carry with him. Valdira moved quickly without striding and I could not keep up. I felt feverish. If I cried out for him to slow down the noise would break the stealth of his hunting. If I did not call, he would keep moving forward and leave me behind. The sun shone on the forest floor through the branches of the trees no more than sixty feet tall. The air was hot and humid and busy with flying insects. I felt faint and walked sluggishly. I decided to stop to rest. After a few more paces, Valdira disappeared among the trees into the patterns of light and shade of the forest. I sat on the ground in the shade.

Many supernatural forces inhabit the forest of the Yanomami. One of these is called a *noreshi*. Animals such as monkeys, lizards and anteaters contain the alter ego of each Yanomami person. Each animal is a person's spiritual shadow in the forest. A woman's *noreshi* might be an anteater; whatever she does, the animal in the forest will also be doing. When she is pregnant, so will be the anteater. If a man makes a journey, his *noreshi* animal will also travel. *Noreshi* animals live far from their specific human counterparts, so there was little danger of Valdira shooting the *noreshi* of his family or neighbours. Humans can lose the part of this "soul" within themselves; a child's *noreshi* may pop out, for example, with hiccups or if someone takes a photograph. Then it must be found and put back. If not, the child and the forest *noreshi* will die.

The most sinister supernatural forest creature is called *poré* or *onka*. They are Yanomami painted black from head to toe who wander in the forest seeking people to kill with their special poisons. There were said to be none in the forest near Coatá but this was soon to change as the threat of the *nabe* looking for gold came closer.

I slept comfortably in the shade until woken by the tickling of ants crawling over my arms and legs. Valdira had not yet returned and suddenly I thought he might be walking in a circle and would not come back the same way. I waited, thinking the songs of birds might be him calling, but when he didn't come I decided to walk back alone to the canoe. The trail on a return journey never looks the same as it does going. Trunks of trees stand in a different relationship to one another. Sunlight catches broken branches from other angles changing their character. Markers you made coming out have blended into the forest's shapes and colours. It's a sobering experience to be lost in the forest and I moved cautiously watching and checking for the faint trail of snapped twigs and broken leaves. I found the way more by instinct than conscious observation, perhaps because I was feverish or still drowsy, and went astray only twice before reaching the canoe. There was no sign of Valdira so I stripped off and jumped into the cold *igarapé* for a swim.

Dozens of white butterflies fluttered into my hair as I sat in the canoe to try to fish. I could feel them stepping over the wet strands like dainty ballerinas until they were overflowing and fluttering round my head like a living halo. But suddenly they took off and flittered away like stars dancing over the black water of the *igarapé*. I waited for Valdira.

"Success!" he exclaimed when he arrived and lowered a large, dead, female armadillo into the canoe and let fall dozens of *custirim* fruits from his T-shirt used as a sack.

"No fish," I reported. "They eat the bait but they don't want to leave the water." Valdira laughed, underscoring my own sense of uselessness at having fed fat worms to the numerous fish around the canoe without getting more than a nibble or an empty hook. "You must teach me to fish," I said.

We checked the gill net at the mouth of the *igarapé* but it had caught only dead leaves. We took it home, motoring down the middle of the river like a small stately barge in the swift current. Valdira sat as usual in the bow with his feet tucked under the low bench. The sun shone with a bright, silver light on the leaves and branches along the banks. In this early afternoon light, the trees were hard, colourless sculptures. This was the time of day I disliked the most. Its harsh light, its flat river surface, robbed of the movement with which water celebrates itself, its lone flies buzzing round like obsessional thoughts, mirrored too exactly my own mindless state while the sun was high. Valdira tied a noose round the wizened neck of the tortoise gathered from the forest and hung the creature over the side of the canoe to bounce on the water as we travelled. Its four legs flapped uselessly all the way home trying to escape its torment. It didn't die but was killed the next day and roasted on the fire.

I told Domingos and Piarina of my sleep in the forest and that I was ill with fever and weak. My greatest fear was that the sickness might pass on to the Yanomami, who have never known these illnesses until now and who have no resistance to diseases from the outside. Whooping cough, for example, killed more than half the children in the communities on the Marauiá in 1982. Domingos suggested Jacinto, the chief *shaman*, should examine me. He said also that as yet they had found no cures for the fevers of the Whiteman's diseases. Jacinto came when I was laying in my hammock. He put his hand to his own throat, "Sick here" he asked in broken Portuguese. I nodded. He smiled and moved his wrinkled but firm hands over my hair and down over eyes, ears, throat, neck and chest with deliberate attention. Then he nodded and left me to doze.

Domingos was gathering my T-shirt and towel from the clothes line outside as the sky darkened with the approach of rain. He saw me watching and brought a stool to sit beside me in my hammock. Lightning flashed across the sky. "Do you know there are people in the sky?" he asked in Portuguese.

"I didn't know."

"Oh yes," he said with that wide-eyed expression of someone who doubts his listener could possibly believe the truth. "It's where the Yanomami go who have died," he said.

"Is it like here? Is there forest?" I asked.

"Oh yes, it's just like here but above the sky," he answered.

"I'll be going there soon," I said, feeling so weak and feverish.

I was sleeping in my hammock next morning when Gabriel shook me awake to tell me he was back with Renato and their kinsmen. Renato greeted me with a wide smile. His open arms squeezed me in a tight hug that, literally, lifted me off the ground. "Martins told us you were back! Dennison! My friend!"

Gabriel and I also embraced tightly. "How are you?" I asked, looking into his dark, glad eyes.

"I am well now," Gabriel replied with the loud chuckle that ended every remark when he was happy. He embraced me a second time and told me again that he was well. "Are you making me ill?" he had once asked me when we faced each other, as we did now, with his arms on my shoulders and looking into each other's eyes. "I have dreamed of you," he'd said.

"How are you ill?" I had asked him.

"I have pains in my stomach."

"My friend, I can give you pain in your throat, or in your nose as a cold, but I cannot give you pain in your stomach," I'd told him, though he had not been convinced.

Dreaming reveals a heightened awareness of good and bad spirits. Domingos was greatly disturbed by my sleep-talking during the first few days of my stay. He said the nocturnal chatter was proof of the creatures attacking to make me ill.

Gabriel and I had liked each other from the first time we met when he, Renato and seven others discovered my camp on the river below the fifth waterfall and asked, with shotgun in hand, "Who are you? What are you doing here?"

"I thought you were a *garimpeiro*," Gabriel told me one day. "But now I know you're not." He kept my straw hat at the end of my first visit after laughing and pleading for me to give it to him. "I'll build a house for you, also of thatch!" he'd said as his final offer for the silly hat he coveted. Exchanging a house for the hat was a fair trade, according to Yanomami values.

"Where's my house?" I asked him now, standing together in bright sunshine.

"Ah, Dennison, it's so much work," he replied with serious face.

"You promised, my hat for a house."

"I did!" Gabriel said with a chuckle. "But Dennison, you can live in my house. I'll build your house when you have a wife!"

The third mention of me taking a wife came after breakfast. Domingos and Valdira were taking lessons on operating and steering my motor canoe, so that they could go on their own upstream to Apuí, the community's main village, to fetch manioc and bananas from their gardens. Only Renato and some of his kinsmen had planted gardens at Coatá, their temporary camp from which to gather *to-o*. I was too sick to go anywhere, but offered to show father and son how to handle the canoe on their own.

"I hope Martins buys the gasoline with the money I gave him," I said when we came back after Domingos had almost capsized the canoe in his enthusiasm to go fast. He never steered the canoe again. "I'm a *shaman*, I'll keep to my work," he said excusing himself.

"I'll be furious if Martins doesn't buy the gasoline," I said, topping up the tank ready for Domingos' outing.

Domingos giggled, "You should steal his wife!" he suggested. His face fizzed with giggles.

Martins did buy gasoline but only five litres, just enough for a day's travel. He brought me a little change but he'd spent most of the money on himself.

"Well, you can cut my hair," I responded, hiding my annoyance with a shrug. I was feeling ill again, feverish and listless. I wanted only to sleep, to drink water, not even soup. My cough was bad and made an awful noise. I could not yet give any serious thought to making the journey through the forest.

The distribution of trade goods from my sacks took place late the same afternoon after Domingos had returned safely from Apuí with baskets of *farinha* and stems of ripening bananas. Jacinto and other men, all of them *shamans* or in training, finished their chanting and dancing with the spirits. Women came back quickly from bathing in the river as the sun sank near the top of the trees. Domingos spread the blue sheeting from the canoe on the ground in front of his home. Valdira carried out the two sacks and helped with the unpacking.

Renato brought his low stool to sit at the head of our stall. His chairmanship was vital to a more or less orderly and fair distribution of the goods. I couldn't afford to bring every item for everyone but there was enough, I hoped, to share among all twelve households.

The shopping list was long and varied: four machetes, four small knives for cutting meat, six barbed forks for spearing fish, one kilometre of nylon fishing line, 250 fish hooks of assorted sizes, 500 metres of parachute cord, three flashlights for hunting alligators at night, a dozen flashlight batteries, a dozen spare flashlight bulbs, six T-shirts, six cotton dresses small enough to properly fit the women, three dozen packets of tobacco, packets of barrettes for girls' hair, marbles, sewing needles and reels of assorted cotton threads, four long bars of laundry soap, packets of coffee, sugar, spaghetti and rice. All of these were from the shopping list from our journey to Manaus with the *garimpeiro* seventeen months earlier. A few special requests, such as a skirt for Renato's wife, were kept separate with my own possessions.

People came from every household; the older men sitting on low stools round the edge of the sheeting, the young men behind them, watched by their wives and sisters. Children crammed themselves beside their fathers at the front or poked their heads wherever they could. Every man tested the sharpness of the knives with his fingers and the youths examined the brightness of the flashlights in the palm of their hands. Girls held up the dresses for their mothers. Eager hands reached to open and feel everything. Shouts to open this packet and to see inside another spiced the gathering with excitement.

"All these things are gifts, except for the machetes, which cost real money. I would like to take some baskets and feathers to my land to exchange for these," I said, before standing at the back behind the women with babies in their arms.

Jacinto claimed two machetes. Gabriel took another and one of the small knives. Renato began counting fish hooks from the little boxes to decide how many to place in the outstretched palms of the youths and boys. A dozen arms reached for the six T-shirts and another dozen grabbed the six dresses.

"Calm, calm," said Renato, or words in Yanomami to that effect. But the hands withdrew and the voices were quiet only until a person saw what they really wanted – and, with a cry, leaned over everyone else to grab it!

"Do you have a flashlight with three batteries?" someone asked, adding that the smaller flashlights were too dim for hunting. "Have you not brought scissors to cut our hair? – You only brought six T-shirts for so many people? – How can I get a knife, I need a knife! – Dennison, I've received NOTHING." Accusations flew like children's arrows. I could only repeat what I'd brought and gently shrug my shoulders. It was best to keep quiet and make a mug of tea.

Every youth wanted fishing line from the big reel of nylon thread. The distance there and back to Gabriel's home across the arena, about thirty yards, was set as the standard measure. People quickly cleared everything from machetes to sewing needles and, either pleased or disappointed, carried home their trophies just before sunset.

Renato, Domingos, Gabriel, Jacinto and half a dozen other men of the community stayed behind to hear the message Davi had recorded for them. A few remembered meeting Arí, Davi's brother-in-law, in Barcelos, a town on the lower Rio Negro, a year earlier but no-one knew Davi. However, they were curious to hear the messages, partly because my tape recorder was a novelty and it was miraculous to hear people speaking Yanomami from inside such a small black box. There was a radio in the village but it spoke only Portuguese or strange music.

Davi was from the Toototobi River, a tributary of the Demini River. The Demini flows south into the Rio Negro, parallel and about 300 kms east of the Marauiá River.

"Do you know Toototobi?" I asked Domingos.

"It's a long, long way from here. I don't know where," he replied.

"Would you like to go there?" I asked.

My mind returned to the evening two weeks earlier in Brasília when I'd met Davi Kopenawa Yanomami and heard him explain what was happening in the *shabonos* in the east. This was the first news the outside world had received of the epidemics and mass deaths brought by the *garimpeiros*. All doctors, nurses, missionaries and anthropologists – anyone who might be a witness – had been taken out of the area by the Brazilian army in October 1987 on the orders of Funai. It was only later that I realized how much of what was to follow for me personally came from this chance meeting with Davi.

"We all know that this meeting is not taking place, what with conditions in Brazil today. We know to give support and help to the Indians is a subversive activity," said the organizer of the meeting between Davi, a Brazilian journalist, a Funai doctor, several other Brazilians and four Yanomami men with Davi. They were travelling to a school to learn about Brazilian laws to protect Indian lands. "If I stay ignorant of the Whiteman, I won't know how to defend the community," one of the young Yanomami men told me.

Davi sat in front of the journalist's tape recorder, tongue-tied and overcome with emotion. "I'm very worried that the children are dying," was all he said, naming empty *shabonos* or those where all the children and old people were dying. "They're ending. I am very sad," he said.

"The government is using the *garimpeiros* to invade our land, to take the gold. I've already asked President Sarney three times to pull out the *garimpeiros* but nothing has happened. He's weak. He fears the military who, in various ways, give him his orders what to do. This is my thinking," Davi replied to the journalist's questions.

"The Red Cross would have been summoned if this was a war," said one of the Brazilians. "Only here, it's an undeclared war. A dirty war."

The Funai doctor was both reluctant to endanger his job by speaking out and horrified by the deaths and misery he was witnessing daily, including epidemics of malaria, influenza and venereal diseases.

"Generally everyone gets sick at the same time when the *garimpeiros* arrive in a community. An epidemic like flu brings pandemonium; it batters their resistance, they aren't able to move, it's a completely unknown disease. So one half of the community dies, always the weakest.

"Only seven Yanomami were treated [by Funai] in Boa Vista [capital of the state of Roraima] in 1987. Now, seventy Yanomami have arrived in the past month," he said.

"How many *garimpeiros* are dying of malaria?" asked the journalist.

"Murder is the first cause of death in the whole territory of Roraima, principally the capital, Boa Vista. The second cause is transport accidents and the third is sexual diseases. Until 1987, sexual diseases were in first place," replied the doctor without mentioning malaria.

The journalist clicked off his tape recorder after half an hour and went home to write the first news story about the spreading catastrophe. Davi and the four other Yanomami went with me into a quiet room to record a message to the people of Ironasiteri on the Marauiá river. Each man spoke in Yanomami and their messages were translated afterwards. Davi later gave me permission to publish this abbreviated version of their private letter:

"I am Davi from the Alto Demini river. I'm going to speak to you in my language. Renato, and you who live on the Marauiá, listen to me. Don't allow the *garimpeiros* to enter. The Whites only speak lies to you. They give many things to cheat you.

"My forest is far from you. I'll tell you how it is in my land; *garimpeiros* are there in the forest looking for gold. They're dirtying the water, finishing the fish, and there's no more game. It has fled. The Yanomami become perplexed when the Whiteman comes. They're sick all the time and catch a lot of malaria. Epidemics of great poison come. The Yanomami don't hunt any more. They don't plant the gardens. Davi is anguished because of this. This is what I'm saying to you. Do not think that I am lying even though I send this message with a Whiteman.

"I didn't know the Whites when I was a child. But I know them now and I'm defending my land and I'm not afraid. Let us defend our land, our forest together.

"You should fear to allow *garimpeiros* on your land. You should defend your land. You should order the Whites to leave, but without firing arrows. If you use arrows, it will be bad. If you only order them to leave you are not going to die. If you use arrows you will be killed. This is what other Yanomami did at the head waters of the river and they are dead.

"The Whites want to arrive giving money and presents and want us to become Whites. Tell them that we don't want to become Whites.

"Before they came we had the spirits of Nature. We have them still today. Don't despair of them. Don't throw them out. If you despair your sons will not be good sons.

"You are my friends, to whom I am sending my words. Maybe, with time, I will go there to visit and to know you. Now I've finished speaking."

After Davi had finished recording his message, the other three Yanomami spoke into the black box, repeating his warning to the people of Ironasiteri of the threat of the Whiteman and calling on them to unite in defence of the Yanomami land.

It was almost midnight when Geraldo, one of Davi's brothers-in-law and the last to speak, took the tape recorder. "I don't know well your Yanomami language but [I will say] I don't think the Whites are good.

"In the beginning they give food and then they give illnesses. Do not think that this food and these objects they're giving are good. It's a lie! They think they speak the truth but they are liars. Do not be ignorant of this!" said Geraldo. Arí, Davi's brother-in-law, leaned over to say into the machine, "Geraldo's speaking uselessly". Geraldo laughed because it was true and handed the machine to me.

"We of Ironasiteri can record a message," said Renato in Portuguese when the tape ended. The decision to do this came a few days later, although the group of men immediately discussed in Yanomami Davi's warning about *garimpeiros*.

Afterwards, I spoke about my motor and canoe and so I unwittingly began my enormous blunder that was to bring so much distrust. "Last year I said that the Whiteman never gives something for nothing. He always has a price. So I will not say that I can *give* you the canoe and the little motor. They are very expensive. I will exchange them with you. My price is not money, nor baskets, nor bows and arrows, nor feathers; though they are beautiful and I would like to take four or five to show the beautiful things of the Yanomami to the people in my land. I would like to stay here two or three months and to record on my machine conversations with you about your lives and how the life is changing. Then I will leave my canoe and motor with you, for all the community to use. You will have to buy the gasoline for yourselves but the motor will make travelling easier to go hunting and fishing." The men nodded but said nothing.

Exchanging something of great value to the community for what I wanted seemed to me a fair and straightforward trade. I could never have guessed the trouble and danger the suggestion would bring to the community and to myself.

"We can talk later," said Renato, being tactful about my offer of the motor canoe. A Yanomami *tuxaua* leads by wise advice and cannot give orders. The other men often murmured against Renato but always let him speak for them with outsiders. He often spoke as if only he had a worthwhile opinion, yet the other people usually followed his advice in dealings with the Whiteman. The post of *tuxaua* is more or less hereditary though an unsuitable candidate would stay in his hammock. Renato's advice to me was good but mistimed.

Once made, the offer of canoe and motor needed to be explained publicly to everyone from the centre of the *shabono* and not discussed round only one hearth to leave others to mutter at home in annoyance. "If we don't tell everyone that the motor canoe is for the community, they're going to say that I'm not exchanging anything with them and that you're keeping the canoe only for yourself," I warned Renato. The anger against me because of this mistake did not erupt immediately – I was to trigger it myself by impatience one afternoon but I felt the first tremors of misunderstanding within a day. I knew then that my offer of the canoe and motor was a monumental blunder in the community. But the offer could not now be withdrawn nor its eventual consequences avoided. Attempts to explain the offer better only caused more confusion and greater rancour. Ignorance and naivety were the hallmarks of my eagerness to do the right thing. This error of judgment still runs like a seismic fault through our relationship.

I liked staying with Domingos, Piarina and their family. They were relaxed with one another and eager for me to be comfortable with them. Often, towards the end of the day, we lay in our hammocks and chatted. Mateus, their youngest son, often lay swinging with me in the hammock examining my fountain pen or teaching me Yanomami.

"When Aoria had a baby, it came out like a little ball," said Piarina one afternoon when Domingos asked me about a small knot in the lower intestines of his daughter-in-law. Aoria and Valdira lay listening in their hammock. My excellent medical reference book *Where There Is No Doctor*, suggested the knot could be a hernia. Piarina called Aoria for me to feel the slight bump at the top of her thigh. "If you're worried, she should go to the doctor in Santa Isabel. It's better to know before she has another child that there's no problem," I said.

Domingos and Piarina nodded. "When?" he asked.

"When you next go to Santa Isabel."

"Next month?"

My reply produced loud laughter. "Well," I said, adopting their frankness, "is she going to get pregnant in the next month?"

"I don't know," said Domingos, unable to contain his giggling. "Only her husband knows that!" he said, producing a further eruption of merriment in which we all shared.

Red howler monkeys were calling from the forest behind us at dawn and by the time Renato invited me to have coffee in his house, one of the troop of monkeys was being roasted on a fire in the *shabono*. Renato wanted to borrow the motor canoe when I showed him how to run it, but he crashed head first into the river bank before more or less catching the idea of what was required. Daniel, his middle son, learned right away and went off with Martins and a couple of boys for a day's fishing where Valdira and I had been earlier.

Domingos and I settled to stripping *to-o* while Piarina joined a group of her kinswomen peeling manioc. She came home in the middle of the morning to change into a purple swimsuit and paint her face with red *urucú* before gathering with the other women and many younger children.

"Spirits!" Domingos said to explain what was going to happen. The women went out chanting into the garden of manioc round the *shabono*. Next, we heard them singing at the edge of the forest before they burst into the *shabono* in a line, beating and sweeping the ground with brushes of green leaves. The women sang and danced one behind the other sweeping first through Renato's home then round the *shabono*. Domingos and I stayed beside the pile of *to-o* and Mateus in his hammock, all of us unobserved by the dancers busy with their house-cleaning. Boys ran ahead of them, leaping into rafters to shriek like monkeys and squeal with delight until the ghost-busters came with their brooms. The women went right round the *shabono* then danced out to the manioc plants once more, and came back calmly to collect their babies left safely out of the commotion at the entrance to the *shabono*.

Little was explained of this spiritual house-cleaning, except for Piarina to say, "We dreamed. We felt so many pains. There's a lost soul here. So we do this. We run and we sweat and we sing and we won't dream now. We're tranquil now."

We ate armadillo soup for lunch, then Valdira started up the motor to grind *farinha* and Aoria and other women came to grind up the manioc they had peeled in the morning. I retreated from the noise to sit with Renato and Gabriel who wanted to record a message.

"Davi, are you listening?" asked Gabriel. He spoke in Yanomami then paused for Renato to translate into Portuguese for me to understand. Gabriel said he couldn't explain himself properly speaking Portuguese. "We're not wanting the *garimpeiros*. We're not accepting anything. No-one wants them. I'm saying this for you to understand us and to combine with us. We're all understanding about our land and we don't want the Whiteman who comes here looking for riches. *Garimpeiros* don't come any more. They are liars."

"The area of the Yanomami is ours, because we are securing [it]. I will not loosen my hand. I have my word and will defend my land," said Gabriel to Davi.

"The Whiteman has to understand me. He has to obey me as well as I have obeyed him. The Yanomami have entered into an agreement with the Whiteman. So the Whiteman must enter into an agreement with the Yanomami as well. They have to respect the area of the Yanomami and make consideration for them. I've finished now," said Gabriel.

Martins cut my hair later that afternoon while we squatted face to face on logs for over an hour. I felt feverish. *Pium* and other flies covered our backs in bites and the fallen hair itched on my sweaty skin. Martins worked with patience, trying to cut and comb my curly locks into the same pudding-basin style and fringe on the forehead that looks so elegant with straight, flat Yanomami hair.

Piarina came as I lay dozing in my hammock after sunset to tell me to take off my shirt. "Domingos is going to 'think you'," she said, using the Portuguese word "*pensar*" (meaning to think) for the shamanic exorcism of the bad spirits making me ill.

Domingos told me to sit on a low stool facing into the arena at the front of the house. "Whoosh!" he cried in Yanomami, attacking the air with his arms to strike the spirits around us. He clasped his hands tightly round my ankles, determined to draw out all spiritual pus from the patient's body, then seized my legs, then my chest, squeezing his hands up through my head, thrusting out the poisons and throwing them away.

"Bad people have got inside you, inside your chest, but I will pull them all out," he said later. Domingos snores loudly at night, like any contented man, though he denied the charge, despite Piarina and Valdira agreeing with me with laughter. My own habit of sleep-talking, often so loudly that I wake myself up, was not a matter for light-hearted complaint. Dreams tell us our enemies, and much else, the Yanomami believe. Domingos said my chatter and cries were evidence of bad spirits trying to get into me. "But do not worry. I will pull them out, Dennison," he said.

"What did you discover when you 'thought' me?" I asked.

"I found a little creature, this size," he replied, pointing to the top of his small finger.

"How did it get inside?'

"When you lay in your hammock like this," he said putting his head back with his mouth open. "That's how the little creature got inside."

"But why attack?"

"He wanted."

I was struck by the similarity between Domingos' shamanic diagnosis and the Western medical explanation of infection. Domingos offered me tobacco to suck at night. "To stop sleep talking?" I asked, to which he nodded and laughed. "Do you want to stop snoring?" I replied. Domingos' shamanic work left me more settled but the fever during the night remained as strong.

The last of my physical energy and, at the time, it seemed also my mental energy, was used up by a trivial affair a few days later. The little event is comical in retrospect, but the deep apprehensions exaggerated at the time by illness, created by my illegal presence with the Yanomami, never subsided on future journeys. Only the trust in my hosts gained strength from this petty half-hour incident one hot morning.

"The padre from the Mission must not find me here," I had said to Renato and Domingos, having been told in Santa Isabel that the Salesian priest would be leaving his mission station on the Marauiá to go for treatment for rheumatism in Manaus. He might very well denounce me to Funai and possibly to the Federal Police if he found me in Coatá when he came downriver. I knew I was defying three Brazilian prohibitions by being with the Yanomami.

Firstly, a large sign above the second waterfall on the Marauiá declares an "Indigenous Area" prohibited to all non-authorized persons. It is illegal to enter any Indian reserve in Brazil without the permission of Funai, based in Brasília, the country's capital 2,600 kilometres south-east of the Yanomami. I knew I would never be granted official permission, for I was not a missionary, doctor nor an anthropologist but a lone traveller curious, in a serious sense, to know this Amazonian tribe.

Secondly, the Brazilian Army, as part of a greater project kept secret for three years, declared in 1985 a corridor 150 kilometres wide along the country's northern border as an area of national security under military jurisdiction. The corridor runs from Brazil's border with Colombia in the west to the Atlantic Ocean in the east. The project to "secure" this area is called the Calha Norte project – meaning the northern ditch or moat project. It is, in theory, to stop possible invasions of cocaine growers, gold miners and settlers from Brazil's neighbours crossing into the Brazilian forests and savannas in the north. The hidden purpose of the Calha Norte Project is to "open up" the region to settlement and development by Brazilians, mainly landless families from the north-east and south of the country. All earlier colonization projects in the Amazon have failed, for many reasons, and left the poorest Brazilians yet poorer. It is taken for granted in the planning of the Calha Norte project that by design or by deliberate neglect, the Indians already in the region will die off or be penned into little reserves. Few Brazilians know the extent of this infamy being done in their name.

Thirdly, the Yanomami area was "closed" by order of Funai and the Brazilian Federal Police in 1987 after a "massacre" of *garimpeiros*. The Federal Police, Army and Funai officials blamed missionaries for inciting the Indians. This was a pretext to take out missionaries, anthropologists, doctors and nurses – any White who could witness the open invasion of *garimpeiros* and the infection of the Yanomami with malaria and other diseases. Nothing was done to take out the illegal *garimpeiros*. The massacre story was later revealed as the deaths of four Yanomami and two *garimpeiros*. Catholic missionaries were allowed by court order to remain in areas without *garimpeiros*, such as on the Marauiá.

These triple prohibitions, from Funai, the Army and the Federal Police, each legal yet each only partially enforced had one result. Far from protecting the Yanomami, they gave open season to the businessmen and politicians controlling the *garimpeiros*, to continue their illegal invasions and illegal mining.

My own journeys among the Yanomami were not sanctioned by the Brazilian authorities but I did have permission. Davi in Brasília had asked me, "Do you have permission of Funai to go to the Marauiá?"

"No," I told him, "not of Funai. But I asked the *tuxaua* to be able to stay. And now I have the invitation from the community to return. Who should I ask, a bureaucrat sitting in Brasília or the leaders of the *shabono* to be able to stay as their guest in their homes?"

Davi nodded and was pleased with the answer.

Renato and Domingos entered into the fun of deceiving the padre, a man they did not respect because he did not help them. "He always says, 'No,' when we ask for a ride in his canoe when he goes to Santa Isabel. The late padre Antonio always took us in his fast fast motor boat," said Valdira, speaking of the Brazilian priest who was the first

Whiteman to visit them. People always spoke of him with affection and respect. Padre Francisco Laudado, from Italy, received no warmth from the people, though it was to be seven months before I met him and found out why.

Valdira hid my canoe up an *igarapé* the night before the padre was expected and my hammock and other possessions were hidden after breakfast.

"Motor! Motor!" came a small boy's cry mid-morning to start our farce.

Renato took me to the only place with four walls in the village. It was a small room that his eldest son had built, "Just because he wanted," said Renato. "Stay here. We will come when the padre has gone," he told me. The room stood next to Renato's house, on one side of the *shabono* and the sounds of the padre's speedboat slowing as he turned into the landing place entered with the beams of sunshine through the gaps in the thatched walls. I lay in the hammock in the room, suppressing a hoarse cough from my lungs.

Father Francisco's visit to Coatá was brief because he was eager to reach the main mission at Santa Isabel. He stopped at the entrance to the *shabono* to talk to the men and women, then started to tour the families at each hearth. I could hear him talking with Samuel who lived at the entrance, next to Renato. Then he was asking Francesca about her baby and how many people lived in the house. He would come next to the room where I was hiding. His voice, and the quieter replies of those around him, turned towards the room. I waited, half expecting the blue sheeting over the door to be torn away by an inquisitive arm. But the group passed in front of the room without pausing on the way to Domingos' house.

A second visitor, the driver of the padre's motor canoe, lingered in Renato's hearth. "What's here?" he asked suddenly, standing within arm's reach of my door.

"This is my house," said Renato's eldest son quickly. "But it's empty now."

Padre Francisco gave small packets of tobacco to each family as he toured their homes and with laughter threw a couple of handfuls of boiled sweets into the air for the children. Then he was gone, and Renato's son fetched me from the gloom of his room. We heard the priest roaring down the river in his aluminium canoe and we laughed at the success of our little deception.

My relief was short-lived. I knew that I had to leave and go down river to see a doctor. Renato said I wasn't strong enough to walk through the forest to Santa Isabel and told his middle son Daniel to take me in my canoe down the waterfalls to the town. Alberto, Jacinto's son, said he would come with us and both would return home with the canoe.

"We will come to bring you back here after a week," Renato said. I agreed while dreading having to leave and the possibility of having to go to Manaus for treatment and thus having to delay much before returning.

I slept in my hammock until we left early the next morning and slept across a bench in the canoe going down the river, except for passing the waterfalls. How trivial my sore throat had seemed on the boat up the Rio Negro from Manaus only a few weeks earlier, yet all hopes and plans were now ruined by being ill.

2

The pneumonia responded immediately to strong antibiotics given by a nurse at the small hospital in Santa Isabel. The Yanomami promised to fetch me after a week or so and went home up the Marauiá with the motor canoe, leaving me in the care of a family who knew me from my earlier visit. I slept for a week in a hammock slung across their living room, until the dreadful weight of disease lifted from body and mind, and I was left exhausted but no longer ill.

The illness and antibiotics depressed me greatly. When appetite began to return, the antibiotics turned my stomach into a petulant little boy. I could swallow only particular foods that were not easily available and my stomach threatened to vomit if I tried eating anything else. Meat of any kind gagged in my throat. *Farinha* stuck like glue. Fish had too many bones. Tea and fresh fruits were all that my stomach would allow without painful spasms or hours of nausea. The tea I always carried with me as my one luxury, but fresh fruits were not available in the town because few people bothered to grow them. My hosts looked after me well but we ate fish or meat from tins each day mixed with *farinha* and boiled beans. I'd stayed with Paulo and his family before, briefly, on my first journey when they'd been living at a tiny outpost called Santomé (Saint Thomas) on the Rio Negro. They had since moved to Santa Isabel where Paulo was now a town councillor, with a salary, and his wife worked as a nurse in the cottage hospital.

I craved mental stimulation and became mind-achingly bored. Will the Yanomami come to take me back to the *shabono*, as promised? I wondered, though I knew I'd temporarily lost the physical capability to make the long journey through the forest. Why am I here? I cried to myself, in that universal plea of the lonely traveller.

My depression fed on many demons, principally boredom and doubt. Once swallowed, these horrid twins gnawed in my stomach to weaken resolve and dissolve hope. They sustained themselves by consuming my physical energy until all my mental energy had gone as well.

Santa Isabel is a place with little to do and where the people take all day doing it. It's an outpost, a stockade against "What's out there", and the town waits for something to happen, something to arrive; what does not come from the big cities like São Paulo or Rio de Janeiro is despised in Brazil. Dependence on tinned foods and television are hard proof of the mental poverty of the small towns in the interior of the Amazon. Wonderful fruits grow well but it is not the custom to plant them. Townspeople queue before sunrise to buy up the few fresh fish for sale on the river bank. *Caboclo* families – the Brazilians who live in small houses along the rivers – grow *açaí* and peach palms only for themselves. No-one thinks to farm turtles or alligators for their meat, as early European travellers reported of the tribes. Today, the wild populations of turtles and alligators have been devastated. It's this impoverished culture of dependence that self-sufficient, self-confident Indians are expected to join.

I wanted to go home to Europe and I massaged my excuses to justify giving up. However, the excuses were always countered by that small voice which speaks from our soul to defend personal truths. "What will you want to do if you go home now?" asked the calm voice each day. My answer was always, "To return to the Yanomami."

Renato, Domingos, Gabriel and six others arrived in Santa Isabel after two weeks to take me home with them. Their embraces and enthusiasm cleared all my doubts as easily as sunshine brightens a gloomy sky. The Yanomami went shopping in the morning for laundry soap, shotgun cartridges and rice. All these were provided on credit by several storekeepers. Renato and Domingos promised to return within one month with dozens of bundles of *to-o* to pay for what they were taking. People in Santa Isabel murmured that these Indians had lost their culture because they came to trade fish hooks for *sorva* and because Renato had once or twice been drunk with *cachaça*, the fire-water of Brazil. Like everything with the Yanomami, the truth is more complex and more fascinating. What threatens their existence comes from the outside, not from their desire for trade goods.

All the Yanomami on the Marauiá come from time to time to trade with Santa Isabel, bringing *to-o, sorva* or rubber to exchange for fish hooks, line and mirrors. The challenge for every community is to weave these irregular strands of contact with the *nabe* so that the new colours may lie without conflict beside the familiar fibres of traditional society.

I was aware now of my own arrogance on my first visit to the Yanomami when – if I am honest – I'd come in search of "true" Indians; people to fulfill my own ideas of what was an Indian: The Whiteman often puts Indians into a time-lock as if their cultures cannot, should not, or do not change. Even the gallery of Amazonian Indians at the American Museum of Natural History in New York does not show a metal tool or a cooking pot in its displays, 450 years after the Spanish first descended the Amazon River.

A Whiteman called Simon LeFevre arrived with Gabriel and the others, having walked through the forest from Coatá with them. We'd not met before but we settled into easy conversation in Portuguese. Simon bubbled with enthusiasm and punctuated what he said by stroking his ginger beard. He was a strange bird to have migrated from Belgium at the age of forty to live among the Yanomami. He had been an architect at home but came here to serve the Yanomami as a volunteer of the Catholic church and sponsored by the Belgian KWIA, an organization similar to Survival International. He had been only the second Whiteman seen by one community up the Padauari River when he'd gone with a Frenchman, Henri Ramirez, to live there for two years in 1986. He talked of them with the same practical appraisal as a master carpenter talking of his apprentices. "What an impression to arrive there. Hah!" he said with a chuckle. "We were very well received. We lived in the *shabono* for the first four or five months. We wanted to live always with them like that but perhaps it was Utopian, a little idealistic. It was hard because the Yanomami way is to watch everything. We're accustomed to our privacy and it's difficult to change, so later Henri and I built a house and moved outside.

"It was beautiful there; a plain closed round by mountains. The Yanomami had arrived only three or four years earlier from Venezuela and had never before had contact with Whites. Nothing! Though all the Yanomami know that they're such people from whom come the metal pots and such things," said Simon.

"Did you wear clothes?" I asked.

"A loincloth. This was positive. Maybe ten or fifteen out of 150 people wore shorts or long trousers traded from other Indians. All the rest were nude. Not one woman had clothes so it was positive to arrive there with a loincloth, because they always want everything in the way of the foreigner. I'm not going to say the Whiteman, but the foreigner. Later, of course, they changed. Now they've met other Yanomami and they know we have long trousers and so they want. There, they were walking round in long trousers while we were still totally nude," Simon explained with a laugh and tug of his beard. "They were more authentic than us!"

"They weren't afraid of you?"

"Not at all! The children were afraid but not the adults. I can say they are wild, valiant. Well, you know how it is – they looked into every sack. You have to say, 'Okay up to this point, but that's enough.' But without violence. I had some quarrels with one man about this because he wanted to show his authority.

"It was an apprenticeship with the Yanomami to learn their language because they understood nothing at all of Portuguese. I can't say this group was 'primitive', but authentic. They didn't have any contact, no influence from the Whites."

"What's acculturation?" I asked.

Simon tugged his beard. "What's culture? I don't know. Culture is like religion. Religion is in every corner but you can't see it. You can't say, 'This is no longer their own culture,' just because they're wearing clothes. Perhaps the clothes will be used in another way.

"Look at glass beads; they've entered the culture and they're truly Yanomami. There's not a Yanomami without beads. Beads are part of the Yanomami culture but they're made in Czechoslovakia. It's not the material but the way they use things that makes their culture," said he.

Simon was going to Manaus, then to Belgium for a few months for the first time in two years. He planned to build a school in Apuí when he came back.

There was no problem on the return journey upriver to Coatá, except that so many men and youths came to Santa Isabel to welcome me back that there was no room for me in the canoe. Domingos reacted angrily when Renato told him to walk home through the forest and eventually some of Renato's kinsmen said they'd walk home.

The slow life of the *shabono* caught me in its embrace once again when we returned in pouring rain. We lay in our hammocks with the water pouring outside off the thatch roof, while Valdira told us he'd shot a buffalo.

"Buffalo?" I said, "but there's no buffalo here."

"Yes, buffalo," he insisted, while Domingos and Piarina giggled at my confusion.

"Buffalo? Really?"

"*Xama*!" said Valdira triumphantly.

"*Xama*? So big?"

"So big!" he said, holding up his arm to claim an animal as high as his own waist. *Xama*, called "*anta*" by Brazilians, is prized by every hunter because there's enough meat for a feast. The *Xama* was sleeping in the forest when Valdira found it. "I shot him in the chest and he died," he said, taking for granted the firepower of the family shotgun.

Valdira and Carlino, Renato's nephew and Alippe's son, had also killed thirty-seven *arakú* (a fish) in one night with their new barbed spears. "We nearly died of the cold in the rain," said Valdira.

Jacinto brought a plate of plaintains soon after we returned and gave me a tight hug. And other people came in the days that followed to ask if I was better. "Illness gone!" they exclaimed.

Other men went out in the rain to fetch the kidneys, liver, heart and offal of the *Xama* while Valdira, the celebrated hunter, stayed in his hammock. These were easy to carry and would have been the first to rot. The rest of the carcass was left submerged in an *igarapé* in the forest to eliminate the scent that would attract animals during the night. Every family received a cut of the huge liver and other offal. The head alone, when it arrived next morning in the *shabono* strapped with ribbons of tree bark to a man's back, was as tall as the children watching.

The use of steel tools has changed the way in which meat is distributed in the community. Piarina explained: "The meat was cooked whole by the wife of the hunter and then divided for the men and for the women and she gave the head for the children. And when there are many heads, she gives them to the other mothers.

"They didn't have spoons. They ate with just their hands. Only with their hands! And only soup with baked banana. We drank *habrua* [a drink made by boiling and mashing *custirim*] the same way," she said, lapping with fingers and tongue.

The arrival of *farinha*, brought to the Marauiá by Salesian missionaries, was love at first sight. "No-one knew what it was," said Piarina, "when padre Antonio brought the first basket."

"Some fell on the ground and I wet my fingers to pick up the pieces," said Domingos. Piarina did the same thing with her tongue. "We didn't have anything. No spoon, no clothes. Everyone nude. We didn't have. We didn't know. Now we've learned," she said.

How did the outside world burst in on the Yanomami? The answer, at least on the Marauiá, is that the Yanomami went in search of the outside world. This is what Renato talked about on the first morning after my return, when we sat together on low stools at the front of his house. Renato had agreed to speak first in Yanomami and then to translate little by little into Portuguese. Stories would be far more dramatic and told with more detail in his mother tongue. However, our arrangement was not a success.

A Yanomami story-teller lives inside his story. He becomes all the people of his story. He speaks all their words. He moves from scene to scene. He dramatizes the action in shouts and sounds. He delivers his own commentary. He moves at the pace of his story and he does all this without taking a breath. Stopping to translate phrase by phrase disrupted the flow of each story worse than any waterfall interrupts a river. So Renato switched to Portuguese to tell the story of how his father first met a Whiteman. Renato took the wad of tobacco from his mouth; the children were told to keep quiet and they leaned behind the hammock, not quite sure what was going to happen when I brought out my small black tape recorder.

"How did your father in the *shabono* know the Whiteman existed?" I asked.

"There was a signal. One day at the headwaters of Marauiá river, my grandfather saw three people in clothes. He was frightened. He was thinking they were people; *nabe*. He went to warn our *shabono* and the Yanomami went out but they didn't catch them. The *nabe* would have died if they had been caught, like the Yanomami always die as well. The *nabe* left clothes. This was a signal."

These *nabe* were almost certainly members of the commission surveying the Brazilian-Venezuelan border in the 1950s. Renato's father decided to descend the Marauiá river from the headwaters.

" 'Let's go to meet a Whiteman,' he said to his nephew and to his brother-in-law." Renato gave few details about his parents, except to say his father was, "very strong, all white, as the white of your body. He was not a White, he was a real Yanomami, but white white [in colour]." Renato was going outside the traditional taboo against speaking of the dead after the necessary rituals to break their links with the world of the living. I asked him his father's name but he would only say his father was called Sabbá by the Whiteman. "I can't speak anything of their names in Yanomami," said Renato. Yanomami names cannot be spoken aloud because bad spirits might hear and know where to do harm. Instead, people were called, mother of such and such a child, for example, as this was not dangerous. Christian names have been adopted to fool the bad spirits because these nicknames are not real names so the spirits do not know them.

"The nephew and brother-in-law accompanied my father through the forest, by the bank of the river, until one day [after a month] they met an old man at the mouth of the Marauiá. This was the discovery of the Whiteman.

"They wanted to shoot their arrows. They didn't know how to speak Portuguese, but they called, '*Shorima! Shorima!*' That's to say, 'Friend, friend!' So they met with the man and they all embraced. The Brazilian gave them machetes, axes and old pans which they carried home.

" 'We've discovered White people, so we'll never again suffer as we're suffering now,' shouted my father. 'Thanks to Omam! I've brought machetes, axes and knives. He gave everything,' he said. Everyone was delighted! All the tribe of Ironasiteri was delighted with these things," said Renato.

A group of about twenty-five men returned through the forest to the mouth of the Marauiá a month later. "A motor boat of a river trader came," said Renato making the sounds of its motor – te-te-te – "bringing a man who said he was the priest from the mission of Santa Isabel. The mission was a little thatched house with no zinc roof. Today, it's a little city out of the forest. So the motor took dad – te-te-te – he disappeared," said Renato.

The Brazilians received Renato's father with gifts and food, much like the hospitality given to visitors in his own community. He was self-confident in Santa Isabel, curious but unaffected by his hosts' habit of covering their bodies, even in the midday heat, while he himself walked freely. He knew the stories, told by his fathers round the fire at night, of the cowardly Yanomami who had fled in a flood long, long ago. Now these people were back, with their language and appearance degenerated. Their *shabono* was broken and every family lived alone in their own small enclosures. They no longer used *ebene* but talked of knowing a Great Spirit. This spirit had his own big house in the village though no-one ever saw him, even when all the people went into his house and called to him by name.

Renato's father may have felt superior to his hosts but the power of the *nabe*'s tools impressed him greatly. "The padre gave him boxes of machetes, of axes and ten baskets of *farinha*. He gave tobacco too and left my father – te-te-te – at the mouth of the Marauiá. Everyone was delighted. My father distributed everything and they returned up the Marauiá and arrived home after one month. Everyone was [so] delighted, they hit themselves with sticks. The *tuxaua* was happy. Everyone was happy. They brought *farinha* and showed it. I didn't know what it was; a little animal, a little yellow thing; fragrant, delightful. Well, today, we make it as a common thing. But then I chewed it with my parents. It tasted like sand on a beach," said Renato, who was about eight years old when his father returned.

Delight with their discoveries and a natural hospitality and eagerness to please continued when padre Antonio Goes came to their *shabono*, bringing yet more cases of metal tools and now clothes to cover the nude Yanomami. Like other Indians, the Yanomami have always recognized the difference between being nude and being naked. To be nude is to wear no clothes. To be naked is to be bared, to be sexually available. Traditionally men kept the foreskin of their penis tucked under a string belt and women walked and crouched without exposing their clitoris. This was nudity. To let the penis fall was to be naked and this was unacceptable.

"Why did the Yanomami want to wear clothes when they didn't have before?" I asked Renato.

"Because the padre gave to them. He wanted them to use clothes so he gave them," replied Renato.

"But why did the Yanomami want the clothes?"

"They thought they were beautiful and also to escape insects biting. Padre Antonio gave clothes not to see the 'thing' of women. My father took off the trousers when he slept. All the old people were nude. Today, I don't go nude," said Renato, though I knew many people still took off their clothes when the *piums* vanished after sunset.

I asked Domingos the same question, "Why did the Yanomami accept the clothes?"

"The late padre Antonio wanted to give clothes. In his thinking he didn't like to see 'things', so he gave everyone clothes," he said.

"Why did the Yanomami accept padre Antonio?"

"They accepted because, as I am saying, they didn't have anything! Not even a machete. The late padre Antonio gave them machetes, axes, pans for us not to continue any longer *shorima* [true Yanomami]," he giggled.

"What did people think when the padre started speaking about Jesus Christ?"

"They thought to stay with him to gain axes. He spoke like this when he gave the machetes: 'With this machete you are going to garden. It's not to cut up people. It's not to cut your heads. A knife is to cut *maroha* [a fish] and meat,' he explained for them. And he brought out a machete. 'Now there's a machete, I've brought for you to cut your hair, like this.' And he taught them all about it. So they were thankful to him because they hadn't had before. It's a big change," said Domingos, bursting with giggles.

"And what did people think about this?"

"They thought all this was a discovery of Omam [the creator God of the Yanomami]," he said.

The power of steel tools to draw Indians peacefully to the outsiders has been used since Pero Alvares Cabral stepped ashore from Portugal on 22nd April, 1500. Rows of machetes, tin pans and shiny mirrors are still used by "pacification" parties trying to contact isolated Indians. Washing lines of gifts are left for two or three days then revisited to see if anything has been taken or any baskets or other gifts left in exchange. Making these contacts requires patience and great trust by everyone involved until, if ever, the two peoples meet face to face, body to body. What is the power of attraction of these strange objects in the forest? To people from industrial societies, with our minds accustomed to the function of machines, it seems obvious that the great attraction of steel tools is their usefulness. Have you ever tried to chop down a tree with a stone axe?

An alternative view is given by French anthropologist Dr. Bruce Albert, who has spent fifteen years studying the Yanomami. He told me that the apparent desire of the Yanomami for metal tools because they are useful is only the *nabe*'s wildly inaccurate interpretation. The real reason for the insatiable desire springs from a wholly different world-view.

"The desire for metal pots is something of an optical illusion by our economic culture. The Yanomami like the metal tools as a way of exchange. What's of interest [to them] is not the object but the exchange. When they see a Whiteman who has a mountain of things, stockpiled, not circulating, this, for them, is an economic scandal. So they ask for these things until they have emptied the stock. It's not to reconstruct a stockpile but to circulate. I know that two minutes after I trade something it's gone. A knife is ten kilometres. away by the next day. It's a black hole for manufactured objects with the Yanomami. Tons of goods enter and are gone, they're finished also because the Yanomami don't take care of them; they've no interest in this. When people die, all their possessions are destroyed systematically. So, when they're asking for these objects it's not for the reason we think," said Dr. Bruce Albert.

"But they use the knives," I said.

"Of course, but they ask for many more than they use. I'm not saying there's no value in the utility of the objects but that the esteemed value is for circulation. You could give ten tons of knives to one person and there wouldn't be one remaining three days later. I was in a Salesian mission where they've provided 30,000 machetes in fifteen years," explained Dr. Bruce Albert.

The second gift of the *nabe* to the people of the Marauiá arrived soon after their joyful discovery of the Whiteman's miraculous tools from padre Antonio. The second gift was death by unknown magic. Epidemics of the *nabe*'s diseases swept up the river like vengeful spirits. Measles, whooping cough, influenza, tuberculosis, river blindness, malaria, yellow fever, smallpox – none of these diseases existed in the Amazon before the Whiteman arrived, and they have killed more Indians than bullets and slavery combined.

"I think more than 300 people died," said Renato. This first epidemic was measles. "My uncle told me that this death did not exist when I was born. It hadn't appeared. Only war with arrows killed people. But the measles came when I was growing up, about ten little years. Measles killed almost everyone.

"Everyone was with fever and starting to fall and began to die. People fled saying, 'Let's stay in the forest. Let's stay on the edge of the mountains.' And the disease went killing, killing, killing. The *pajé* [shaman] couldn't deal with this. He died with many others. It was a disease of the Whiteman. When the measles ended it had killed half the Yanomami. Ended! Ended! They didn't bury the dead. All the bodies rotted. Everyone hid themselves in the forest. Everyone was afraid of what had happened to the Yanomami. Later, after more than two months they burned all the bones to be able to hold the festival of the dead," said Renato. He paused then added softly, "I tired of seeing my family dead."

"When it was finished, they went to hunt *shama*, forest turkey, monkey, pig and everything. A huge amount of animals, roasted! After one week, when they were going to hold the festival, they broke the bones of the dead, made a funeral pyre and burned them all until they were powder. Then they sieved them to mix with the banana porridge," Renato explained.

"Like a birthday party?" I asked.

"Like a birthday party."

"Do you still do this when a person dies?"

"It's done, but now I do it a little differently. Today, I do it with fireworks! We didn't have these but today we've discovered to buy rockets," he said, laughing loudly. "Rockets! To brighten the party! Everyone's invited and they come from all over," he said.

Renato whispered that Jacinto, the leading *shaman*, would be drinking the bones of his nephew when the plaintains ripened next season. Renato invited me to attend. "Jacinto kept the bones?" I asked.

"They're here, buried in the earth."

"Buried?"

"It's like this. We die and we bury in the earth and we take out the bones already cleaned after two or three years and then we burn the bones."

"Why did you change?" I asked. "Was this connected with Christian burial?"

"It wasn't White people who discovered this!" retorted Renato. "It's our responsibility. It's not necessary to burn the body. The *shabono* becomes ugly. Roasting like a pig – zzzzz – I didn't like this. So now we bury, then we take out the clean bones," he said.

"What did people in the *shabono* think when padre Antonio started talking about Jesus Christ and God?" I asked.

"The old men said they didn't believe in Jesus Christ. Others believed. 'God never existed. It's a wrong belief,' the old men said. 'It's not him who made the sky. It was another man who did this when he was a bird,' they said. All animals were once humans, according to the Yanomami.

" 'God didn't do anything. Jesus Christ didn't do this, nor Saint Paul, nor Saint Peter,' said the old men. The padre told them, 'You're speaking badly with me. One day you're going to be punished. One day the Yanomami will die. Those who don't believe in God will die, all of them. But the ones who do believe will still be living.' The padre spoke like this," said Renato.

Everyone I met on the Marauiá always spoke of padre Antonio Goes with affection and respect because he helped them. Domingos, for example, said how sorry he was the padre had died away from them in Manaus and was buried in Manaus. "How could we drink his bones?" he asked. "I could have gone to the cemetery when I was in Manaus. But there was no reason," he said. Padre Antonio came from the north-east of Brazil and lived for ten years amongst the Yanomami in the little mission house he built beside the river three days farther upstream. He brought them manioc plants and taught the people how to make *farinha* and tapioca. He exchanged the trade goods they wanted for work in his own fruit and vegetable gardens at the mission and he encouraged them to gather *sorva* and rubber in the forest also to exchange for trade goods.

"Why does the Whiteman have all these things and the Yanomami don't?" I asked Renato, eager to know how he reconciled the disparity of tools between himself and the Whiteman.

"I've been thinking about this," he replied. It was Omam, the Creator god of the Yanomami, who gave the Whiteman all his tools. "Omam left us to use *ebene* and to be *pajés*. His spirit is in our bodies, even though you don't see anything. It's in my head. It's very strong the spirit of Omam. And he stayed over there! where the sky ends, where it descends," said Renato.

It was Omam who gave the Whiteman his shotgun, his motor, ammunition and flashlight, though the *nabe* are ignorant about their benefactor. "Omam taught them to do many things," said Renato. "It was Omam who discovered the aeroplane," he said. The other men sitting listening nodded their agreement. "Omam flew about and he gave this to the Whiteman to fly about," said Renato.

I asked Domingos and Piarina, on another day when we were peeling *to-o*, "Why did Omam help the Whites with these things and not the Yanomami?"

"Omam didn't teach us because his journey was fast and he missed us out. He went quickly. He would have lived here but [when he came to a feast] his nephew frightened him and he went away," explained Domingos. "All the grilled meat for the feast became rocks. All rocks!" he said. Omam taught everyone everything they know, even the Whiteman how to use his tape recorder.

"Why didn't Omam teach the Yanomami?" I asked.

"It's like this," said Domingos, putting down the length of *to-o* to try to explain to me the saga of Omam's journey across the world. Wherever he paused, Omam made a factory – a factory for cooking pots, a factory for axes, a factory for machetes. Omam didn't stop long enough with the Yanomami for them to receive factories but he gave them the animals and fruits in the forest and he taught them to take *ebene* to become *hekura*. Thus the job of the *nabe* is to produce tools, while the work of the Yanomami is to maintain the spiritual world in order.

The idea of factories being ready-built by God may be far from today's Western theories of evolution and geological ages, but the essential notion is the same as the seven days of Creation told in Genesis. One profound difference is that the Whiteman believes he was thrown out of the garden of Eden for disobeying God. In contrast, the Yanomami accepted what Omam gave them (and thus have lived without knowing sin or guilt). The marvels of Omam's creation were already perfect; they were only waiting to be discovered by the Yanomami, like heavy fruit on the peach palm tree. This sense of discovery is very strong with the Yanomami. The encounter with the Whiteman by Renato's father was only one more example, among numerous, of their important discoveries that have changed their world.

Fire, for example, was discovered by Iwa (an alligator) though he tried to keep it just for himself. "It was in the time when animals were people. Iwa discovered fire and he didn't tell anyone but his wife," explained Renato. Everyone else ate their food raw, while Iwa ate meat cooked secretly. He kept fire hidden in his mouth. But one day the others found a few burnt pieces of meat so they knew Iwa was hiding something.

Several animals tried to amuse Iwa but he never opened his mouth. Then two hummingbirds flew down and round and round in front of him. Iwa laughed and the birds flew inside his mouth to snatch the embers of fire and flew off into the branches of a tree. The Yanomami have eaten cooked meat ever since.

Renato and Domingos were boys when their father returned from his expedition with proof of the existence of another people by bringing knives harder than any wood and cooking pots that wouldn't break even if you dropped them. I wondered on whose shoulders the weight of these discoveries would have fallen most heavily. Men like Renato's father or his half-brother Jacinto, were adults with their beliefs, explanations and mental maps of the world already drawn. They would have fitted the discovery of the *nabe* within this already formed vision of the world; hence the counter-assertion to padre Antonio by the older men of the *shabono* that the world was not created by God nor by Jesus Christ.

Their grandchildren take beads, axes and metal pots for granted, having grown up with them in their homes and with an awareness of the *nabe* down the river. Valdira, Aoria and Daniel, Renato's son, for example, want what is useful but are not enthralled by the Whiteman. Distance and time have allowed their generation to adapt. Valdira talked much more often about training properly to become a strong *shaman* like his father than he asked about Santa Isabel. This third generation accepts the world they were born into just like their grandparents, for they both missed the revolution that still swirls through the minds of their parents' generation.

The world of the *nabe* still weighs heavily on those who were children when the giant, bearded Whiteman whom they later called padre Antonio came into their homes and it is they who are gullible to its endless tawdry charms. His size, his charisma and his great power deeply impressed the children approaching puberty.

The strongest impact fell on five of the children who were taken away by padre Antonio to the Salesian mission school in Santa Isabel. They lived there for several years with a few Yanomami from distant *shabonos*, children from other tribes and children from the town.

If it seems strange that Yanomami parents should have agreed to send some of their children away with the newcomers, perhaps it is because we unconsciously think of Indians as passive, as being acted upon, and not as members of dynamic societies curious about the outside world and open to change to improve their lives. Is it not natural for them to ask, "By what power do the nabe possess their knives, their big canoes that hurry through the water without men paddling?" No prudent leader would lose an opportunity to find the source of the new powers. No courageous man could turn away from the marvels, just as no expert hunter would abandon the forest trail of an animal he did not recognize. There was, above all, the need for some members to learn the language of the newcomers to be able to communicate.

No-one could be better suited to learn about the new powers of the *nabe* than the *tuxauas'* own children. They should go to live a while with the *nabe* and return to share with their relatives all they have learned of the new language, the counting (the Yanomami had only three numbers – one, two and more-than-two), the drawing on white leaves bound together and the rituals of the great spirit giving such tools and power to these people.

Two of the children from the Marauiá died in Santa Isabel. Domingos, Piarina and Renato all came home after several years. Their experiences touched each of them differently.

"Didn't your father think that you weren't going to return?" I asked Renato.

"No!" Padre said, "Your son will return, let me bring him to stay in the college." I went with Domingos.

"Five-thirty – ting-ting-ting – the bell to wake and take a bath. Then we put on clothes and went to the church for morning prayers. After prayers came *farinha* porridge; then we went to work in the garden, cultivating, planting, cutting grass. Nine o'clock, have a snack and go to the classroom," said Renato.

"What did you learn?"

"I learned Portuguese, the alphabet and counting. Eleven o'clock, lunch. After lunch we went to the playing field. Football. We took a bath after the playing field. Three o'clock, a snack and then we went to the garden until five o'clock. We returned and took a bath.

"Dinner at six o'clock and from there we went to study at night. Nine o'clock striking on the clock and we went to church. Midnight, going to the dormitory to sleep. We lived like this. It was too much a devoted life," said Renato.

"What did you think of the stories of the Bible?"

"I believed them – that Our Lord existed; Heaven, angels. The padre taught this for a long time," he said.

Jacinto's shamanic chants sounded across the *shabono* like a counterbalance to the intrusion of the Whiteman's regime, completely alien to the Yanomami way of raising and educating children. There's a fundamental difference in the treatment of children among the Yanomami that changes the objective of their education. A child's self-confidence is nurtured as much as possible by allowing him or her to explore the world without restraints – four-year-old boys go fishing alone in small canoes, babies play with knives. The dangers are great but mothers let children play in peace. They do not distrust their sons and daughters by always assuming they'll be up to mischief. Children can turn to any adult for help yet the adults rarely interfere in what the children are doing. People grow up with a robust self-confidence that serves them well as adults responsible for daily hunting and gardening to feed their families.

Self-confidence springs from within. Confidence is not something gained from outside the individual, because it's never taken away. Children learn all by imitating and participating. They play and work in the gardens. They wander in the forests with the adult. There is no school but they learn the complete taxonomy of animals, trees, plants and fish. They learn where and when to hunt, to gather and to fish. Young women learn from their mothers how to use magic plants and many others from the forest, how to cook, make baskets and deliver their own babies. Young men are initiated as *shamans* and train their *hekura* to serve the community.

Renato's studies ended abruptly. "The padre said – and I'll speak the way he spoke; 'You don't obey your padre, you don't obey us. You have to respect the padre, to come every day to the college, to pray all the time. Don't forget this. If not, don't come any more. Remember what God has given you.'" So Renato returned home.

Going to school was a radical experience for Renato. He is deeply impressed by the ways of the Whiteman and is eager to please and to be considered an equal by the *nabe*. So he wears a wristwatch and tells other people what to do. "They are not knowing," Renato often said to me to explain his own superiority.

"I have the Elector's Card [to vote], a Brazilian Identity Card and I have the Birth Certificate. Only I have these. The others don't have. But I don't want to leave the life of the Yanomami, no. I use everything," Renato told me.

I asked Domingos and Piarina why their fathers sent them to school in Santa Isabel.

"They wanted to know things," Piarina replied, smiling at the foolish question.

"I think for them to understand. Dad wanted to let me study, but some [other parents] did not allow. When I arrived in Santa Isabel, I thought, 'Sad!'" Domingos said with a long face that cracked quickly into giggles.

"You cried?" I asked.

"I cried five hours! Five hours of crying. I was homesick for mum and dad and all the relatives. I drank porridge in the morning to please the Salesians. I liked it and I drank and I stayed," he said.

"What was the food?"

"At first I didn't think the food was good. Every day tinned meat! I didn't know it was good. I was afraid to eat the food of the Whites. So I ate only banana. Later, I got used to it.

"And milk! I had already heard that they took it from a cow. The Salesians took me to the cowshed and said, 'Drink this.' They mixed it with porridge. It was still warm and I drank it," said Domingos.

"And what did the padres teach in the school?"

"They taught us to learn ABC, the letters of Brazil. Everything was in Portuguese. There was nothing in the Yanomami language. Nothing. So we went slowly learning the ABC," he said.

Domingos stayed for four years and though he remembers the letters of the alphabet and can sign his name, he has forgotten almost everything else that has no application in the *shabono*. "Was it worthwhile going to school?" I asked.

"It was worthwhile."

Domingos did not return straight away up the Marauiá but went to another *shabono* at Maturacá, on the river Cauabarí, where he wanted to marry one of the girls but he was forbidden by the *tuxaua* and had to leave. "The padre said, 'Look, Domingos, come to study again.' So I returned to study in the college. There were girls there and I sent notes to them when they passed. One girl left a little letter in my place. So she was my girlfriend. Heavens, how beautiful!"

"Another one!" I exclaimed with mock horror.

"Another! The padre discovered me with this girl. He said, 'You're depraved. You're no good. It's better you go back to the Marauiá. Don't come to study any more.'" Domingos laughed. "I was fifteen years old when the padre expelled me. I never returned," he said.

"Are your sons going to attend Simon's school here?" I asked.

"They are!"

"Why?"

"They have to learn how to read a bill because the traders rob us a lot. Poor us! If the children learn in the school [then] later they can go to the college. This is what I say to my sons. Valdira is married, so he can only learn here. But if Mateus [the younger son] learns in the school then I'll put him in the college. If it's his desire," said Domingos.

"Why didn't you send your sons to Santa Isabel?" I asked.

"I wanted to send Valdira, when he was unmarried, but he didn't attend, and so he has grown up without knowing," said Domingos.

"He knows hunting."

"He knows! He says he wants nothing more. He hasn't asked any more about the school," said Domingos. (In fact, the Salesian mission no longer takes boarding students.)

Piarina went to work, not to study, when she was taken to Santa Isabel. "I stayed in the kitchen, cooking with the two sisters. Later, I stayed in the bakery to make bread, biscuits and cakes for the padre," she said.

Piarina laughed. "I was a small girl here on the Marauiá river when the padre wanted me to go to Santa Isabel. I stayed such a long time," she said. Piarina eventually returned home when her mother died.

Our conversations were not all in one afternoon, but lasted over several days for an hour or two each as we peeled *to-o* –the task was endless – or lay in our hammocks after meals. We went over and over the same subjects as I tried to be sure I really understood what people were saying. Straightforward story-telling produced the deepest responses. Direct questions were best avoided because they too easily provoked answers that were out of context. For example, I asked many questions about the missionaries' teaching of God and Jesus Christ before realizing that the questions were presupposing an opposition between believing in Omam and accepting the Christian God. Unconsciously, I was assuming that you couldn't say yes to both.

The assumption of Domingos and Renato, on the other hand, was that Jesus Christ was a powerful *shaman* whom they hadn't heard about before, but who they had now added to their own pantheon. It was natural for Domingos, Piarina and Renato to be baptized by the bishop while at school. And they wanted their children to be baptized also, but the two Salesians who replaced padre Antonio at the mission would not allow this, according to Domingos.

"How can you do the work of the *pajé* and also be a Christian?" I asked.

"I can. The padre doesn't complain," said Domingos.

My assumption of opposites or at least of incompatibilities extended also to sickness and medicine. "How does the work of the *pajé* go with the work of the doctor?" I asked.

"It's like this. The *pajé* thinks, 'Could this be a disease of the doctors?' If the sickness is coming from the Whites, then we ask for medicine and it is cured by the medicine. With diseases of the *hekura*, you're going to feel pain! here in the liver, because they have shot an arrow. It's hidden in here. That's different and you stop eating.

"You can go on eating if it's a disease of the Whites. With the work of the *hekura* you don't eat. You're going to say, 'I want only water. I'm very thirsty,' " explained Domingos. The purpose is not to feed the bad spirit in your body.

"Is a woman ever a *pajé*?"

"There are! But not here," said Domingos. The chirps of a pair of green parakeets, the size of budgerigars, called from the neighbouring section of the *shabono*.

Renato's account of what happened when his mother died in the hospital in Santa Isabel attests to the continuing force of traditional practices and beliefs, side by side with the new credence. It's also evidence that the Yanomami have not always had easy reflections with the missionaries.

"My mother's buried in Santa Isabel. She got ill here and went to the hospital. She died within one week. I was there alone with my sister. I stayed crying with the body of my mother, holding her. I didn't want to allow them to bury her. They made a big box for her and buried her in the cemetery in Santa Isabel. She's still there today."

"No-one drank the bones?" I asked.

"The padre didn't want to allow. He wouldn't allow me to burn mum. I was very small. I didn't know how life passes. I was thinking that everyone was cremated, including the Whites," he said.

The padre took Renato and his sister back up the Marauiá to tell the sad news to their father. "But I was crying when we arrived and so he knew already. Everyone in the motor was crying. The padre took machetes, *farinha* and axes to please my father, who was very angry. Dad leapt out and wanted to cut off the padre's nose. Dad wanted my mother's bones. 'Padre! Where is my wife? If not, I'll kill you,' he shouted. And he would have killed the padre with his machete. I saw it well," said Renato.

" 'Let her stay there,' the padre said. He was afraid. He almost died and then he went downstream rapidly," said Renato. "My little sister died one week later. Dad cremated her. We went to look for plantains, but at that time there were none [in the forest] but the Whiteman in Santa Isabel had the big ones for cooking. So dad went down the river to ask for plantains to drink the bones of my sister," said Renato.

His welcome in Santa Isabel was not what Renato's father expected. "This Yanomami wants to kill me," shouted the padre when he saw him. And the padre thought to give the *tuxaua* a scare. "He told students to throw stones at my father – peh! – to frighten him – peh! peh! Poor dad! He suffered with fear. The students chased him, throwing stones almost landing on his head to crack it open. Dad ran and ran," said Renato. His father escaped by jumping into the river and swimming away. "It was television! Real television!" exclaimed Renato, having seen the magical box in Santa Isabel.

"Time passed – te-te-te-te – we stayed a long time at Irapajé [the site of an earlier *shabono* between the waterfalls]. There were lots of plantains, oranges, mangoes, *açaí*," said Renato. It was here that Renato's father, the chief of the community and discoverer of the *nabe* fell to the arrow of a *hekura*. "The *pajé* tried to save him but couldn't, so my father was lost and he died," said Renato. The body was cremated and later the *shabono* destroyed. "We knocked down everything for nothing to remain because he'd died. We had to leave," he said. It's the custom to abandon a *shabono* when a chief dies and the furious *hekura*, dwelling in him, is released.

"Dad said to me, 'My son, you can't live here. It's better for you to go away.' He feared his spirit would kill us. He was a strong *shaman*, very strong. Everything was cut down when we left. Alippe and I came up the river with our families," said Renato. Alippe was so different in temperament to Renato, as a toucan is to a chattering parrot, that I hadn't realized he was Renato's elder brother. He had never been to the *nabe*'s school so let his brother talk about the Whiteman on his behalf. He retained a graceful rhythm whether gardening, attending the fire or inebriated with *ebene* and chanting and dancing each afternoon. Alippe rarely spoke to me but would nod while listening to the conversations with other people and called me sometimes to his hearth for a bowl of boiled smoked *peccary* (wild pig) or to share a plate of plantains.

Alippe's reticence contrasted sharply with Gabriel's self-assertion and noisy laughter. Gabriel was Renato's brother-in-law and the two men spent much of each day in each other's company. The relationship of brother-in-law is the closest between two men in the *shabono*, closer than even brothers, who may have competed with each other to gain their wives. Renato and Gabriel shared meals, planted their gardens close together and their families sometimes went to gather *to-o* together. Gabriel liked to wise-crack but this only partially disguised his serious temperament. He refused, for example, to talk into my tape-recorder in Portuguese because he said he didn't speak the language well enough to explain himself clearly. Yet sometimes, he would answer casual questions with a humorous candour. I asked him on one occasion what he thought about the life of the Whiteman.

He laughed. "I think he has a lot of food," Gabriel replied. "But I don't want to live there; only to eat! And then we come home. I don't want to be like that, to lose my Yanomami life. Only to travel there and get a few little things, [such as] clothes and hammocks. I have to return to my land. I grew up here. I wasn't born there," he said.

3

Every day in the *shabono* was a week of experience, though the hours often seemed to pass slowly. There was time for every task yet we did nothing in a hurry. Howler monkeys often started our days at dawn when the horrific shrieking of rival mates pierced the mist to proclaim their own troop's feeding area. These baritone howls, produced from under vast drooping chins, might carry the distance of an hour's walk in the forest. They served as alarm calls to summon young men in the *shabono* to go hunting, while the rest of us lingered, reluctant to exchange our snug hammocks for the chilly morning air.

Piarina, Domingos or Aoria usually made hot coffee (from my sack) and tapioca porridge for breakfast. This warm glutinous mess appeals more to the stomach than to the eyes. "It's hot frogs' eggs!" I joked to Domingos each time he brought the big gourd bowl. "Croak, croak, croak! Jump about! Jump about!" I exclaimed to everyone's merriment. Tapioca was one food I could still eat without my throat or stomach rebelling. I could barely swallow chunks of smoked *xama* liver at meal times and instead sipped its meaty soup mixed with *farinha*. My physical energy and optimism were recovering steadily after the pneumonia but it was a curious side-effect of the antibiotics that I only wanted to eat scones with lots of sultanas or fresh fruit salad. My underpants hung loosely round my waist and my arms looked like poles. I didn't know what to do with myself, yet was barely content only peeling *to-o* every day.

Renato usually sent his young son José to call me for a second breakfast in his home each morning. "Midnight. A child was born," Renato announced suddenly one day.

"Whose child?" I asked foolishly.

"My child. A girl," he said. Francesca, his wife, smiled over the edge of her hammock near the back wall, away from the sunlight, where she lay with her new-born baby. She rested that day, nursing her daughter and directing the other four children in cleaning and cooking. So little drama surrounded the baby's birth, though Piarina told me later she had heard Francesca's cries during the night, that the child might have been brought to the *shabono* by a bird. Kinswomen came to see the daughter but no men came for several days. I presumed it would not be good manners, as a man, to ask Francesca about the birth. The usual custom is for a mother to leave the hammock when her waters break to have her baby outside the *shabono* either alone or with an older woman as midwife. A deformed baby would be killed at birth, before it had gained its spirits, thus becoming a human being.

Sharing meals with the families of both Renato and Domingos revealed a friction between the two men. They treated each other as cousins not half-brothers, and rarely sat in each other's hammock. Both wanted me to be staying with them; both wanted to know what the other was telling me. They seemed to be straining against the ties of family, position and experience that bound them together, however they might behave in public. Both seemed irritated by the same attitudes – both Yanomami and *nabe* – that they exhibited in themselves.

Each man warned me about my foolish offer to leave the motor canoe with the community. The offer had seemed a straightforward exchange, but now I knew I'd blundered but couldn't think how to remove the anxiety without breaking my promise. I wanted Renato to tell everyone in the *shabono* that the motor canoe was for the use of the whole community, not just himself as Domingos was murmuring.

"Don't leave the canoe if he behaves like this," Domingos warned me more than once.

"Domingos talks a lot but he doesn't *know*," replied Renato. "It's your canoe, you must do as you think," he said, though his voice told be he'd be offended if I did this.

"If he doesn't know, then you must teach him," I replied. A wiser man would have kept quiet.

The disruption the canoe was creating reminded me of the Coca-Cola bottle in the film *The Gods Must Be Crazy*. Perhaps we could sink the motor canoe, I thought, just as the Bushman had thrown the bottle from a cliff at the end of the world because it brought too much disharmony to the community.

Renato only nodded, adding to the enigma of his character. He was the person who had originally invited me to the *shabono*. On that occasion, he'd defended my presence against the suspicions of others, notably Domingos and his kinsmen. He was still patient in excusing my gauche social manners and ignorance of Yanomami. He seemed to enjoy trying to explain the Yanomami cosmology to me and the day-to-day life of the *shabono*. We discussed the issue of the motor canoe at length so it was inconceivable to me that Renato would not have told Gabriel that the community was gaining the motor canoe in exchange for working with me but, in the end, it was Gabriel, and not Domingos, who was to erupt against me with furious hostility.

Almost everyone went out of the *shabono* during the mornings to hunt, to fish, to plant plantains or carry home baskets of manioc roots. One morning, Valdira suggested after breakfast that we should go downriver in the canoe to gather *to-o*. I readily agreed. Nine people and the dog called Três Cruzados, climbed into the four-metre canoe to go on the trip. "We won't be able to bring back any *to-o*," I muttered to myself, but if so many people wanted to go, then let's take them all!

We motored about two miles down the middle of the mud-brown water until Domingos pointed in to the right-hand bank and we drew under the dark roof of branches extending over the water. Everyone helped themselves to the plantains and *farinha* we'd brought before starting in single file into the forest.

"Honey," exclaimed Valdira after walking a hundred yards.

"Honey," repeated his younger brother Mateus, pointing thirty feet up a tree. I nodded but couldn't see either bees or hive. Valdira started chopping at the base of the tree with the axe he'd brought while the rest of us continued deeper into the gloomy trees which quickly absorbed the thuds of Valdira's work. Walking in the forest with the Yanomami was always like going into the January sales with experienced shoppers. Their eyes glanced everywhere, for more honey, for *to-o*, for magic plants, for *açaí*, *custirim* and other palm fruits, for the perfect stems of a reed with which to make arrows, for lines of fire ants that have a nasty bite, for spines and serrated leaves that can cut your feet. They were listening too for the chomping of wild pigs eating fruits, or the chattering of monkeys high above our heads.

"Pull this," Domingos told me when we stopped. He held out a thin vine hanging from high over our heads. I pulled. Nothing happened.

"More!" he said, giggling at my weakness. I sat down with the vine under my backside hoping my weight would jerk the vine free from the high branches where it was rooted. Suddenly, the vine snapped. I fell over backwards onto the soft forest floor of rotting leaves. Domingos laughed loudly and helped me to my feet.

There's no safe technique for pulling down *to-o* from the branches of the trees, though a gradual pull is better than one yank; otherwise the vine falls like a released spring bringing down a shower of small branches, leaves and creepy crawlies.

"They don't bite," said Domingos, the first time a drizzle of black ants fell with a vine. They were *cona-cona*; harmless, Domingos said, but respect is the best form of self-defence in the forest. The smaller the ant, the bigger the bite. The leaf-cutter ants, one of the largest of the thousands of species in the rain forest, have such large claws that some Indians have used them as sutures to close cuts.

Piarina and Valdira's wife wandered together for several hours gathering plants in a wide circle around us and calling from time to time to tell us where the *to-o* hung the thickest or where the palm fruits were ripe. Mateus, being only a boy, wandered at will with his catapult. He aimed at small birds to take home as pets but caught nothing. "I'm a hunter," he boasted when Piarina asked what he was doing.

"Then where's the meat, dear boy?" she replied. Thunder growled as we worked, though Domingos dismissed my anxiety not to be soaked again in a rainstorm. "It'll not rain," he said with a smile, "because I've 'thought' of it."

The thunder came closer and the light in the forest faded into twilight while Domingos busied himself chopping down a palm tree heavy with ripe fruits.

The rain was upon us with a single breath of wind like God exhaling; falling first with a pitter-patter on the leaves high over our heads. Several minutes passed before the rain reached us on the forest floor. Domingos by then was dancing with his arms outstretched like a whirling Dervish, and singing, then running through the forest round us. Shrieks and sudden laughter came from his mouth while his head rocked from side to side. He ran round, then fell on his back on the forest floor and his eyes watched the rain while he giggled with the spirits.

The rest of us huddled under a little shelter of long palm fronds hastily built by Valdira's wife. I kept my T-shirt down the front of my trousers, hoping to keep it safe from the heavy cold rain. Domingos came to crouch with us in silence when his dance eventually ended. Valdira crouched face to face with his wife, their heads relaxed on each others shoulders and their arms round each other in intimate embrace. Sometimes they kissed or laughed together. No-one spoke while the cold rain ran down our bare bodies.

We were all shivering, with no sign of the rainstorm slowing, when Valdira said softly, "Let's go back." He led us through the trees, first to gather a basket of palm fruits, then the pot filled with black honey from inside the trunk of the tree he'd felled, and finally to the canoe. Thankfully, someone had covered the motor with its plastic sheet. We left the bundles of *to-o* to be collected the next day and motored home through the hard falling rain.

"How can there be so much water in the sky to rain like this every day?" I asked. An explanation came from Alippe, Renato's quiet brother, when we were back in the *shabono*. "The moon's filling. This brings more rain," he said.

How welcome were the crackling fire at home to dry our bodies and the hot meal of smoked *xama* meat, rice (from my sack) and *farinha*. Hours of rain brings calm to the *shabono*; everyone lies wrapped in their hammock or occupied with small jobs. Piarina sat in her hammock making a large basket in her lap. Valdira was binding bright blue feathers (from the sides of parrots) into small bundles to wear dangling from his arms when he danced. Domingos and I continued stripping bark from *to-o* gathered earlier.

"My mother was a hunter not like other women," said Piarina when she started to talk. "Mummy looked like a man. She killed alligator and armadillo. Mummy was a hunter, she was strong, she didn't have affairs. For this she was so good, a mother who did everything," said Piarina.

"And the men accepted?" I asked.

"She went with dad and so they brought home so much game. Dad loved mum a lot for this. It was all like this. My aunt was like this as well. Two hunters who were women. They gathered everything, fruit trees and honey. We were never hungry," she said.

"You've not continued as a hunter?" I asked.

"I'm her daughter and I don't know why I don't hunt. I don't go to the forest often because I look after my garden," she said.

"Is the women's work the same today as long ago?"

"It's the same thing. Well, cooking has changed. Now it's [done] cut up. It's easier now," she said.

"And the division of work between men and women?" I asked.

"The same thing today as long ago; the men don't help the women. The only man who helps me is Domingos. My son doesn't help because he goes out to hunt for game and to fish. When my children were small, Domingos used to hunt and fish in the morning," she said.

"Now he has Valdira to do this," I said.

Piarina laughed. "Valdira is a very good hunter. So I don't allow Domingos to work like that, only to work in the garden cutting down trees. The others don't help their wives. They think to let their wives do the work. This man is a better man for me," she said.

"The other women have a lot of work," I said.

"They suffer. The women have to work more. 'Go fetch water to take a bath.' This is what the men say to them."

"Why do the women accept? Why don't they say, 'No! You want water, then go to the river!' "

Piarina and Aoria laughed loudly.

"Why don't you speak like this?"

"No, if the wife says, 'Go take a bath!' the man will say, 'No, I'm not going. Fetch me water here.' And he wants me to fetch water," said Piarina.

"But why does the woman accept? Why don't you say, 'Take a bath in the river!' ?"

Piarina laughed again. "No, we don't say."

"The men are soft," I said.

Piarina laughed. "I won't allow Domingos to learn to do this. 'It's better you go to the river,' I say to him and he goes to take a bath there."

We talked again of land; of what in Yanomami is called *urihi*, meaning "land as a place where you belong". I was told so many times that a land belongs to the people who were born there, that I could find no reply when people asked me to tell the Brazilians that they, the Yanomami, were already living here.

"Why does the Whiteman want the land of the Yanomami," asked Domingos.

"To take the riches of the land and because the Whiteman's like that. He always wants more," I said.

"Don't the Brazilians have their own land?"

"Yes, but they want all the land."

"He can't want!" replied Domingos. He said that Renato didn't believe what was being said about the land being taken. 'It will not happen,' he says. 'I believe it will,' said Domingos. He suggested sending a reply to Davi from all the chiefs of the Marauiá river.

"It would be good to go from here and to visit Davi, to see with your own eyes what he's saying," I suggested. This was the 250-mile journey from *shabono* to *shabono* through the forest that I wanted to make with people from the communities on the Marauiá river. My hopes soared that Domingos might be willing to make such a journey to bring together leaders of the scattered communities from east and west. Domingos nodded to my suggestion so I left him to think about it.

The rain stopped late in the afternoon leaving the sky a dull grey. Three women were sitting in the shallows of the river washing their young children, while the older ones followed me to bathe before dark. We plunged into the tepid water like happy ducklings, splashing and diving, glad to be free of the *pium* flies in the air.

"Throw me!" shouted José, Renato's younger son, followed by lots of others shouting, each with their arms outstretched, to be hurled and dropped like stones into the water, with their fingers plugging their noses. Each one bubbled to the surface with giggles of delight and holding up their arms to be thrown again and again. The young girls stood alone in the water watching our fun. "Do you want?" I asked. One girl nodded and laughed, and waited to be thrown then came up wiping her face and laughing again. Everyone who wanted had a turn and when we tired of it, my back became their ladder and my shoulders the platform from which to jump. The mothers in the shallows laughed with delight to watch a dozen children chasing the *nabe* and my own arms outstretched like a monster's, splashing and chasing them in the water.

A grandmother appeared suddenly on the sandbank, hands on her hips, her whole face painted red, her breasts drooped almost to her faded pink shorts. She stood shouting at us all, then she pointed to me, then she shouted again. The children stopped in silence. "We're in trouble," I thought while she shook an arm at the children and at me, then marched back up the path to the *shabono*. One of the young boys translated: "She was saying if we climb up your back and jump off your shoulders again and again, then you'll be ill again in your chest!"

We ate boiled fish, *farinha* and rice for supper, sitting in a circle on low stools and helping ourselves from the pots in the middle. The air was warm and clear of *piums*. A dozen fires blazed like beacons marking each family's home in the darkness. A million stars shone so brightly that they lay like a blanket over the trees. Whatever was happening in the forest in the east seemed remote from Ironasiteri; Domingos referred to it as the region "Over *there*!"

The fires at night discouraged vampire bats and provided a warmth that was welcome during the middle of the night when the air was damp and chilly. People lay in their own hammocks or with relatives, or sat on low stools after supper, beside burning oil wicks, until the conversations waned and they went home to sleep. Each day's activities left me weary and glad of the long sleep during the nights which lasted as many hours as the days (being on the Equator).

Living with the people of Ironasiteri was often like riding a roller-coaster with high rides and plunges between our two cultures. What impressed me most was people's courage in tackling the challenges brought by their discovery of the *nabe*.

Henrique, one of Jacinto's sons, did not think it incongruous when he told me he wanted to exchange his radio-tape recorder for a canoe. He was sitting at the front of his house, with the back of his radio open on his knees, cleaning out dust from inside with a short length of *to-o*. It was a surprise to see the radio and I couldn't imagine what Henrique wanted it for.

"Why a canoe?" I asked.

"Because I don't have a canoe," he said with an apologetic smile, "but I must exchange the radio outside [the *shabono*]."

"Doesn't anyone here have a canoe to exchange with you," I asked.

"No. They don't want the radio here. They say it brings sickness when I hear people speaking. I know that it doesn't, but they say, 'Don't switch on the radio, it will bring malaria and other sicknesses.' So no-one wants the radio here," he said.

I tuned into the BBC World Service on his radio one day, to hear news in English about the Berlin Wall.

"What's this?" asked Henrique.

"It's a big wall," I explained slowly in Portuguese to the incredulous faces gathered round us. "It's a big wall built by the leaders in another land to keep their own people inside the land," I said, myself unable to believe that such an absurdity could be true.

"Why don't they change their leaders?" someone asked.

"They can't."

"Why don't they kill them?"

Our talk faltered because I couldn't explain about armies of hundreds of thousands of men with guns, nor about a dictator coercing millions of people. Yanomami *tuxaua* were leaders by eloquence and example, not by force; for when the Yanomami go to "war", they send a volunteer raiding party of a few dozen men.

Although Henrique is Jacinto's son, he belongs to the generation that has grown up handling metal tools and clothing, as *nabe* children today might grow up with computers. He takes the tools for granted and is keen to learn to read and write Portuguese.

"I want to know how to count and about the money so that the *patrão* doesn't rob me when I take *sorva* and *to-o* to exchange," he said.

"What contacts do you want with the Whiteman?" I asked.

"Coffee!" he replied with a broad smile. "Well, to sell *to-o* so we can buy the things."

"You don't feel there's a danger that you'll become a Whiteman yourself if you buy many things from the Whiteman?" I asked.

Henrique paused for several minutes. "Uuuhmmm," he murmured in polite disagreement. "You think we're going to stop using *ebene* and become Whitemen but we're not. We use *ebene* to be able to save ourselves. We can't abandon it. Medicine serves for malaria, for tuberculosis, for fever and after fights (i.e. injuries), medicines serve for these, only these.

"Medicine doesn't cure everything. If it's the *hekura* wanting to kill my son, so then I'll take *ebene* and – sh-sh-sh – ready! And I go 'thinking thinking'. And my son becomes well. If we abandon *ebene* we shan't be able to cure and we shall die. We'll die quickly," he said.

"How old are you?"

"Me? I don't know," Henrique chuckled. "I don't know what a month is, so for this, I want to study," he said.

I left him to take photographs of Jacinto's three wives sitting in their hammocks making baskets. A man may marry as many women as he can cope with and for whom he can properly provide. Jacinto married his wives after the deaths of their husbands to whom he was related. As in the Biblical tradition, a man must look after his dead brother's wife. How else will they have a man to hunt for them?

"Oh, Dennison," said Paulo, who was Jacinto's neighbour, "You can take photos of the women working but not of these things here," he said, touching rows of "sacred" objects hanging on string from the rafter at the front of Jacinto's home. I readily agreed not to photograph what looked to me like pieces of alligator bones.

"They're a sign," said Domingos when I asked what they were.

"A sign for what?"

"This is for sickness. When we're breathing like this," he explained, breathing noisily as if suffering tuberculosis, "then the *hekura* sees when he comes and he stops."

Valdira came home dragging a bundle of *to-o* but with neither game nor fish for the cooking pot. He was sweaty and went off immediately to take a bath in the river.

"Now we'll have honey," announced Domingos with the same mischievous giggle with which he announced all such treats. He took a chunk of black honeycomb from a pot and stirred it in a pan of water. "We drink it pure," he said when he started to pour the juice through a sieve to strain out the dead bees and pieces of wax comb.

Valdira came back from his bath already dry from the hot sunshine, cut a sliver of *to-o* and sat down on a stool facing the arena. A small basket at his side contained his mirror and a few pods of *urucú* with their oily red seeds. He held the mirror in his hand and began to paint his lips and lines curving across his face. Next, he put on black armbands, made from the scalp feathers of the forest turkey, and took down scarlet macaw tail feathers from the rafters to insert inside his armbands along with the clusters of parrot feathers prepared a few days earlier. The purpose of this decoration was to look beautiful when he took *ebene*, transformed himself into a *pajé* and danced to the *hekura*. Valdira was still in training, but eventually he would attract one of these humanoid spirits to live within himself as guardian and helper.

Only Valdira and Renato would allow me to take photographs of them dancing and chanting as *pajés*. Gabriel and Domingos explicitly forbade it, saying such a thing would be dangerous when their "souls" were exposed like this. I respected each person's wishes about being photographed, including the women and children, and never took a picture of people sleeping if I did not have their prior consent. One sneak photo would have destroyed all trust between us.

"You must drink all of this," said Domingos passing a large gourd bowl to me. "Take as much as you want." The brown opaque liquid tasted like bitter-sweet lemonade and quite different from other honey mixtures.

"*To-ti-hi ta-wi*," I repeated, meaning delicious and wonderful!

Valdira painted my face when he was done. "Now you're Yanomami," he jested. Domingos took my photograph, as if to make sure I got an equal dose of whatever came from the machine or whatever amount of energy was taken from real life to make the image. Mateus then blew *ebene* powder up his brother's nostrils and within twenty minutes Valdira was chanting and dancing and had become his *pajé*.

I lay down in my hammock to sleep again, prompting people when they passed to ask, "Are you ill again, Dennison?"

"Lazy," I replied, though feeling weak and irritable and still not eating properly. I knew many people wanted me to take the *ebene* snuff, as I certainly did myself, but not while still recovering from pneumonia.

Mateus climbed into the hammock with me to tie a string of beads round my right wrist while his brother's chanting called across the *shabono*. "For friend," he said, swaying in the hammock with me. I still wear his gift today.

"They're beautiful, that's why we want," answered Domingos to my unspoken question.

"Worth a ton of shotguns," was how Renato had once described his long necklace of tiny red, green, blue and yellow beads. They were traded from the Salesian mission at Xamataweteri, farther up the river, and it was a source of frustration that the padre no longer exchanged beads with them. Aoria worked skillfully at a small frame in her lap threading intricate squares of beads that I'd brought. She never spoke to me, perhaps because I spoke little Yanomami, but she was aware of everything going on and once exclaimed with laughter, "He's looking at me!"

Renato called me to his home later in the afternoon to talk more about recording a message to Davi. I'd mentioned several times about going to visit Davi but Renato only nodded at the suggestions.

"I want to say, 'I'm not a *nabe*. I am Yanomami. Real Yanomami. I know I'm speaking Portuguese now but I'm true Yanomami. A Yanomami all the time. My *ebene* doesn't stop. It's Yanomami; the life of the Yanomami. I'm speaking to defend myself from the White, because I graduated from school but I'm not going to leave the Yanomami [life]. It's not abandoned, no!' " said Renato. He paused to watch Gabriel dancing and chanting in the centre of the *shabono*. His legs paced gracefully back and forth to the rhythm of his singing, with arms outstretched as if in broad embrace and his erect head catching the full strength of sunlight.

"Each person sings a different music," replied Renato to my question. "We teach only our music at first to someone who has never taken *ebene* and wants to study to be *pajé*. After about fifteen or twenty days, then he's going to sing his own songs, according to what we have already taught him. He'll sing for himself and he goes singing his own song."

"Where does the music come from?"

"From the spirit of the *pajé*. At the moment, we can see nothing, so we take *ebene* up the nostrils. You [become] like being drunk with *cachaça* only *cachaça* is poison and *ebene* is not. Wait twenty minutes for the effect and then you ascend [transformed into your *pajé*] and you're ready to sing. The music appears in our mouths; well, it doesn't appear, it's just music in the front of our mouths. Open your mouth and the music comes and then a man goes singing," he said.

We sat watching Gabriel in silence, before Renato suddenly started saying aloud what he was thinking. "No-one's going to let go of the old life. We continue always, as the Whiteman continues his life. I also want to live the life as the first Yanomami. Today, I speak Portuguese, I wear clothes, but in the business of what I feel, well, my penis is still tied up under my belt," said Renato.

We laughed at this sudden reference to the traditional male posture of wearing the foreskin of their penis tucked under a string belt. In fact, most men of Ironasiteri now wore underpants. "The belt really hurt so much, so I took it off," said Renato.

Gabriel was by now sitting down with the other men taking *ebene* and Valdira stepped into the sunshine in the arena to continue the dancing. This is whom we saw, though he was already transformed into the *pajé* within himself and had gone through the portal of the *shaman*'s labyrinth. These shifts between the dual realities of human and *shaman*, of natural and supernatural, happened so easily, so obviously for the people of Ironasiteri that they hardly ever mentioned the transformation. The distinction between the realities was clear to everyone, except myself.

"Jacinto has gone to Manaus," said Gabriel when he came to Renato's home after an hour and lay in his brother-in-law's hammock. "The *shaman*'s gone to the city," he said.

"To Manaus? How?" I asked, sensing I was missing his real meaning. Renato explained that Jacinto-as-*pajé* had gone into the forest to study and he had descended from there to a place in the underworld with many many people like a city. Manaus is the only city Gabriel or Renato have visited and so, in an effort to help me understand, they'd compared the place with many many people where Jacinto had gone, to the city of Manaus.

We woke early in the morning a few days later, to the rhythm of Jacinto's chanting, unwavering despite a drum-beat of hard rain hitting the ground. His lone voice sang with a low pulse by which every murmur and movement of the community was unconsciously regulated. I do not know what he sang, for the words only "came into his mouth", as Renato had explained, as his spirit pleased him within a general pattern of song. No other voice was heard from the circle of families while we lay wrapped in the snug folds of our hammocks, waiting for *farinha* porridge to cook on the crackling fires. A grey sky seemed to be hanging over us like a tombstone. I had no idea then that my conduct that day was to kill any chance of the journey to meet Davi.

Valdira and most of the other men left the *shabono* to fish or hunt when the rain paused in mid-morning. There could be no lunch until they returned with fish or game. Groups of women and some men took big baskets and machetes to go dig up manioc in the gardens. I was feeling exhausted and fretful and stayed home with the older men to strip yet more *to-o* bark.

I was alone and listless and did not work long before laying down again in my hammock to doze. My stomach was still not settled and I could not yet eat a meal without the food I *knew* I liked gagging in my throat. Valdira returned with a few fish to boil for lunch at midday. I lay afterwards in my hammock to sleep. *Pium* flies bit at my face and hands. I felt lonely and was bored.

I woke to the drone of a motor canoe on the river. "Who's that?" I asked the children nearby, knowing that no-one had asked permission to take my motor canoe. We all went to the river bank to discover my canoe, loaded with children, racing round and round the river. "Joy-riding! And without my permission," I cried, suddenly flushed with anger. I didn't wait to see who was in the canoe but went back to my hammock to wait for the guilty party to return.

"Who asked permission to use the canoe?" I asked Renato.

"Didn't Gabriel come?"

"No! If people want to use the canoe they only have to ask, but they must ask," I said, angry and determined to stand my ground.

Gabriel laughed when he did come back and told me he'd forgotten to ask. His smile infuriated me.

"Well, I'm going to padlock the canoe and then no-one can use it!" I exclaimed and marched across the *shabono* to get the key from Daniel, Renato's middle son who looked after the canoe. Daniel's calm reply could have warned me of my madness. Instead, I went down to the water and padlocked the canoe to a tree.

"You shouted," said José, Renato's youngest son as we returned to the *shabono*. His surprise could have been a second warning. I lay in my hammock hardly conscious that everyone was waiting to see what would happen. Renato came over with Gabriel with his eyes glaring at me. "I asked you yesterday when you were recording Yanomami. You said, 'Hm, hm.' Today Daniel was teaching me how to go with the motor," rebuked Gabriel.

I didn't remember and I didn't believe him. "Then if we listen to the tape, we will hear you asking," I replied. Domingos smiled. Gabriel stood with hands on his hips, shifting his weight from one leg to the other as energized with rage as I was.

"I'll leave the canoe when I go but I'm still the owner now and responsible for the canoe," I said. "I don't take your shotgun without permission!" I said. None of what I did makes sense now, so perhaps it was fatigue and boredom that caused my mind to snap that particular afternoon.

Gabriel's anger was inflamed further by whatever I said. "You think I'm a child. Well! I'm grown up too. It's not just the Whiteman who's an adult! No! You come here recording our stories, taking our photographs. And you'll earn money from this and the Yanomami will gain nothing," Gabriel shouted. "Whites are all the same. You talk a lot but you don't help the Yanomami!"

I sat in stunned silence, with my head bent forward, listening without reaction and wondering what to do. Sunlight faded from the *shabono* as a thunderstorm gathered overhead.

"No more recording! No more recording! You recorded me. I want it back," shouted Gabriel. Everyone in the *shabono* had stopped their work or play and was turned towards us. "No! You keep the recording but the clothes, the machete that's enough [payment]. No more." Gabriel was no longer even glancing at me but marching back and forth in front of Domingos' home with his anger pouring out. "You can go. You can go. Take the canoe. We don't want you here," he was screaming for everyone to hear. "I respected you, Dennison. But no more. No more!"

I sat in my hammock, watching Gabriel, stung by what he'd said with such vehemence, waiting for him to finish, with no idea of how to answer. His rage flooded the community, flooded over me like a dam of venom that I had inadvertently burst. I was cold with fear at his harsh voice, his hand pointing in my face, his legs bent and taut ready to fight. Goose-pimples rose on my legs and arms. Nothing I could do would change whatever was going to happen. I waited, knowing my life depended on the reaction from the whole community.

"I'm not afraid. I've said I'll break the machines of people who come here. I'll destroy your photo machine and your tape recorder," Gabriel shouted.

The thunderstorm in the sky never burst over our heads but the grey light of twilight gathered in the *shabono* and Francesca and the other people who lived opposite Domingos faded into a half-light until only the orange flames of their hearths were clearly visible. When Gabriel finally stopped shouting Renato said calmly, "Dennison erred. He should have waited to hear all Gabriel's explanation. If they went only to teach Gabriel to use the motor, no harm is done."

I nodded my head. "I became suddenly hot, too hot," I said softly. Gabriel was no longer listening. "I acted too quickly, but I have not said, 'No!' to anyone to use the canoe. Maybe Gabriel did ask permission but I cannot remember," I said.

No-one spoke for five minutes. "I've spoken and that's all," said

Gabriel and walked away to his hearth. No-one else spoke. Everyone watched and waited. I felt as isolated and as vulnerable as an *agouti* in the forest (a South American rodent the size of a rabbit).

Jacinto came over to Domingos' home, gave me a big smile, crouched on his haunches and asked in Yanomami, "What has happened?"

Domingos explained. Jacinto looked at Gabriel in his hammock and at me without smiling. He nodded his head, muttered a few words and then paced slowly home.

The silent tension snapped abruptly when Henrique spoke in Yanomami to Renato. Then Domingos spoke and all of a sudden five men were shouting at each other across the arena. I understood nothing and, not understanding, imagined something yet more terrible was about to happen. This only showed how little I understood of their hospitality. I'm going to be expelled by the community before nightfall, I thought. If not, Gabriel may destroy the canoe and my tapes and films during the night.

Domingos suddenly spoke in Portuguese in the midst of his shouting across the *shabono*. "He's denied nothing!" he exclaimed, before the quarrel reverted to Yanomami and I was isolated again amid the storm of anger. The quarrel seemed to be dividing according to kinship around Domingos and Renato, revealing the importance of allies and the vulnerability of being alone.

Jacinto came back to Domingos' home in silence about twenty minutes later holding a small white plate with three plantains. Without a smile or a word, he handed the plate to me then turned away and walked back to his hammock. By this generosity, he signalled his support to the *nabe* and his impatience with the bickering. The arguing faltered. Renato returned to his own hearth.

I sat in my hammock in silence until after nightfall before I thought it was safe to speak. "I'm going down the river tomorrow," I said.

Domingos nodded. "It has to be your decision," he said.

"If you want to gather medicinal plants for Piarina, let's go up early to Apuí and then I can go downstream after midday. If two people come with me, they can bring the canoe to the community," I said wearily.

Domingos nodded.

"You're leaving tomorrow? Why?" asked Valdira when he heard.

"I don't want to stay in the middle of a quarrel. It's better to go," I said.

"And the motor?" he asked.

"If you come with me to Santa Isabel, then you can bring the motor back here as I promised. I know I've recorded many stories and taken photographs and when I came I said I'd leave the canoe and the motor. I will do what I promised," I said to Domingos and Valdira and to the other men who came after supper.

"Stay. This is nothing. Gabriel's not from here," said Piarina warmly. We sat near the fire, in darkness except for the reflected glow of flames on our faces. I was silent. Domingos said he'd warned me what would happen about the canoe. "I once took the padre's motor canoe without permission and he was furious when we returned. He hit me on the head so hard that I cried until the night," said Domingos, giggling at his escapade. His story did little to lift my sombre mood.

Valdira reinforced my unease when he slept in his hammock at the front of the house, next to mine, rather than repositioning it beside his wife's for the night near the back wall. Will Gabriel attack during the night, I asked myself? As a precaution, I put all my tapes, film and notebooks into my hammock to sleep with them.

Despite my fears, it was a strange paradox that I actually felt drawn closer to the Yanomami. The argument had revealed the cohesion of the community. Gabriel's anger showed me his deep dislike of the Whiteman's arrogance. His fury and threats expressed courage according to his manner. I no longer doubted that he would defend his own way of being against the mean, uncivilized people from outside. Probably he would not have believed me, nor have cared, but his forthright way and independence seemed the very qualities needed to protect himself.

"Is it certain you will come back?" asked Piarina.

"No. I don't know. I don't know if I will be welcome," I replied.

"Of course you'll be welcome," said Valdira and his parents repeated his words.

Domingos asked about shotguns. "Can you bring a shotgun on your next journey?" he asked. It was a relief to talk about anything except what had happened.

"A shotgun's very expensive," I said.

Domingos nodded and his smile was amplified by the half-light in the dark.

"I've been thinking again that if I come back, I'd like to travel up the Marauiá to the headwater and then to travel through the forest to visit the other *shabonos* to go visit Davi at Toototobi. I've been thinking I'd pay a guide for every day of the journey and if we reached Davi I would pay also a shotgun. Extra," I said.

Domingos nodded his head and drew a map on the earth floor with a stick, marking the Marauiá, its headwaters and the *shabonos* we would have to visit. "I will take you. We can go together. Don't tell Renato," he said.

In this simple way, at the end of a day of stupidity, fear and dog-weariness, Domingos and I teamed up to make a 250-mile journey across five rivers through the forest. We planned to play Davi's message in all the communities on the way and to visit Davi in his own *shabono*. "I'm a chief, I will ask the chief in each place to send a youth with us to the next *shabono*," said Domingos.

I repeated that the shotgun would have to be a bonus if we reached Toototobi. "I'll be travelling illegally," I said, and I knew the journey might be hazardous. I promised to provide all the food, tobacco for the journey and to leave supplies with Piarina so that nothing should be lacking while we were away. We agreed to meet again in Santa Isabel during the first week in April, five months away, when I could return from my land and when Domingos could come to collect me in the motor canoe.

"I want to go to see the places and to meet Davi," said Domingos. "And it'll be good to have a shotgun."

Domingos, Henrique and Mateus took me upriver to Apuí early the next morning. Tall grasses and weed bushes blocked the path from the river to this other village, the main *shabono* of the community of Ironasiteri. Separate houses were built round a circle twice or three times the radius of the temporary camp at Coatá. Shoots of grass coloured the earth of the arena. No-one had stayed here for three or four months, yet the place did not seem empty of spirits. We gathered stems of ripening plantains, pineapples and a magical plant to cure the pains Piarina was feeling in her back. Domingos and Henrique showed me the closed house where, they said, the dead were buried until their bones would be clean enough to dig up. We travelled a little farther upriver, using precious gasoline, to their gardens cleared in the forest and clambered over charred, felled trunks to inspect their crops of manioc, *macaxeira* (sweet manioc) and maize.

On the way back we sat on the huge granite rock half-buried in the river bank at Apuí, eating plantains and a pineapple before going downriver again.

"Renato wants to keep the canoe to himself," said Domingos.

I repeated that the canoe and motor were for all the community and that Renato knew this. "I wanted to explain this to everyone, otherwise they would say I'm recording your stories and you're gaining nothing. And now this is what Gabriel has said," I said.

Henrique listened and watched my eyes.

"It's a surprise to me that there can be such a fight about the canoe and motor," I said, genuinely baffled to think that a community of sixty-five people could not arrange to share one motor and canoe. I had expected the leading men to be able to control when and who could use the canoe and motor. My assumptions of "community" were wrong because I had completely underestimated how much freedom the Yanomami enjoy among themselves.

Henrique gave a simple reply that expressed this profound freedom in which the Yanomami live as individuals within communities. No-one controls other adults. "They will say, 'I am not a child. I will go where I want in the canoe. It is not your canoe to order,' " said Henrique.

Our gasoline ran out half-way towards Coatá so we drifted down the river in sunshine, with Mateus paddling leisurely, until we reached home late in the afternoon. By then, it was too late for me to leave to go down the waterfalls to Santa Isabel, as I had said I would.

"Are you all right?" Renato asked me when he came to Domingos' house in the early evening after chanting and dancing.

"Yes. More or less," I replied.

"We want to record a message for Davi and Arí," he said. This request came after Henrique had talked to Renato and to the other leading men, and after Renato had also gone from hearth to hearth to speak to them. I took out my tape recorder and cautiously followed Domingos to where a circle of the men were gathered.

I sat on a low stool face to face with Renato who wanted to speak first. All the messages were recorded in Yanomami and later translated. Five men spoke. Edited excerpts are given here:

"Davi, pay attention. This is Renato speaking of Ironasiteri on the Marauiá river. We're knowing what you're saying about the *garimpeiros*. I don't want the *garimpeiros*, as you also don't want. We don't want them here to search the earth. I know they bring sickness, that everyone dies, that malaria comes and I also do not want to accept these.

"I know they bring many things – ammunition, clothes, sicknesses – [but] I don't want. Today I don't want *garimpeiros*, no-one here on the Marauiá wants. I don't want them as you don't want them.

"Good. The Whiteman who comes from far away, who comes to record, to take photos who brings some little things to please people, for the Yanomami not to lose confidence, I accept a Whiteman to do this. But as you're speaking about the land, to defend the land, I also know that the Whiteman wants to take all our land. I'm opening my eyes! I'm thinking to converse with the Whiteman about all that you're saying.

"Davi, you often go to the city, to Brasília to speak with the Whiteman. One day, I shall also arrive there. Don't think that I'll only stay here. I know that one day I shall appear there and we'll converse, us two together.

"Today I have learned, and don't want to know any more about the *garimpeiro*. So Davi, don't worry. I already have my thinking. We have all to meet, to look for our defence. I consider everyone [to be] a family. Only this I wanted to say," said Renato.

Domingos came to sit on the low stool facing me and I held up the tape recorder to record his message.

"I also don't want any *garimpeiro* here. That's my reply. If I allow one to enter and if he discovers [gold], he's not going to tell me. It'll be hidden. He'll say, 'Let's take the land.' So I don't like and I won't accept. Today, I am awake.

"We're hearing what you're saying about the land, to secure your land. Of course we can speak out. I've studied in Santa Isabel with Renato my cousin. Those who've studied have to speak out. We have to speak in Portuguese, not just in our language, otherwise the Whiteman isn't going to understand anything.

"I am defending not just Apuí but all the people of the Marauiá because the people up the river don't know anything. The Yanomami don't know what is gold. They don't see gold," said Domingos.

I had tried to explain that Brazil would shortly be electing a new president – the first elected president since the military takeover in 1964. President Sarney, appointed at the end of the dictatorship in 1985, would soon be leaving office.

"Look, one day we'll go to speak to the president, not this José Sarney who's leaving, who is taking all the Yanomami area. We're not going down river yet. We'll go to speak to Collor if he is the president. This is what we shall say: 'Why do you want to take the land. Don't do this. You are rich already. We are not going down the river to divide your land. Finish with this business. This is all shameful. The Yanomami don't come from far to divide your land. This is what you must think because at the moment you are thinking erroneously," said Domingos.

"Davi, I want an agreement with the president about the land. The Yanomami are poor. 'You are not poor. You are rich. Leave the Yanomami alone,' I shall say to him."

Domingo nodded that he had finished and called Jacinto to the low stool to speak to Davi. "I am Jacinto, the old man, who is speaking," he said to begin his history of the people of Ironasiteri. It was a complicated story of *shabonos* long since abandoned and giving the names of communities who have since divided.

Jacinto then addressed himself to the leaders of the *nabe*. "I have not studied. I don't know the pen. Why are you wanting to take all our land? You're wrong. We live here already on the land. I want to fight with the *garimpeiro*. I don't like them because they are liars. I want to break their heads with an axe," said the old man in a voice charged with anger.

"Domingos and Renato can go to Brasília for us to converse, for you all to defend our land. Go to the city. Speak to the chief there. That's all I have to say," said Jacinto.

Alippe, Renato's elder brother, repeated what the others had said about not dividing up the land and not wanting *garimpeiros*. "I don't know what gold is. I've never seen it," he said. "The *garimpeiro* doesn't divide the gold for us after he finds this in the area. He's not going to say, 'This is for you to get something for yourselves.' He's not going to say [this] for us, so for this we don't want him here."

Henrique called me to his home after supper to ask if it was true that I was leaving. I told him it was. Renato came to invite me to eat grilled *xama* liver. This is a delicacy and the invitation seemed like a peace initiative.

"You're going downriver tomorrow?" he asked when we'd eaten. "Have you lost your confidence in us?" asked Renato.

"No!" I gasped. "Well, a little," I admitted.

"Don't," said Renato, putting his arm round my shoulder. "You're a great friend. When will you come back?"

"In April, if it is possible."

"Yes, come when the plantains are ripe."

Domingos and the others accepted my wish to leave, though I no longer knew why I was insisting after the row with Gabriel had cooled, but the decision felt right. My chest ached and I was still losing weight. It would be better to return refreshed after a few months, at a time when there would be abundant food in the weeks before the start of the rainy season.

Jacinto came to Domingos' home in the morning when my hammock was already rolled and my other possessions put away in the sack. He brought a large basket, flat like a fruit bowl and decorated with red *urucú* dye and strands of black *to-o*.

"*To-ti-hi ta-wi*," I said in Yanomami, meaning beautiful. Other men arrived with baskets or slender red macaw tail feathers or arm bands made from the black scalp feathers of the forest turkey. I held each item in my hands, turning it slowly to inspect the handiwork, watched by the men and women gathering for the presentation in Domingos' home. Piarina sat quickly crushing the red *urucú* to colour the basket she made for me. Her rushed work made me realize the inconvenience of my hasty departure. Renato gave me a polished stone axe-head, with a broad sharp edge. "I found this in the waterfall of the *igarapé*," he said.

Domingos took down his beloved headdress of black fur made from the tail of a squirrel monkey. This was too much in payment for the trade goods I had brought him, but I'd spoken too much already and didn't know how to say, "No", without giving offence. Jacinto fetched more feathers from his home. Henrique brought a second basket. Valdira took down his pair of forest turkey armbands with scarlet and orange toucan feathers and gave them to me with a smile. Other men brought bows and arrows in response to this competition of their generosity.

Gabriel was the only man who didn't sit with us in Domingos' home but he came at last with a basket and a pair of black armbands. "If I didn't come, you will tell the people in your land that I robbed you," he said.

"I would not. Thank you," I replied, taking the items from him. "We're friends."

"I am not angry with you," he said slowly.

"I know. We're friends," I repeated and shook hands with him and we embraced and held each other tightly.

Jacinto brought me one of his slender tubes for blowing *ebene* up my nostrils. Henrique offered me his personal container of *ebene* powder.

"Thank you, but if I take this to my land, I'll not come back. It's forbidden. I'll be in prison," I said.

Everyone laughed. "What is prison?" asked Henrique.

"If I take *ebene* the government will say, 'You are a bad man!' and they will lock me in a house for a long time," I replied.

"Oh. We will come to get you out," he responded.

Several men asked me to bring a machete for them when I returned again. Francesca and Piarina each wanted a dress for themselves. Renato said, "We've exchanged what you are taking for what you brought. And we would like a few more small things." So I wrote out a shopping list of requests and noted the calibres of the shotgun detonators. "That's all," said each man when they finished giving me their family's shopping list of four or five items each.

The farewell of the Yanomami is simple and short, as if visible sadness might attract bad spirits. Children gathered on the river bank with elder sisters while their brothers organized the loading of the canoe. Older men and women waited to embrace those who were leaving. I embraced or shook hands with everyone and then the three young companions and myself paddled the canoe into the pull of the river's current before starting the motor, watched by everyone of the bank until we were out of sight down beyond the trees.

Alberto steered the canoe through the swift water in the middle of the river and, for most of the time, looked out for rocks and floating obstacles. Valdira, Mateus and I sat on the benches, silent, except when one of them pointed to birds or a beehive. We were lulled half to sleep by the harsh light on the trees on the bank and wakened by rain showers and for our tedious portage over the five waterfalls. We paused for a few hours at the third waterfall for Valdira to catch and grill three big fish for lunch using water weed plucked from the rocks as bait. We reached Santa Isabel before nightfall.

My young companions returned home the next morning with the motor canoe, more gasoline and gifts of tobacco. I paid my passage on a cargo boat going down the Rio Negro to Manaus. I knew I had returned to a different world because the deck of the boat was stacked with crates of empty Coca-Cola bottles. The Bushman in the film threw the Coke bottle off the cliff at the end of the world. And by then, I knew that we should have done the same with the motor canoe.

4

Davi Kopenawa Yanomami left his forest *shabono* in early December to go to London, England, to speak out about the deaths of his people and to ask for money for medical aid. His arrival in Europe – bundled in thick sweater, blue anorak, scarf and heavy boots – was an admission that the government of Brazil was not resolving the illegal invasion by *garimpeiros* despite a federal court order to withdraw the gold miners.

Davi travelled with a determined woman called Claudia Andujar who was the national coordinator of the Commission for the Creation of the Yanomami Park. Both she and Davi were invited to London as guests of Survival International. This British-based organization was receiving the Right Livelihood Award, often called the alternative Nobel Peace Prize, for its twenty-year fight in support of threatened tribal peoples around the world. The prize was founded by a young Swede who sold his stamp collection to start an award more relevant to the practical solution of the world's problems. Davi would receive the Award on behalf of Survival in the Swedish Parliament, the day before the Nobel Prizes were presented.

However, before going to Stockholm, Davi and the six other Award winners gave a press conference in the British House of Commons. It was held in the Jubilee Room, at the back of St. Stephen's Hall, beyond the security machines that are today's guardians of our democracy. A wardrobe-sized machine sniffed for explosives like a mechanical dog and the X-ray machine examined briefcases and tape recorders as they moved along the conveyor belt.

Inside, the polished corridors of carved stone and stained glass echoed with the whispers of awe-struck visitors pretending to be admiring the statues of famous men and the painted ceilings, but hoping all the while to spot political celebrities. Davi came wrapped in his blue anorak with lines of red *urucú* smeared on his cheeks and orange toucan and black forest turkey feathers in his ears. He may not have been impressed by the sombre colours of the halls and corridors, but he must have intuited the presence of prestige and power that permeates the Palace of Westminster like a vapour. Political advantage is the coinage of this labyrinth of rooms and he may well have asked himself, "What will these people care for my relatives in their thatched communities in the forest?"

From the head table with other Award winners in the Jubilee Room, Davi began his speech speaking in Portuguese, and pausing between sentences for Claudia Andujar to translate. "This is the first time I've left Brazil. I'm here to tell the problem of my people. I came here to seek support and your help because I believe that you are important people, you are authorities and you have the possibility to intervene.

"I want you to know that the Brazilian government today is not taking care of the Yanomami. They're leaving my people dying, and without help. They've let in many *garimpeiros*, without control, and now our reserve is completely invaded and the river is polluted.

"My people are contaminated with malaria, dysentery, worms, pneumonia, tuberculosis, and other diseases which are arriving. Our worries are very big. How we can cure these diseases?

"The rivers also are contaminated; the fish, the crabs, the shrimps, the game that we eat has disappeared. The forest is destroyed.

"They're doing this to us to finish us off. I am Yanomami. A son of my people. I don't want all my people to die. We want to live as you also live, because we are people too. We want to live on our land, we want to live in peace; because if the government doesn't resolve our problem I think that all my people will die.

"I've already asked our Brazilian government to pull out the *garimpeiros*. Nothing has happened. So I want you also to help me by putting pressure on our Brazilian government. It was only this that I wanted to say. Thank you," said Davi.

Claudia told the journalists that 45,000 gold miners, called *garimpeiros,* had invaded the Yanomami area since 1987 using 156 airstrips cleared in the forest. "The government could have taken them out if there'd been the political will at that time. Today, it's a real social problem," she said. President Sarney was doing nothing, despite his promises. He'd been appointed at the end of twenty years' military rule in Brazil and was due to retire within a few months. There was no doubt that the invasion by *garimpeiros* was illegal. Clear statements in Brazil's new Constitution made mining illegal in

Indian areas without the specific permission of Congress. A federal judge in Brasília on 20th October had already ordered Sarney's government to take out the gold miners pending a final definition of the Yanomami area. Action to defend the Yanomami by upholding the country's new Constitution was coming from the Office of the Attorney General of Brazil.

"Until today there's been no response. The Federal Police have suggested that the Army and the Air Force should be involved, because it is impossible for a very small group of policemen to do this job. We're waiting to hear," said Claudia Andujar.

An initial reaction to this request for assistance to take out the illegal *garimpeiros* had already come from Brazil's military leaders. *O Globo*, Brazil's main newspaper, quoted Brigadier Sócrates da Costa Monteiro, Comandante Geral do Aeronáutica (General Commander of the Air Force) saying that he considered the operation impossible and "an impropriety to think that the minister should be responsible for the closing of the airstrips."

Salvation for the Yanomami would have to include relocating the small-time gold miners to other places, "where they can work and live as human beings as well," admitted Claudia Andujar.

"Were British companies involved?" asked Member of Parliament Max Madden.

"No," replied Claudia. This is not entirely correct. Almost one year later I saw an invoice for fuel from Shell on the desk of *garimpeiro* leader José Altino Machado. The fuel depot, decorated with a large Shell sign, stood only three yards from his office at the airport in Boa Vista, capital of the *garimpeiros*.

This revelation, alas, was in the future and was typical of the problems of investigating and piecing together what was happening both inside the large remote forest and inside Brasília's bureaucracy 2,000 miles from the Yanomami. The details of people, places and companies and of where, when and what acts of negligence or duplicity were being committed came only as a trickle during innumerable interviews and from newspapers, reports and personal observation. This was one of the frustrations of the public campaign to defend the Yanomami. Argument could only be made with facts – and facts were difficult to uncover and to verify.

However, so much is being done in secret or by deceit to destroy the Yanomami, that every opportunity such as the House of Commons press conference, was important to reveal the truth.

Late in the afternoon, after the House of Commons, we gathered with mugs of tea in the cramped offices of Survival International above the rush-hour traffic on London's Edgware Road. British playwright Ray Connolly was to interview Davi for one of the series of features about childhood he was writing for *The Times*. During this interview, and throughout Davi's visit to Europe, the difficulties of mutual non-comprehension between the Yanomami and the Whiteman became apparent. Our philosophies of living contrast so much that even sympathetic individuals are sometimes baffled by the other culture's different attitudes and approaches to being human. Plain ignorance enlarges these gulfs and doubles the challenges of either Yanomami or Whiteman helping or explaining something to the other. Ray Connolly wanted anecdotes and facts about Davi's upbringing with which to highlight the threat to Yanomami children today. His questions were sincere yet they seemed often to be missing the point. Davi was tired.

"So if you could tell me exactly where you were born, and the kind of lifestyle you had?" asked Ray pressing the record button of the tape recorder then looking down in his notebook for the next question.

"I don't know very clearly where I was born," answered Davi, with Claudia acting as interpreter.

"He's a chief I understand," said Ray.

"No, he's not," replied Claudia like a helpful schoolmistress.

"That's wrong," said Ray, with a low whistle of exasperation.

Davi was born about thirty-five years ago in a place called Maracana (the name of a bird in the parrot family) and later moved downstream with his family when the New Tribes Mission built an airstrip and a station.

"Did they move because of education?" asked Ray.

"At first there was no mission. They came looking for us. We Yanomami do not need the mission," said Davi.

"The missionaries asked them to get nearer to the place where afterwards the mission was established," added Claudia in English. "It was an attraction. His people moved there and I suppose they find it to their advantage to be near a place where there is a mission."

"Can you tell me how many brothers and sisters he has?" asked Ray.

"I don't know if he will know it," said Claudia, "because during a lifetime there are various types of marriages that can take place."

"An American taught me to write and read and also taught me Portuguese. And we caught illnesses. I had a sister, a brother, they died there of chickenpox and measles," said Davi.

"Could he describe the daily routine of a child growing up in the rain forest? I know it's very difficult, isn't it?" asked Ray.

"You know these are questions, well, that can I tell you? They don't have it systematized like this," explained Claudia. She plunged into Portuguese. "When you were this age [showing a photograph of a child of seven years], did you accompany your father on the hunt?"

"My father had already passed away. I met only my mother," said Davi.

"Your father died of what?" asked Claudia.

"I don't know! I don't know!" replied Davi, his voice rising with annoyance and fatigue. "It's a secret. This is not explained when the people die, because our customs are different to yours."

"Yes. Was it an illness of the Whites?" persisted Claudia.

"I don't know, nothing was explained. I was very small. I was one or two months old."

"Ah!" Claudia turned to Ray. "He doesn't know. In Yanomami society, when somebody dies, they do everything to cancel out all his memory. You cannot speak about the person any more. You can't even say his name any more," she said. "Who took your father's place to bring you up?" she asked, turning to Davi.

"My uncle Roberto."

"Your mother married Roberto after your father died?"

"She stayed with my uncle Roberto," replied Davi, disgruntled by the tedious questions.

"What happened to your mother?"

"She died of measles."

"What age was he then?" asked Ray.

"More than ten years old," said Davi.

Another question followed each answer, back and forth like the click-clack of a shuttle in a loom handweaving a cloth. Every answer needed a new question to clarify or double-check the meaning.

"How old was Davi when he became a warrior?" asked Ray.

"What do you mean?" replied Davi.

"When did you feel that you were no longer a child?" explained Claudia.

Davi chuckled. "I don't know. When we reach fifteen years old we feel to be a man," he said.

The interview meandered like an out-of-focus dream for another half an hour, despite the mugs of tea. We all wanted Davi to tell his story and to make a good impression, yet the seemingly neutral contrivance of a journalist's interview was confirming the gulfs between our two cultures. Every question confined Davi to answering within our own priorities and outside his own context. For example, Ray asked about Davi's religion – something that doesn't exist for the Yanomami as a concept separate from being alive and hunting and having babies.

"Is Davi Protestant? He went to this Protestant mission," said Ray.

"No, he's not Protestant! He has the beliefs of his people," replied Claudia tartly.

"Ah, good. What are those?"

"He's a *shaman*. A spiritual leader," replied Claudia.

"Him?" asked Davi, thinking Claudia meant Ray.

"No! You!" Laughter broke some of the tension.

"Maybe he is too as well, I don't know," answered Claudia.

"I'm a writer," said Ray.

"Yes, I am a *pajé*. I'm a *hekura*," replied Davi.

"Does God choose him? Is it a vocation?" asked Ray.

"Did someone speak to you to be a *pajé*?" Claudia asked Davi.

"No-one spoke with no-one. We want to become a *pajé* to help the people. We work with the old *pajé* who knows very well how to call [the *hekura* spirit]," said Davi.

"Did that entail leaving home and going and doing something separately?"

"No," replied Claudia. "All learning among Indians is done by imitation. Nobody tells you, 'Go here, do this, don't do this.' He hates that. All the Yanomami hate it. You learn by observing how another person behaves. And shamanism is also something that you learn by imitating and by hearing the older person talk to you and talk about the myths and so on. It's in the village because it's the *shamans* of the village who teach the young ones."

"What's the oldest memory you have of when you were a child?" asked Claudia.

"I remember my relatives. I feel them very much. We lived very well, free, without problems. We lived quietly. Nothing was happening. There weren't *garimpeiros*, there were no invasions," replied Davi swiftly.

"When did the first Whites come?"

"The first I saw was when I was six years old; a person from the Comissão Limite [the Commission to survey the border between Brazil and Venezuela]. I fled. I was afraid," said Davi.

"When did he first see a car?" asked Ray.

"He wants to know everything!" joked Davi in Portuguese. "I'll become curious and ask him questions!"

"You can do so!" said Claudia. Davi had been about fourteen years old when he'd first seen a car in the small town of Barcelos on the Rio Negro.

Davi was not like a rehearsed propagandist wearing an easy half-smile or self-righteous indignation. He yawned when bored by the questions, and laughed at absurdities or sat with both his hands grasping the chair when listening. Minor changes in his mood were not hidden when he let his mind wander. This seemed rather rude but it was refreshingly honest and appealing. It also repeated the wrong impression that has become a stereotype about many Indians, that they are "child-like" because they do not mask their emotions nor repress their feelings.

It was soon time for the photo call; Davi was reluctant but consented with the reassurance that the picture would help his people and not just be thrown on the fire. "I don't like to have many photos taken because it damages our health and our energy," he said.

He turned to Ray Connolly just before leaving the room to say, "If you have a strong soul, if you are a real *shaman*, you have to help me."

Davi left the office of Survival International to rush to a public meeting in one of the large halls of Regent's College in Regent's Park. The college's lights shone like beacons through the dark and cold foggy winter's night. I arrived with two companions who'd come specially from Belgium; Simon LeFevre, whom I'd last met in Santa Isabel two months earlier, and another man called Daniel who was one of the volunteers of KWIA, an organisation like Survival.

The six winners of the Right Livelihood Award faced 400 people when they looked down from the long table on a platform at one end of the hall. Here was Davi's chance to tell his story in his own way. Stephen Corry, the director of Survival, talked first about their work. Then Davi began to speak of the invasion of the *garimpeiros* and the arrival of diseases and death.

"You do not know me. I am a true son of the Yanomami, I'm wearing clothes because the Whiteman doesn't like a nude Indian. We are few who speak Portuguese. The majority of the people don't. We're few and we learned the Portuguese language in order to defend our community.

"I want you to be interested in helping us as friends because we are people just like you. We are human beings. We want to live in peace, in good health also, we want to preserve our place, our land," said Davi in Portuguese, to be translated phrase by phrase. The gulf from the afternoon, that Grand Canyon between his views of the world and ours, seemed to close tightly, like friends embracing, as Davi spoke.

"If we don't struggle, the people of the forest are going to become less. I know this is the work of the Brazilians. They don't want to respect the Yanomami," he said.

Davi spoke to the audience about Simon LeFevre, Daniel and myself. "They work on the [river] Marauiá and speak a little of our language. I want them to continue helping my people so that not every one of my relatives will die.

"I am a Yanomami who thinks, and Yanomami thinking is something different. We don't think like the Whiteman thinks. My interest is to preserve my land and the game, fish and health and the Nature that created us. To preserve also our customs, our religion; a religion that's also different. Our creator is Omam, whom only the *shamans* can see.

"We are children of Omam, not just me, but you too; black, Indian, white, we are children not of God; for us, it's Omam. He is not a destroyer, he is not like President José Sarney. He is the spirit of the Indian, he looks after us well.

"This is my work. I have a good thinking to preserve our forest, our land, our place, and our health so that we can live. Without land, without life. I love very much my forest because I am of the forest.

"My fight continues to the end, even if the Brazilian government does not change. I live a long way from here and I wish you not to forget me. Help me so that we will work to take better care of the world, if we want," he said.

Davi asked a question near the end of the evening that was misleading in its apparent simplicity, because it also brought us to one of those portals of the *shaman*'s labyrinth through which so much more of the Yanomami cosmology might be revealed, or by which we might so easily pass without noticing. "Do you want all the Yanomami to die?" Davi asked simply.

Claudia translated this into English as, "What do you think will happen if all the Yanomami die?"

"Part of us will die too," a woman called from the back of the hall.

Claudia translated this for Davi as, "If the Yanomami die, a part of humanity will die also."

"That's true. Not only the Yanomami would die. The Whites are going to die. We would all die," he said.

The audience applauded the words and the evening meeting ended.

Several months later I read a transcript of conversation in which Davi took anthropologist Bruce Albert into the labyrinth of the *shaman* to explain what he meant when he said the *nabe* would also end when the last Yanomami dies. Bruce Albert asked Davi about epidemics and the pathogenic smoke that causes them. It was typical of Davi's wider perspective that his reply explained not only the sicknesses but also the worldwide burning of rain forests and global warming due to the burning of fossil fuels.

"I will tell you what we think. We call these epidemics *xawara*. *Xawara* is what kills the Yanomami. Now we know the origin of the *xawara*. At first, we thought that it propagated itself alone, without cause. Now it is growing a lot and spreading all over. What we call *xawara*, our ancestors kept hidden for a long time. Omam keeps the *xawara* hidden. He keeps it hidden and doesn't want the Yanomami to interfere with it. He says, 'Don't play with this!' And so he hid it in the depth of the earth. He also said, 'If this comes to the surface of the earth all the Yanomami are doing to start to die for no reason.' Having said this, he buried it deeply. But today the *nabe*, the Whites, after having discovered our forest, have been overtaken by a frantic desire to take out this *xawara* from the depth of the earth where Omam had guarded it. *Xawara* is also the name that we call *booshike*, the substance of metal, that you call "ore". We're afraid of this. The *xawara* of ore is [the] enemy of the Yanomami, and also of you. It wants to kill us. If you start to be ill, then it kills you. We Yanomami are very worried because of this.

"All is well when the gold stays in the cold of the depths of the earth. All is really well. It's not dangerous. When the Whites take the gold from the earth, they burn it, they mix it over a fire as if it were *farinha*. This makes its smoke go out. Doing this creates the *xawara* that is the smoke of gold. Afterwards, this *xawara wakexi*, this 'pathological-smoke' goes spreading in the forest where the Yanomami live, but also to the land of the Whites, to every place. We're dying because of this smoke. It becomes the smoke of measles. It becomes very aggressive and it kills all the Yanomami when this happens.

"A type of smoke escapes when the Whites guard the gold inside tins. This is what the oldest people, the most venerable who are the great *pajés* have said. A smoke starts to come out when the Whites put gold inside tins, with well-closed lids, and leave these tins exposed in the heat of the sun; a vapour you don't see that spreads and starts to kill the Yanomami. Whites also die, in the same way. It's not only Yanomami who die. The Whites may be very numerous but they'll all end up dying. This is what the Yanomami say amongst themselves.

"When the smoke reaches the shoulder of the sky, the sky also begins to become very ill; it also starts to be touched by the *xawara*. The earth also becomes ill. Even the *hekurabe*, the helping spirits of the *pajés*, become ill. Even Omam is affected. God also. We're very worried because of this.

"There's also the smoke of the factories. You think that God can chase away this *xawara*, but he cannot repel this smoke. He also will be dying of this. Even though he's a supernatural being, he's going to become very ill. We know that things go like this, so that's why we're telling you these words. But the Whites don't pay attention. They don't understand this and think simply, 'These people are lying!' It's because of this that there are no *pajés* among the Whites. We Yanomami have *pajés* who inhale the powder of *yakoana* [also called *ebene*] that's very potent and thus we know of *xawara* and we're worried. We don't want to die. We want to stay numerous. But now the *garimpeiros* have come to us and come close to us.

"Despite the fact that Omam has guarded the gold under the earth, they're excavating the floor of the forest and taking out great amounts of it. The *xawara* has grown a lot because of this. It's much higher in the sky and has spread very far. It's not only the Yanomami who die. We're all going to die together. The sky is also going to start dying, like a Yanomami, when the smoke fills as far as there. So, when the thunder's ill it's going to be heard without ceasing. The thunder is going to become ill and is going to shout with anger, without stopping, under the effect of the heat.

"The Yanomami *pajés* who have died are already many and they're going to want to take revenge. When the *pajés* die, their *hekurabe*, their helping spirits, become very angry. They see the Whites making the deaths of the *pajés* [who are] their 'parents'. The *hekurabe* are going to take revenge, they're going to want to cut the sky in pieces for it to fall down on top of the earth. The sun is also going to fall and all is going to be dark. When the stars and moon also fall, the sky's going to be dark. We want to tell all this to the Whites, but they don't listen. They are another people and they don't understand. I think they don't want to pay attention. They think. 'These people are simply lying.' This is how they think. But we are not lying. They don't know about these things. So that's why they think like this.

"The Whites appear to increase a lot, but later the Yanomami will end up having their revenge. It's for this that the *hekurabe* are with us and the sky also, with the spirit of Omam, who says to us, 'No! Don't despair! Later we're going to have our revenge. The *garimpeiros*, the government, these Whites who don't like us . . . they are other people, and for this they want us to die. But we have our revenge, they will also end up dying' . . . this is how the *hekurabe* think.

"We, the *pajés*, are working for you, the Whites. So when the *pajés* are all dead, you will not be able to free yourselves from the dangers that only the *pajés* know how to repel . . . You'll be alone on the Earth and you'll end by dying. There won't be any more *pajés* to secure the sky when it becomes really ill. The Whites don't know how to secure the sky in its place. They only hear the voices of the *pajés*, without knowing about these things, and they think, 'They're speaking uselessly and are only lying!'

"As long as the *pajés* are still alive, the sky may be very ill, but they're going to manage to stop it falling. The *pajés* keep the sky in place even though it begins to fall towards the Earth and would like to fall. This is because we, the Yanomami, are still existing. When there're no more Yanomami, then the sky is going to fall once and for all. It's the *hekurabe* of the *pajés* who secure the sky. It can start to crack, with a lot of noise, but they manage to repair it and make it quiet again. When we, the Yanomami, are all dead, the *hekurabe* will cut the spirits of the night and they will fall. The sun will also end like this. The sky once fell [like this] when it was still fragile, in the first times. Now it's solid, but despite this, the *hekurabe* are going to want to break it. They're also going to want to rip up the Earth. One piece will be torn from here, another from over there, and yet another from another direction. All will fall, all will fall from the other side of the Earth and all will die together. This is how things are, and so we're very worried. But the great *pajés*, the oldest, tell us, 'Don't be worried! Later we'll have our revenge! We will procure their deaths in the same way that they are making us die.' This is how the *pajés* speak.

"The *hekurabes* are very valiant. They get very angry to fight when their 'fathers' die, who are the old *pajés*. [The *hekurabes* reside in the *shamans* while they're alive.] They want revenge. And so they begin to cut at the legs of the sky. But the other *hekurabe*, who belong to the *pajés* who are still alive, stop them by saying, 'Don't do this! There are still *pajés* living. The young *pajés* are taking the places of the oldest *pajés*!' Speaking thus, they manage to stop the fall of the sky," explained Davi.

"What will happen to the Yanomami if the *garimpeiros* are not taken out of your lands?" asked Bruce Albert.

"The Yanomami are going to die. We're really going to be finished. Only a small group of us will survive. No more Yanomami are going to be created after the *garimpeiros* have killed us all off. It's not going [to happen]. Omam has already gone far from this world and he's not going to create more Yanomami," replied Davi. "The *garimpeiros* don't like us. We're another people and so they want us to die. They want to work alone. They want to stay alone with our forest. We're very afraid because of this," said Davi.

"Do you want me to translate anything else?" asked Bruce Albert.

"You're going to give these words to other Whites. Then tell how it was when you were there [with us] in the beginning; how we were in good health, not dying for nothing. Tell them how we were really happy, how we hunted, how we held parties. You saw this. We held *pajélanças* to cure [people]. Today, the Yanomami don't make their great *shabonos*, that we call *yanos*, they only live in small *tapiris* [thatched houses] under a tarpaulin of plastic. They don't make their gardens, nor go hunting any more, because they're ill the whole time. This is how it is today," said Davi.

The purpose of Davi's visit to Europe with Claudia Andujar was to appeal for help in putting pressure on the Brazilian government to take out the *garimpeiros* from the area of the Yanomami, in accordance with the Brazilian federal court order. Journalists and the general public were sympathetic to the Yanomami plight, especially after Davi spoke, yet we live at a hectic pace today and I wondered how long it would be before the newspapers' stories would be wrapping fish and chips. The haste of interviews and meetings seemed such a contrast to the miserable slow deaths of dozens of Yanomami every week as malaria and other "unknown" diseases spread from community to community. The media tour was necessary, in the *nabe*'s contemporary world, if the Yanomami were to gain support, but its cruel superficiality and brevity added farce to the tragedy.

This was especially true when, at dawn the morning after the meeting in Regent's Park, we travelled north by train to the BBC television studios in Manchester. Television has done much to make us aware of the diversity and beauty of the planet and rekindle concern. But television is also a demanding beast. It feeds on a diet of only the richest foods from the choicest cuts. This diet must be specially prepared by a team of trained flunkies and served in pre-weighed portions to ensure easy digestion. What appears on our television screens is as far removed from everyday life as *nouvelle cuisine* is from a vegetable garden. Davi did not do well in this unfamiliar world where his message needed to be packaged and labelled with catchphrases.

Over breakfast on the train, passing through the mist-covered landscape of industrial England, we rehearsed what he was going to say on the programme "Open Air" at eleven o'clock. Davi spoke eloquently. The breakfast was small but still our table filled with discarded "disposable" garbage. "These people look sad and hungry," said Davi as we trundled through stations lined with commuters on an early December morning. "Is there no food for them? So much concrete. Planting concrete does not grow food for people," he said.

The train was late into Manchester and we rushed through the traffic to the studio where Davi and Sue Branford, his interpreter (and BBC World Service broadcaster on South America) were taken off to be prepared. Make-up came first. Then they were led out to the sofa on the studio-set to be wired with microphones. Davi waited to speak. "What did you have for breakfast?" asked a voice from a speaker to check their voice-levels. They were ready. They were standing-by to go live on air. Television jargon rolled. Davi froze. He answered the first question with six words that left Sue Branford to fill in during her translation by repeating what Davi had said on the train. Davi did not get much more of a chance to speak because his co-guest David Icke (spokesman for the fledgling Green Party, and sports broadcaster) gave out ecological catchphrases like discount shopping coupons, and two telephone callers told us what they thought about concern for the environment. It was difficult to imagine any situation more remote from people talking together in the *shabono*. Our ever-smiling host Eammon kept "it" moving all the time by repeating those two words that will be television's epitaph, "Quick point. Very quick point!"

Davi relaxed on the train returning to London and spoke more about the plans and projects of the Brazilian military for the Yanomami lands. "The Calha Norte project is working with Funai, the government and other authorities and people from outside, to divide up our land. It's working to kill the Yanomami Indians. They think it's good to give islands to us."

Communities on the river Demini, where Davi lives, would be confined to 33,000 hectares. "It's not enough for fishing, hunting, working, visiting others, for changing places when one *shabono* becomes old. We want our land demarcated in a single, continuous area for the Yanomami only, without mixing with the Whites.

"The Calha Norte [people] think the land is big. They think, 'What are the Yanomami going to do with this land. The Yanomami don't do anything, the Yanomami are lazy, they don't know how to do anything.' This is what they think. And they fly in a helicopter to count the Indians. I believe they count less in order to speak a lie. To say, 'The Yanomami are few, so let's divide them up and give them only a little.'

"We're going to lose our land if there's no fight to defend. That's why they want to make the islands, to constrict us like a *jabuti* [tortoise] in its shell, like a chicken-house to become prisoners. We don't want anything of this. We want our large single area.

"The biggest problem is health; medicines to save the lives of my people. We're needing and asking for money to be able to charter an airplane, to be able to buy a Toyota, and for an electric light generator to be able to work at night.

"The other *tuxauas* don't know the problem. They're dying because of this. *Garimpeiros* arrive in the *shabonos* to speak with the *tuxaua*, saying they're friends, saying they'll give food, shotguns, clothes, old hammocks, and the *tuxauas* believe them so the *garimpeiros* stay.

"The *tuxauas* don't speak Portuguese. They don't know how to defend themselves. They think the *garimpeiros* are their friends, but they are not their friends. They're only friends of gold. They make promises to the Indian but they give only illnesses to the Yanomami to kill them. The *garimpeiros* are like termites. They scatter when you throw water on them but then they come back.

"I'm afraid of gold. If I dig for gold my spirit will be hurt. I don't want to be hurt, digging a hole like an armadillo," commented Davi.

"Everyone is ill far inside the area, where no doctor goes, where I don't go. There are no children. They're dying directly of malaria, flu, dysentery and gunshots," said Davi. (The incidence of malaria in one area had risen to 91% from 3% of the population.)

"What do you think of the reply of the Whites?" asked Simon LeFevre, who, like me, had come on the train with Daniel, his Belgian colleague, as the only way to speak to Davi between his engagements.

"The reply of the Whites is only to promise," said Davi. He told us of the Assembly of the Yanomami that he'd organized between several communities in 1986, before the invasion of gold-miners. "[It was] for us to stick together to defend our land, not to allow the Whites, the *garimpeiros* to come in," said Davi. Guests included Brazilian senator Severo Gomes, who had worked for years to get a guarantee of Yanomami lands, and CCPY, Funai and the Federal Police. "They saw that my work was strong, they were frightened, so they prohibited it," said Davi. One year later all non-Indians who were witnessing the invasion, epidemics and sporadic shootings were expelled from the area by the Federal Police. No action was taken to expel the *garimpeiros*.

Davi had a couple of questions for us. "I'm asking whether you have any interest in secretly prospecting for gold and cheating my relatives."

"I have none; only pen and paper to tell the story of the Yanomami. I'm only a writer," I replied.

"We don't know how to look for gold," replied Daniel.

"It was only this that I wanted to ask. Also, are you married?" asked Davi.

"Yes, I'm married. I have two sons," replied Daniel.

Davi said he didn't want us mixing with the Yanomami women, nor marrying them and taking them away, like American anthropologist Kenneth Good who returned to the US with a Yanomami bride. "This is bad for you, because the newspapers will say that foreigners are creating sons in the Yanomami houses. I'm fed up with this," said Davi.

Simon said he was going to start a school in Apuí, though Renato wanted to move farther downstream.

"Hm. Downstream. Fleeing to the prison," remarked Davi. "It's not good to live beside the Whiteman. You have to stay separate," he warned.

I gave Davi the taped messages from Ironasiteri and talked of their desire to meet him. He welcomed my proposal to travel through the forest from *shabono* to *shabono* with a group of *tuxauas* for them to see for themselves the devastation brought by *garimpeiros*. Davi promised to welcome us to his community if we arrived in April.

Davi's last public meeting before going to Stockholm was organised by Survival International at a Quaker meeting-house in central London. About 250 people filled the room for the meeting chaired by Dr. John Hemming, board member of Survival International and Director of the Royal Geographical Society.

Claudia Andujar spoke about how she had first met the Yanomami on an assignment as a photo-journalist from her home in São Paulo. It was during the building of the Perimetral Norte highway by the Brazilian army through the middle of the Yanomami area in 1973. Construction brought epidemics of flu and measles to the Yanomami. "Half the populations of villages disappeared within a short time. I was there, I witnessed that. It changed my life and I felt that I had to change my work," said Claudia, in her clear nasal voice. The Commission for the Creation of the Yanomami Park was founded in 1978.

Claudia told us about a meeting in the Brazilian senate, the day before she and Davi had left Brazil for Europe, attended by the president of Funai, some entrepreneurs organising financing and employing *garimpeiros*, doctors, members of Congress, Indian leaders, CCPY and other organizations defending Indians.

"The president of Funai declared in front of everybody and the Press, that they had no power and no ways of handling the situation of the Yanomami. It was an open declaration of total failure and he invited the organizations – whom they'd rejected from the Yanomami area in 1987 – to return and to do whatever we could.

"The entrepreneur spoke as if the Yanomami area was his personal possession. He said, 'Whoever goes into the area is someone I'll allow to enter, and if I don't allow them, he won't enter,' reported Claudia.

"The doctors declared, 'Yes! We have to do something.' But what can they do if the *garimpeiros* continue to be there. As far as we know, about 20,000 gold miners are also contaminated with malaria. It's just one population contaminating the other.

"We agreed, however, that even in this situation something had to be done, and this is how we came to Europe, Davi and I, to make people aware of this terrible situation. We'd like you to contribute in speaking out about what's happening and also we're trying to raise funds to start an emergency health programme without which the Yanomami are condemned; knowing, however, that if the Brazilian government doesn't have the will to take out the *garimpeiros*, the Yanomami will have no chance to survive."

Davi spoke after Claudia. "My Brazilian government doesn't want to hear or to see my Yanomami people. It thinks that we are animals. On the contrary, we are people like you. We have mouths to speak and we have things to say.

"I'm saying that the Whites also suffer like us. The *garimpeiros* are being used by the government. They're slaves. The Brazilian government doesn't worry itself with the poor people of the city nor about us. It doesn't respect and doesn't know how to respect. The government doesn't think of the future, not even of one son or one grandson," he said.

Davi accused both police and military in the state of Roraima of complicity in the invasion and the deaths of his people. "They protect only the *garimpeiros* because the *garimpeiros* give them gold," he said. Since the start of the invasion in 1987, taking gold and tin ore from the Yanomami land had become the main economic activity of Roraima. Local politicians do not want this to stop.

"My work continues. My work will only end when the situation's resolved, the *garimpeiros* pulled out, the airstrips closed, and our land demarcated in a single, large area for the Yanomami to live alone in peace.

"We Yanomami are an ancient people and more Brazilian than they are," said Davi. "The man who lives in Nature doesn't want it destroyed. I'm not a destroyer. I'm a friend of the forest and look after [it] well. I want to teach you, so that you can also think as I think. You cannot think of destroying.

"It was Omam who created all of us – Yanomami, and you English also, except you don't realize it. I know this, even though I don't have books or papers. My papers are in my brain," he said, making the audience laugh.

"I'm fighting to preserve our sacred place, where the *Shabori* lives, where the clean spirit lives. Not a spirit like Sarney or the rich men but a spirit preserving the whole world," said Davi. He then spoke in Yanomami to incant the *hekura*, or spirits, to aid his work.

"The government thinks we're little birds to be put inside a cage. They say this because they're accustomed to living in a chicken coop, for the city is enclosed. But we don't want this, we don't want the cage. We've been free, living without the chicken coop. My struggle was born for this."

Davi was especially critical of Romero Jucá, the governor of Roraima and the former president of Funai. "He claims to know us, to have visited us. He claims to be able to talk about our problems. But he hasn't, he doesn't, he's a liar. It was he who opened the hand (sic) to allow the *garimpeiros* to enter. He's a Boa Vista defending the *garimpeiros* not to leave because he wants to win votes. It's not only him but other businessmen, farmers and others who are with him defending the *garimpeiros* to take out more gold for them to get richer.

"Jucá wants to have the richest city in the world – a gold metropolis. He wants a city like this one [London] – clean and everything made of gold. This is what he wants and he's not going to stop," said Davi. "Let's work together. I want you to continue the fight, to continue to write letters to all those you know and to join our friends who want to help the Yanomami," he said.

Only one presidential candidate in Brazil, the left-wing trade unionist known as Lula, had promised to take out the *garimpeiros* if elected. Fernando Collor de Mello, the right-wing candidate from the small north-eastern state of Alagoas, was making no mention of Indians in his campaign.

"I don't trust Collor. He's a friend of president José Sarney, a friend of Jucá, a friend of the Army," said Davi. But it was Collor and not Lula who was to be elected president of Brazil.

A man in the audience asked, "Is there any [direct] action being taken by the Indians or friends of the Indians against the gold extractors?"

"That's impossible. What would you do, or even all the people here, in front of 45,000 armed people? The Yanomami actually reacted against the *garimpeiros* on the first days of the invasion but, when they started to be shot, they instinctively knew that they were at a loss and had no way of reacting," said Claudia.

Support for Davi and the Yanomami was expressed in many ways. Survival International launched an SOS Yanomami appeal to raise money for medical supplies and doctors, after Funai had declared the problem beyond its capacity and reopened the Yanomami area.

Tam Dalyell, the Member of Parliament for Linlithgow, who'd met Claudia Andujar while Davi had been up in Manchester, gave me two boxes of House of Commons chocolates for the cause. A woman in the audience paid fifty pounds to SOS Yanomami and went home with the chocolates.

The British Government, through its Overseas Development Agency, offered money for a health project. Thousands of people sent donations to Survival and signed a petition addressed to the future president of Brazil. Sacks of letters arrived at the Brazilian embassy in London and other European capitals, or people wrote directly to the Brazilian president and to the heads of the Federal Police and of Funai.

What good would it do? It was surely a leap of faith to support the Yanomami, yet people responded to Davi's appeal with generosity and commitment. It was as if their own humanity depended on the Yanomami survival.

Davi went to Avebury while in England, with Stephen Corry, director of Survival International, and Claudia Andujar. He toured the standing stones, one of the oldest prehistoric sites in Europe, bundled against a misty, cold day, with a sniffly nose and his hands deep in the pockets of his padded anorak. He could feel the presence of the spirits. Claudia explained: "He says Omam put these stones here because they sustain the sky; they don't permit the sky to fall and for the world to end. That's why they're eternal. Some day, in the very far future, these stones will fall and the world will end."

5

The man who leads the *garimpeiros* in the Yanomami area has the sort of head that sculptors like to carve into stone statues. His face is large and hard. His broad forehead is balanced by a greying curly moustache and beard. His olive eyes are sharp and bright. They hold their audience with an unblinking gaze, as a snake might fascinate a mousey victim. His voice is forceful, even when he speaks softly; his sentences sound like orders issued in the expectation of obedience. His large hands tap on the desk and his fingers jab the air to emphasize his points. He explains the situation of the *garimpeiros* and the Yanomami with an absolute conviction that wins supporters and scares his opponents. He is José Altino Machado – the family name means axe – the founder and long-time president of the Union of Syndicates of *Garimpeiros* of the Legal Amazon (USOGAL), founded in 1985 and comprising eighteen unions and four professional associations.

I met José Altino several months after the first operation of the Sarney government to remove the *garimpeiros* from the land of the Yanomami, but what he said later explains much of what happened in the first weeks of January 1990. We met in Spain during a four-day seminar about the Amazon, organized by the University of Salamanca, with two other men from USOGAL who acted as his side-kicks and who operated the video camera with which Machado was recording his performances for party political broadcasts during elections later in the year.

It was difficult not to admire – and to fear – José Altino because, like all great orators, what he said was based on what is true. José Altino Machado did not publicly slur the Yanomami and admitted, "I cannot say the *garimpeiros* are the best thing for the Indians but they're the only [contacts] they receive." He explained the geographical situation with a mixture of facts, statistics and fictions that was overwhelming.

José Altino had come to Salamanca in northern Spain to defend the gold miners of the Amazon, though there was nothing about his swashbuckling confidence to give any sense of being on the defensive, and to explain what he called the "social reality" of the Amazon.

"For all of us, there are three Amazonias in the world. The first Amazonia is the one the Press publicize, fed by the official information; the second Amazonia is the one produced by our emotions, the one our sentiments imagine ought to be. The third Amazonia is much more fundamental for all you of the First World and for all the people of the planet. It is the real Amazonia. It is there for what it is, without excuse [apology]," said José Altino.

"Organizations like Cimi [a Catholic church missionary group] and Survival International don't like to talk with us because we don't allow the right to dream," he said.

Indians were attracted to *garimpeiros* more than to anyone else, he said, because the Indian, "wants to participate in whatever form of consuming. He wants the things that he knows and that give comfort. It's not that the *garimpeiro* is good for the Indian, he's not, but it happens that this is what is transmitted," said José Altino, accusing church and pro-Indian support groups of trying to keep the "Indian" in zoological gardens. "He doesn't want to stay," said José Altino.

"Lamentably, we don't work with the emotions that we feel and even less in the sense to transform those who belong to USOGAL, or all those other peoples who live in Amazonia," Machado told 150 people at the seminar in Spain.

"I'm strongly against the proximation of *garimpeiros* with Indians, but this is not the social world in which I live. This is not how I see these things. I cannot turn myself into a saviour of the world for the *garimpeiros* and for the Indians, because the world in which I live behaves differently. So I have to rationalize and I have to look for legislation and adaptations for the world that's around me," he said.

"There's not a *garimpeiro* side nor an Indian side, but one social reality," he said. "My country is divided in two. We represent the real faces of the country, the face that doesn't have culture, the face that works to produce! And the face that doesn't have the resources of the electronic media, but which is the true face, with its brutality and grossness, but which does produce," he said.

What was the driving force behind this social reality that gave excuse to so much? It was an economic anarchy into which most Brazilians were sinking. Brazil's inflation had taken off again, like some prehistoric people-eating bird, from zero per cent in late 1986 to 7,000 per cent per year by January 1990. You needed 140 of what had been Brazil's largest banknotes in 1986 just to buy a small cup of coffee by 1990. Big companies and civil servants insulated themselves from the effects of inflation by index-linking their prices and salaries. The profits of some companies went up even measured in US dollars. And there was no slowing down in the building of big houses in Brasília, the centre of government of the country. Meanwhile, the amount of food that the minimum wage would buy had actually fallen by fifty per cent. Public condemnation of inflation was common but no-one felt roused to action. Inevitably, tens of thousands of impoverished people fled from the cities and the farms of the Northeast, north into the Amazon. The Amazon has always been Brazil's dumping ground for poor, illiterate, and often ill, people hoping to leave their misery behind.

According to a census conducted by USOGAL, which José Altino quoted without pausing for breath, the number of *garimpeiros* working in the Amazon trebled from 254,000 in December 1986 to 810,000 just five months later. This included, he said, 11,500 Indians also working in *garimpos*.

José Altino separated the men he called professional *garimpeiros* from the newcomers when he wanted to remark on the professionals' good behaviour, but mixed them whenever he argued for the size of the problem. "We were responsible for 400,000 people in professional work and today we cannot be responsible for the behaviour of a country." The newcomers, he said, were "nothing more or less than the rubbish of a national political [situation]."

The Amazon is too vast, and so much of it is too remote, for government, USOGAL or the Catholic church to produce numbers that could be statistically accurate from thousands of isolated mining camps scattered in a forest the size of western Europe. However, it is certain that tens of thousands of men and some women arrived in the Amazon in the late 1980s, continuing the flood started in the 1970s with the bulldozing of the TransAmazon highway. It was a flight from greed, from negligence and the failure of Brazilian society, not a planned flow generated by "development". The people arrived in the Amazon because there was nowhere else to go in search of a better life. In Brazil, this means only regular food, decent clothing and somewhere to live. Most Brazilians don't enjoy these basic amenities despite a thirty-year surge in the country's wealth.

"*Garimpagem* in Amazonia today involves five million people; 1,200,000 direct workers in *garimpagem*, producing in Amazonia two billion dollars a year in gold and maintaining many many industries in the south of Brazil. Our class produces eighty-six per cent of Brazilian gold. Our class is the greatest producer of tin in the world – very important for our government and for the economy of our country," asserted José Altino. Actually, the tin ore and the gold produced from the area both destabilize the legal mining companies by increasing supply and depressing prices.

The Yanomami are not the enemy in José Altino Machado's fight, though they are the people who are being destroyed. For him, the Yanomami are non-combatants caught between White fighters in a wrangle over mineral rights.

The *garimpeiros* take all the risks to discover mineral deposits but the government then hands over their discoveries to the mining companies, he said. This was the injustice which José Altino said he was fighting to stop.

His strategic aim was to discover mineral-rich areas before mining companies – which he called "houses of corruption, houses of chains' – and to keep the companies out by championing the rights of *garimpeiros*. In 1985, he organized an invasion by hundreds of *garimpeiros* of Surucucus, in the heartland of the Yanomami area, when the government leased the area to a mining company, even though the vast deposits of tin ore had been discovered by *garimpeiros*.

"We started fighting immediately. We didn't agree. Hand back to the *garimpeiros* what is ours!" José Altino demanded of the military government.

"The general said to me, 'I'm not very worried if you agree or not. You're not worth anything to agree or disagree.' "

"I'll *show* you that I'm not going to permit what you're doing," responded José Altino.

"And the general replied, 'I'll put you in jail if you enter the area.' "

José Altino organized hundreds of *garimpeiros* to invade the forest near Mount Surucucu where rich deposits of cassiterite had been discovered. "The Indians opened the airstrips for me," said José Altino and the invaders arrived during the excitement of Carnaval on the 13th February, 1985. The Brazilian Army immediately sealed off the state of Roraima and seized television video footage of the *garimpeiros*. José Altino Machado was undaunted. "I presented myself to the air base as a prisoner and I was put in a cell. I said I wasn't going to agree to being imprisoned without a judicial order. A judicial order arrived. I was transferred to the penitentiary and put in solitary confinement. I stayed four days without eating or drinking because they passed the food under the door and I didn't agree with this. 'You should open the door and put the food into my hand,' I said. They didn't, so I wouldn't eat. I stayed twenty days imprisoned by the military government," said Machado with pride. He was released one day before the end of Brazil's military dictatorship and the appointment, by the generals, of the first civilian government in twenty-one years.

Despite the run-in with the military, or because of it, José Altino was respected by military commanders with whom he often met. He claimed to speak for one million people in the Amazon in Brazil, and had set himself up as a protector of the *garimpeiro*. He liked to see himself in the public mirror as a champion of the Common Brazilian Man – the dispossessed, the illiterate, the people marginalized by society, impoverished by inflation and forgotten by the national government whose priority is to benefit the small middle-class.

José Altino accused both the Brazilian and the Venezuelan government of being hypocrites for living off the illegal earnings of the *garimpeiros* while condemning them in public and not providing health or other public services to them. Venezuela lies just north of the state of Roraima and, according to José Altino, eighteen of the twenty tons of gold produced in Venezuela in 1989 came from the work of Brazilians. "We have 16,000 to 18,000 men working inside Venezuela today," he said.

Who is José Altino, aged fifty, that he should stand as the leader and self-appointed spokesman of the *garimpeiros* of the Amazon? He is a self-made tin ore miner, entrepreneur and bush pilot; a true son of the new Brazil of the 1950s when President Kubitschek turned the country's vision of itself from the decadent cities along the coast to the occupation and development of the country's interior by building a new capital on a windswept plateau of scrawny trees 600 miles north-west of Rio de Janeiro.

Uniform office blocks for government ministries, huge paved plazas to amplify the impact of the palaces of Congress and the

Presidency rose from the labours of workers imported from the Northeast to build this dream of a greater, modern Brazil. Brasília would be "the launching pad for the conquest of the Amazon," declared one speaker at the inauguration in April 1960.

Brazilians enthused about Kubitschek's dream of creating a new future where nothing had existed. His vision reflected their own sense of prowess and optimism in the 1950s. No teenager of the 1950s, like José Altino, was likely to forget the black and white film showing Brasília rising from the architect's drawing board as a ready-made city over red earth and coarse grass. Broad avenues and individual zones for hotels, shopping arcades and blocks of apartments were declarations of progress and official conquest. No Brazilian schoolchild forgets the classroom lesson that his country was created by the physical occupation of a large part of the territory divided between the kings of Portugal and Spain by Pope Alexander VI in the Treaty of Tordesillas in June 1494. Progress came from physical occupation. Brasília was the textbook example for the 1950s.

José Altino grew up in Governador Valadares, today a small city in the state of Minas Gerais. The latter name, meaning General Mines, refers to the frenzied gold mining in the 18th century during which the area was colonized by the Portuguese. Two discoveries in 1700 and 1701 started a stampede of adventurers into the forests: "All the gullies and streams were ransacked by prospectors, and many struck gold. In the excitement, no word has come down to us about the fate of the local tribes: they evidently died defending their lands, or were seized to work in the mines, or melted away into forests that did not contain the fatal ore," wrote John Hemming in *Red Gold*. Almost as much gold came out of Brazil from 1700 to 1770 as came from all the rest of the Americas from 1493 to 1850. Golden baroque churches were built by the wealthy new colonists of Minas Gerais but most of the gold went to Portugal and to the rest of Europe.

Most of the prospectors hunted for gold in *grimpas* or hill ridges. Their activity was illegal because the King of Portugal claimed gold mining as a royal monopoly. He, like a modern nation-state, delegated the right to mine to his favoured courtiers and received in exchange royalties from their production. José Altino Machado is proud of the historical link with today's *garimpeiros*. "We keep the name today as we keep our condition of furtiveness in the Brazilian mining sector," he said.

It's misleading to think of José Altino as a prospector with a gold pan in his hand. He owns eight aeroplanes and operates his own airstrip and tin ore mine. "If ever he takes hold of a gold pan or drives the high-pressure water hose to tear down a precipice, it's to maintain the respect of a category [of men] that he controls with cunning, charisma and the voice of command. José Altino is in truth a *garimpo* entrepreneur," according to the Brazilian magazine *Istoé Senhor*.

Machado's colleagues in Salamanca spoke more bluntly than their leader about the conflict with Indians. "Why is the Indian always asking for more and more land? What the Indian needs is not more land but social assistance," said João Feijão, who looked like a handsome wrestler despite the eleven attacks of malaria suffered while with José Altino. "Amazon for us is not a political question. Amazon for us is our own life," he said. He was running as a candidate for the state legislature in the first elections in the newly created state of Amapá, on the north bank of the mouth of the Amazon. A copy of *How to Win Elections* lay on his bed to help him.

The geologist with Machado accused the Church of being primarily interested in mineral wealth. "Why else are the Indians located on the pre-Cambrian shield?" he asked. "The church has more anthropologists than doctors," the geologist asserted.

José Altino is more sophisticated than these men but the message is the same: The Yanomami have not lived in the same place for thousands of years, as their supporters claim, he argued, but arrived after fleeing from the Portuguese priests and colonists who founded Brazil. This was untrue of the Yanomami. They have always lived around the volcanic mountains that now form the frontier between Brazil and Venezuela.

"Take an Yanomami baby and you'll see that he's perfect. He's perfect like any from the civilized world, [but] a Yanomami adult is entirely degenerated because of lack of calcium, vitamins, and foods that in the past he had and which he doesn't have any more," said José Altino.

"It's not because the *garimpeiro* interfered today, it's because the White colonizers centuries ago interfered in the places where they lived and pushed them into the mountains.

"[The] only way [for Indians] to defend themselves was to go above the waterfalls, to leave the sedimentary basins of the Amazon, and the other rivers, because the boats of the colonizers couldn't get up the [rapids and waterfalls on the] rivers. And, speaking geologically, when you leave the sedimentary basin and pass the waterfalls, you're entering the kingdom of minerals," said José Altino. He described the gold in the Yanomami area as, "an open bank of money in the forest."

No-one could be other than impressed by José Altino's physical power and his style as a speaker. He was a true demagogue, thirsty for the challenge of a hostile audience, well practised with statistics like a conjuror with a deck of cards, and charming to sweeten people to his views. He propounded these with shaking arm and a voice carrying his authority to the back of the hall. It was this conviction and his readiness to speak out that had made him one of the best known of the men who lead the hungry *garimpeiros* in Roraima. If you were picking teams, you'd want Machado on your side.

The last great "rush" in the Amazon was for rubber, at the end of the 19th century, when thousands of Brazilians from the dusty Northeast, and foreigners from Europe, sailed up the Amazon on promises of the wealth to be tapped from rubber trees in the forest. Bosses supplied tools and foods on credit from their own stores up the rivers they controlled; then they waited to receive heavy balls of rubber to pay off these debts. Prices were high, interest rates extortionate and the hapless workers never paid off their debts but sank physically and mentally under the load of rubber they had to gather just to stay alive.

The exploitation practised by today's bosses is simpler. The Brazilian magazine *Istoś Senhor* called it, "Harmony between Capitalism and the law of the jungle."

Critics claim that what are called "*garimpo* cooperatives" are, in practice, paid slave camps. Everyone earns a share of the gold or the tin ore but only while fit and working. Most of what they get is paid back to the *garimpo* owner for food, medicines and the airplane ride back to the city. This was the reality for the illegal *garimpeiros*.

"I don't say that the law is bad or that the law is wrong or that the law should be different. I say only that the law is not [in accord] with the social reality existing in Brazil. The laws were made after the occupation, the indigenous areas were demarcated after the occupation," said José Altino, squarely facing the group of a dozen pro-Indian, pro-Amazon supporters in the audience at Salamanca.

The Yanomami area was first interdicted by the ministry of the Interior in 1973, two years before the first geological survey.

"The law came after the advance of Civilised Man in the direction of Amazonia. It was constructed now, without taking account of how the society was already composed.

"We're not trying to continue with the illegality [of *garimpeiros*]. We want only that there should be alternatives. Obviously, we want a space for a legal conformity [to be able to mine], but this should be done in a form of social respect," he said.

Part of Machado's appeal is his strength; part is also an apparent candour and a readiness to confess doubts and his past mistakes. Having explained the situation according to his own colours, he invites his audience to resolve the insoluble tangles he has presented.

One of the greatest errors of his life and one which he always regretted, he said, was with the Kayapó on the Xingu river in the south-east of the Amazon, when he organized the *garimpeiros* to pay a royalty to the Kayapó for the gold being taken at the Maria Bonita *garimpo*. (The Kayapó had campaigned vigorously against the royalty of only one per cent paid by miners to Funai not to the Kayapó themselves.)

José Altino's new deal paid ten per cent directly to the Kayapó. According to him, this gave the Kayapó, "an economic liberty to consume, for which they were not prepared, and gave them a political voice above the other Indians in Brazil that they weren't prepared to have. Many other indigenous communities in Brazil started watching the *garimpos* and wanting lands that had gold in order to attract *garimpeiros*. This increased and transformed the problems in our hands. This was the error that we committed in the past and the experience still pains us today," said Machado. He has since been quoted as suggesting the Yanomami be paid a gross royalty of 0.75 per cent.

José Altino ended his speech in Salamanca with a plea for fair play. The government does nothing to help the *garimpeiros* but sells their illegally-gotten gold, "with cynical smiles in the international market." The government of Brazil sold 137,000 kilograms (worth about $1,657 million) in the first half of 1990.

"This is the form of treatment that we have in Brazil! And this is the fundamental problem," he said. The crisis is not with Funai or Cimi or with foreign organizations in Brazil. "Our crisis is with ourselves and the problem is much larger than a simple crisis in a single area. The problem is the survival of *all* a society. Thank you," he said.

Machado sat down to loud applause, sipped from a glass of water and waited for questions.

According to the meeting chairman, not one Indian from the Amazon had been "available" to come to Salamanca to give their side of the story nor to counter Machado's confidence assertions. So this task was taken up by a loose coalition of pro-Indian and pro-Amazon Spanish supporters from Madrid, Barcelona and the Basque country. These young well-wishers had met for the first time the night before over *paella* and red wine and their coalition was founded on enthusiasm for the cause and desperation to make José Altino Machado answer for the deaths of the Yanomami.

Their impassioned speeches bored the audience and gained support for Machado's "realism". This conflict of images –sobriety versus naivety – was augmented by what the players were wearing. José Altino and his two colleagues wore dark suits, white shirts and ties. They looked like hard-headed bankers. The gathering of pro-Amazon, pro-Indian, pro-Greeners stood up in jeans, T-shirts and blouses in a rainbow of colours that matched their political slogans. Machado handled them with the deftness of a champion fighter.

A young man with Day-glo ginger hair, that seemed to crackle with static as he read his long and angry speech denouncing the sins of the Amazon, could be dismissed with a single question. "Have you ever been to the Amazon?" José Altino asked him.

"No," he said.

The meeting chairman twice stopped the proceedings to remind everyone that one of the purposes of a university was to foster debate amongst divergent views, however unpopular. "It's worthwhile listening to a man [José Altino Machado] who represents a million people," he said.

The well-meaning individuals stood up one after another to tackle Machado in verbal duels, but he always won and the audience grew impatient with their self-importance. José Altino was firmly in control. Each bout was like watching a prizefighter toying with the weaker man before forcing him to submit.

Only one man took on José Altino and gained the cheers of the audience. He was Fabio Villas, vice-president of Cimi; a small, quietly-spoken man who stood to explain to the audience that there were two types of *garimpeiro* working in Roraima; the hungry man working with his hands and the other who owns the airstrips, the camp canteen and the only plane flying in or out, and to whom the workers must pay their share of the gold for each service they use. "I ask Senhor Altino Machado, are you a worker in the *garimpo* or are you the owner of a *garimpo*?"

The meeting chairman ruled the question too personal. People whistled and booed and wanted an answer. Machado smiled and said he was happy to answer any questions. "People without reasonable arguments always make personal attacks," he said. "I want to say that I'm a professional pilot [with 22,000 hours of flying in Amazonia]." He dismissed the suggestion that he exploited people by saying that his secretary had worked for him for twenty-seven years and that the most recent of his sixty-eight *garimpeiros* had been working for him for five years.

Fabio asked about deaths. "You say there's no conflict between the *garimpeiros* and the Yanomami Indians. I ask you, 'What's the cause of the deaths of the Yanomami, where does the malaria come from that's devastating the Yanomami?' "

"Malaria's no monopoly of the Yanomami, nor is the right to life nor access to the resources of the state for health care. It was Christopher Columbus, not the *garimpeiros*, who brought malaria," replied José Altino angrily, adding that 55,200 people had died of malaria in 1989 out of half a million cases.

José Altino told his colleagues in a low voice after the meeting that the protesters had been really "after my liver".

On the late bus leaving Salamanca that night, I asked an English friend, "What d'you feel, now that you've met José Altino Machado? Never mind what anyone said, what do you *feel* occurred?" (It's my own belief that what people would remember the morning after such a meeting varied far more according to their own emotional responses than to the words or the logic of the arguments; this is what gives oratory its power.)

My friend Jane spoke little Spanish or Portuguese and had been much frustrated by understanding so little of what had been said. She was free, therefore, to give an intuitive report of the emotional registers of the evening. She replied, "I feel defeated already. He's so powerful. I felt cold being in the same room with him," she said. "What do you think?"

"I've met people who do wicked deeds, but I've never before met an evil man," I replied.

The last decade of the 20th century began in the state of Roraima with warnings that the *garimpeiros* were not going to quit the Yanomami area unless forced out by the government. Many of them were armed and, according to rumours in Boa Vista, the capital, some had obtained bazookas with which to shoot down aeroplanes.

"We don't want a war but we'll make one if necessary. We may be imprisoned afterwards but we'll not leave what we've taken. The federal government and those lying priests have to learn that the *garimpeiro* is a worker, not a killer of Indians. On the contrary, we help the Yanomami in the villages," said José Teixeira Peixoto, known as "Baixinho" ("shorty") and president of the Syndicate of *Garimpeiros* of Roraima, quoted by *O Globo* newspaper.

His warning passed round the bars where the *garimpeiros* gambled over dominoes and drank cold beers. They'd worked too hard and sweated too much malaria to now abandon the tin ore and the gold dust scattered under the soil of the forest. They'd found it and paid for it with hellish work. And where else could they go? There was nothing for them on the parched land of the Northeast nor in the cities in the south from where many of them had come full for hope of something better in the Amazon.

Newspaper reports in October had been greeted with anger and disbelief in Roraima. How could a judge in Brasília stop all flights into the *garimpos* or order all *garimpeiros* to withdraw from more than nine million hectares claimed by a few thousand Indians? It was impossible. It was impractical. Nothing would happen, nothing could happen, people reassured themselves.

Judge Novély Vilanova da Silva Reis's order of interdiction – sealing the area – was only provisional, until his final determination, but the federal government was required to act immediately to stop all unauthorized flights into the interdicted (closed) area and to withdraw all non-Indians from the forest.

Boa Vista waited to see what would happen. They'd been waiting more than two months already, since the end of the rains in October, to see what would happen but every report of action had proved so far to be only rumour.

Boa Vista (meaning beautiful view) had grown from a population of about 30,000 at the start of the decade to about 180,000 by the end of 1989; thousands of men arriving month after month with little more than an eagerness to work and brash hopes of getting rich. They came by long-distance bus travelling twenty-six hours from Manaus along a dirt road that was red mud in the rains and swirling dust in dry weather. The buses always rushed with axle-breaking speed near sunset to get through the forest of the Waimiri-Atroari Indians, who came out at that time armed with shotguns to close the road.

Other men landed from Manaus, after an hour's flight and a boxed snack, into the noise and activity of dozens of small planes and helicopters hopping about Boa Vista airport. Hundreds of single and twin-engined planes were flying into the *garimpos* from here every day, making it as busy as the international airports of São Paulo or Rio de Janeiro. Drums of diesel fuel, high-capacity pumps and their long hoses, cases of food and the men who worked and dreamed so hard for gold or tin ore had to be loaded and ferried to the *garimpos* half-hidden in the forests to the north and west.

Most of the newcomers came with only a one-way ticket, bought with the last of their savings or from money borrowed from their families, or from the sale of their car, house or business. Some men came with their one-way passage paid for by the mayors of towns glad to be rid of them. They were from the Northeast of the country, the impoverished region that has provided hard-working immigrants into the Amazon for a century. All these men were newcomers to the practices and lores of *garimpos*. Other men were experienced *garimpeiros* from Rondonia, in the south-west of the Amazon, expelled by the competition among miners for places to work and political favours.

Just a few men arrived in Boa Vista with spare money in their wallets for a return ticket. They did not go to the forest to work, but invested in shops, bars, gold-buying or other businesses and hoped to grow rich as gold and tin ore came through the city itself.

No-one knows for sure how much gold has been gathered from the earth and rivers of the Yanomami area by 45,000 *garimpeiros*. Unofficial production is estimated to have been about 2,000 to 3,000 kilograms per month during 1989 (worth $24–$36 million, or $800 per person). Government statistics of production are totally unreliable because the government itself estimated that less than one per cent of the gold was being officially registered, according to the head of the federal government's Official Receipts. According to the law under the Sarney government, all gold had to be sold to the Bank of Brazil at the official price. However, this was below the world price, so most gold was smuggled into neighbouring countries to be sold at the higher world price. Further amounts of gold disappeared into private vaults within Brazil, and probably Switzerland, as honey pots against inflation or revolution. Yet there was no government strategy to combat this enormous tax evasion. "We're only present at the airport and round the gold-buying shops," said Senhor Assis Espindola, head of Official Receipts. The government's lack of concern to collect any royalty on gold production in Roraima was curious. A fortune in gold and tin ore was coming out of the ground every month, yet neither the federal nor the state government showed any enthusiasm to gather revenue from the bonanza, despite lots of political rhetoric about "developing" the state of Roraima. It was as if there was another purpose to all the activities of *garimpeiros*, the flights of dozens of aeroplanes and the social upheaval, separate from the momentary value of the yellow metal.

Boa Vista's asphalted streets and rows of whitewashed houses sprawled over the flat grasslands radiating from the circular *praça* in the city centre towards the serras, or volcanic hills, covered in forest in the distance. No newcomer could doubt the business of Brazil's youngest state; the statue of a *garimpeiro* stooping while panning for gold stands like a bull's eye in the centre of the circular *praça* as both tribute and reminder. The traffic of Boa Vista circled this open grassy arena as if all the cars and trucks loaded with men and mining equipment were fulfilling a superstitious rite. The palace of the governor of Roraima (called the Palace of the Frontier), the building of the Bank of Brasil, the red and white tower of the *Globo* television station, and the Roman Catholic cathedral and residence of the bishop of Roraima, and other public buildings, stand round the rim of the *praça* to overlook the *garimpeiro* who's work is never finished.

Newcomers wanting to join the gold rush waited in bars and hotels down the street from the gold shops, hoping to make new friends who could get them into a *garimpo* and show them the way of working. Many were recruited to work the machines of the *garimpo* bosses – the men who operated the mining in the Yanomami area like regular company businesses. José Altino Machado was one of these bosses and controlled his own airstrip and tin ore mine. (He also ran an air taxi business.) They finance the parties of men searching for gold and tin ore, finance the cutting of an airstrip in the forest and the purchase of pumps and other equipment, and food and fuel. Everything must be flown to their clandestine airstrips from Boa Vista and they must hire men to work for them in their *garimpos*. The bosses must also keep "sweet" the people in power in the military, police, political and administration areas because the operations are illegal. The risks and start-up investments are huge, matched only by the profits.

The miners' scramble for gold or tin ore tears the forest apart; torrents of mud are flushed out with high-pressure hoses to be pumped through machines where the gold, in fine powder form, is caught. Waste pours into streams and rivers, or fills stagnant pools where mosquitoes thrive. Gold and impurities are separated by rinsing them in water with mercury and burning off the mercury to reveal the precious yellow droplets. Fish are killed by the pollution and the miners themselves absorb large doses of the toxic metal.

The workers at a site receive about thirty to forty per cent of the gold (or money based on the weight of tin ore) recovered and this must be divided between the teams of, usually, four to six men. The remainder stays with the boss or *patrão*, who pays for diesel, for the pumps and other expenses of the work. However, the workers must pay their own food, clothing, medicine, shelter and the flights in and out of the *garimpo* every few months. These essentials are available only from the *patrão*. Each man pays for these from his own earnings which may diminish quickly in sites with little gold. If it does, a *garimpeiro* may go hunting in the forest for monkey or wild pigs, in direct competition for the meat with the local Yanomami.

Each meal in the *garimpo* canteen costs one gram of gold ($12). Twenty minutes with the camp prostitute (who may also be the camp cook) costs ten grams. The flight from the forest back to Boa Vista might cost five to twenty grams ($60 to $250) per person, depending on the distance and flying time. Many *garimpeiros* wear a gold nugget on a chain round their necks as insurance for that flight; people who cannot pay in advance must stay in the forest waiting for their luck to change.

By the time his workers get back to Boa Vista most of the gold is back with the *patrão*. The *garimpeiros* take what they have left to the gold-buying shops – painted yellow or white and with a chimney to carry the mercury fumes from refining into the street – to sell at a discount. The shops are supposed to resell the gold to the Bank of Brasil or to pay a tax. The system depends on honesty. One shop was estimated to be buying 300 kilograms per month without paying tax. The workers may not keep much of what they take out of the ground, but it's still a small fortune compared to the earnings of a landless farmworker or a factory worker in São Paulo.

Some men – the more courageous, the more experienced or the gamblers by inclination – pay for a ride to a *garimpo* to work freelance in the forest with a few companions. They pan for gold on the beaches and from the sides of streams with the wide shallow pans that form the traditional picture of a prospector or *garimpeiro*. If they're lucky, they find a fortune of gold. Their corpses are left to rot in the forest if they're not.

Few men retire from the *garimpos* to the smallholding or the city house of which they may dream every day in the mud and noise. The brutal work for fourteen hours each day and their lust for gold exhausts them and eventually they wander home, still laughing, glad to be alive, and as poor as the day they left home. Or they die from malaria and other diseases with only their companions to bury them. Or they die in fights with companions better armed with a gun or a knife. Few *garimpeiros* save what they earn. It's not in the blood: "Spend what you get and you'll find even more", promises one of the *garimpeiros* superstitions.

Why do men come to these hellholes of mud, noise and malaria where they dream of becoming rich and fear death from bullets or mosquitoes? At first, it's courage and desperation to escape poverty. Anything's better than working for years for wages that shrink every month. Brazil is a spectacularly wealthy country – yet most of its citizens are amongst the poorest in the world. The feudal system on which the country was founded by the Portuguese has not fundamentally changed. The massive foreign debt has done little for the country because much of the money flowed through the traditional channels to make the rich richer. Present-day poverty is not so much the result of inflation, as the economic turmoil is proof of people battering against power and wealth still held in the hands of a very few people.

Look round any airport in the Amazon, or many of the rougher bars in its cities, and you can spot the *garimpeiros* in the crowd. It's not the lack of luggage when they check-in for a flight, nor the half-dozen empty bottles of beer already on the table by ten in the morning. Watch their weathered faces. Watch their expressions. Watch their eyebrows and the wrinkles round their eyes. The fine dark skin twitches with tension, yet their eyes are cool and wide and gazing into the distance. They're possessed by a hunger for gold or diamonds or emeralds. "You can't eat, you can't talk, you can't sleep. It's a real thing. I've never seen a Whiteman take a nugget of gold from the ground and not have gold fever," said one *garimpeiro.*

They're courageous men, stubborn in their struggle against malaria, rain, poor food and exploitation, but easily led. They're not put off by talk of the rights of Indians – they want their share of the country's wealth. Gold and tin ore in Roraima have been promoted by unscrupulous men as the way to get it. They're the worker bees in a hive – or wild boars making holes and dirtying the rivers, as Davi Yanomami has described them – yet no-one was asking publicly who were the people who encouraged them to shatter the peace of the Yanomami and to open up this northern region.

President José Sarney knew about the extermination of the Yanomami from detailed reports and briefings months before the federal court order. One of these, in January 1989, from Paulo Brossard, one of his own ministers, catalogued the diseases, violence and deaths, the corruption of public officials, the illegal mining in the Yanomami area and the smuggling of gold out of Brazil. Sarney had twice promised Davi Yanomami that he would remove the *garimpeiros* but nothing had been done. Now, in the last few months of his administration, he was under legal compulsion to act.

The initiative to get a federal court order compelling the government to take action had come from a source that was doubly surprising because it was unexpected and honest.

Brazilians wrote a new Constitution for their country after the two decades of military dictatorship ended in 1985. Specially-elected senators and federal deputies talked and negotiated in the Congress for two years to produce a document that had been praised for including civil rights and democratic freedoms so extravagantly little in evidence in a society of extremely rich and illiterate poor. Several articles confirm the rights of the indigenous peoples within Brazil's borders. Article 231, with eight sections, is the main guarantor of their lands and distinct societies and requires the state to demarcate the areas, to protect them and to respect their riches.

Seven other articles or sections specify, for example, that "lands traditionally occupied by Indians" belong to the State; that only Congress can authorize prospecting or mining on Indian lands or in frontier areas.

Mining and mineral resources are dealt with in eight articles or sections. These include, for example, statements that the State owns all mineral rights; that *garimpos* are legal only when *garimpeiros* work in cooperatives regulated by the government.

The sessions in Congress, in Brasília, to write the new Constitution ran on week after week until they became Brazil's longest running soap-opera. It was easy to ridicule so many politicians haggling over the pension rights of retired civil servants and their country's political organization while millions of families in economic and social misery waited for crumbs. One television commentator satirized each week's proceedings with a "candid camera" showing the hard-working politicians kissing, picking their ears, swatting flies or sleeping during the plenary sessions.

The aspect of pantomime seemed to be confirmed by an appendix of seventy "transitional acts" to bring governments, companies and individuals into conformity with the provisions of the Constitution. Article 67 boldly declares, "The State will conclude the demarcation of indigenous lands within five years from the promulgation of the Constitution." This was more a wish than a promise when the document was promulgated on the 5th October in 1988.

However, the Brazilian Constitution was a serious document, not a political lampoon, because the Constitution was given teeth. And in 1989 those teeth decided to bite President José Sarney.

The Congress gave the Constitution teeth by appointing a Public Ministry to defend its provisions; in practice, a small inspectorate of Federal Attorneys (or Public Prosecutors) to make sure the Constitution was being followed, with the ultimate sanction of impeachment. These Attorneys of the Republic, part of the Attorney-General's office, are appointed like judges and cannot be sacked except by the Congress. "To legally defend the rights and interests of the indigenous populations" was assigned as one of their specific tasks, under Article 129, Section V.

In October 1989, the Public Ministry took the initiative to defend the Yanomami. Lawyers applied to the Federal Court for an order closing the clandestine airstrips used by the *garimpeiros* and a second order to expel all non-Indians from the Yanomami area – all of the 9.4 million hectares. The federal judge granted both orders and required the federal government to take action.

Two weeks later, nothing had happened when the president of Funai received a telegram in Brasília from his regional administrator in Boa Vista: "Situation worsening daily. Indians arriving daily, even brought in by *garimpeiros*. In view desperate situation request you arrange two helicopters and funds from appropriate authorities. Repeat that unless urgent measures taken situation will become irreversible. Situation is beyond our solution."

Three weeks later, the president of Funai called a meeting in the Senate to tell politicians, public health officials, groups supporting the Yanomami and *garimpeiro* leaders, including José Altino Machado, that the health situation of the Yanomami was "hopeless". Davi Yanomami and Claudia Audujar attended just before flying to London. The president of Funai invited the non-government agencies, whom Funai had expelled in 1987, to return to the area to do what they could to fight the malaria, dysentery, malnutrition and venereal diseases.

Five weeks after the court order, the Federal Police reported that it hadn't the capacity to take out the *garimpeiros*, so the matter was passed to the military. The minister of the Army, General Leonides Pires Gonçalves said that withdrawing the *garimpeiros* was "psychologically difficult" and would take a long time. "Those who want the *garimpeiros* taken out are some religious [missionaries] and people who defend other interests," he said, asserting that the Yanomami didn't want the *garimpeiros* taken out. The general had been widely reported in Brazil eight months earlier when he'd told diplomats and politicians in Brasília on the national Day of the Indian that, "there are only 30,000 wild Indians. The rest wear jeans, carry round Panasonics and are actors". The military were to take no part in fulfilling the federal court order.

Dying Yanomami men, women and children continued arriving at the Casa do Indio (House of the Indian) run by Funai, on the outskirts of Boa Vista. Even the local media could no longer deny that the Yanomami were facing mass deaths. No-one dared speak of genocide. The Casa do Indio was supposed to be a hospital for

Indians from all over the state of Roraima, but supplies of medicine and food were poor, and, in practice, patients arrived with one disease to exchange it for another to take home to their families. Many of the Yanomami arrived in Boa Vista in the aeroplanes of the *garimpeiros* themselves; in planes owned by men such as José Altino Machado. These acts of mercy undoubtedly saved many people. They were also used to portray the *garimpeiros* as the friends of the Yanomami.

President Sarney released $1.6 million in early December for an emergency medical plan and the Congress voted $3.8 million to pay for a Federal Police operation to withdraw the *garimpeiros*. José Altino Machado said he didn't believe the Federal Police operation could be successful but he was taking no risks. USOGAL and GoldAmazon, the main gold-buying company headed by Elton Rohnelt, rented three helicopters (one of them a Bell 205, the type used by the Americans in Vietnam) and five small planes to take *garimpeiros* and sixteen journalists to Paapiú on 6th January, 1990. It was a public relations exercise costing about $10,000. The purpose was to show how little damage the mining caused; you can't see diseases nor lack of game animals nor toxic levels of mercury in the rivers nor the people who have already died. However, the staged event did not go off quite as expected.

The Paapiú airstrip served as the gateway for the rush of *garimpeiros* into the Yanomami area and had been built, then abandoned, by the Brazilian military without any attempt to control access. There were now twenty-two illegal airstrips within a radius of four kilometres. It was amazing that, even as *garimpeiros* were occupying the Paapiú airstrip as their main staging post for equipment, Paapiú also possessed a Funai post. Paapiú, for the Yanomami, was the focus of their cataclysm of diseases and death. Ninety per cent of the people in the area were still suffering from malaria though, by January, the main *garimpeiro* activity had already moved north to an airstrip called Baiano Formiga.

Yanomami men thought more *garimpeiros* were arriving when USOGAL's guided tour landed at Paapiú. The men had been drinking *caxiri*, an alcoholic brew. One of them – shouting in Portuguese, "Go back to your own village!" – attacked the visitors with a pole. An Italian television journalist had to fight off the attacker with his camera tripod for twenty minutes until the Yanomami calmed down. The incident was a prelude to the greater travesty.

What few people in Roraima had believed could happen began on Monday, 8th January, when the Federal Police began Operation Canaimé. Forty policemen, in black jackets and carrying automatic weapons, stood out at midday on the hot tarmac at Boa Vista airport to stop planes taking off with food, fuel and other supplies for the *garimpos*. Registration papers of planes and pilots were checked. Every aeroplane that landed was boarded and the *garimpeiros* escorted to the VIP lounge which became the police interrogation room. "Which *garimpo* have you come from? Do you plan to go back? Who are you working for?" the Federal Police asked mildly for twenty minutes. No-one was arrested but the action seemed like impertinence in the capital of the *garimpeiros* and prompted an angry response.

Several thousand men gathered that night round the statue of the *garimpeiro* in the main *praça* in loud protest against the police operation to expel them from the Yanomami area. "Roraima without *garimpos* is a father without a son", was the slogan of the demonstrators. President Sarney was condemned as a traitor. The show of force was part threat to the federal government not to meddle; part support to their leaders, including José Altino Machado and Romero Jucá, the governor of the state; and part plea, as migrants, not to be pushed somewhere else. Anger and frustration were combustible emotions in the atmosphere but it's impossible to judge how serious was the likelihood of explosive violence. Exaggeration was in everyone's interest if the mining was to be allowed to continue.

Anger at being "betrayed" by the police action resonated through a manifesto from the pilots' association, published in one of the local papers. The mass demonstration in front of the governor's palace was, "to repudiate the grand farce that runs in the name of Yanomami. The small population of Roraima wants to alert Brazil to the real facts about the blow struck in the name of the Indians by powerful foreign groups (Japan, the US and others) who have known about Roraima's gold for a long time," said the manifesto.

Foreigners had been working for years, through the Church and false missionaries, many of them geologists, to withdraw the *garimpeiros* and, consequently, for the people of Roraima to abandon the state, said the statement.

"Nine million hectares for one thousand Indians," claimed the manifesto, "Never has the foreigner been so worried for such a small number of inhabitants in a remote region of the planet. It's strange that in money-rich Japan and the United States few worry about Ethiopia or Biafra, where there are more people but no gold, tin ore and other noble minerals.

"The major goal of their so noble mission is simply to separate Roraima, to make it a neutral country, to explore the mineral riches and to rob Brazilians through the greatest act of treason.

"To end the *garimpos* of Roraima is the same as throwing mustard-gas defoliant on all the orange trees of São Paulo and decimating and burning all the soya bean plantations all in one go. Closing the *garimpos* will bring economic and social catastrophe, bankrupting thousands of businesses and harming Brazil itself by cutting this important symbol that can contribute so much to the development of the country," said the pilots' association.

It was almost midnight when governor Romero Jucá, appointed by President Sarney, came out of the governor's palace to address the crowd. Romero Jucá has played a special role – and I choose the words carefully to avoid the dangers of libel – in the affairs of Indians in Brazil. He was president of Funai for two years from May 1986 and was then appointed governor of Roraima by President Sarney. "His name should be a byword for cynicism, like the Marquis de Sade for sadism," according to Carlos Zacquini, a guant and softly-spoken Italian who lived among the Yanomami for twenty-two years. He was expelled from the area in 1987 along with other medical and missionary workers but he continued campaigning for the Yanomami by operating the CCPY office in Boa Vista, a courageous act in the capital of the *garimpeiros*.

Romero Jucá has been accused of selling lumber off Indian lands while president of Funai but nothing was proved. He was also responsible for demarcating more Indian areas than ever before, often by reducing their sizes. For example, while president of Funai in August 1988, he reduced the size of the Yanomami Park by almost seventy-five per cent from the 9.4 million hectares already approved by Funai in January 1985. Romero Jucá was president of Funai when all the medical and missionary personnel were expelled from the Yanomami area in 1987.

The heart of Jucá's Yanomami scheme was to reduce the park's area to about 2.4 million hectares and to divide this into nineteen isolated "islands", based on the groupings of Yanomami communities. The remainder of the original area would become "national parks" –open to logging and mining. The Yanomami would be corralled within their own area, on parcels of forest too small for them to survive by hunting and planting gardens. The plan was denounced as "genocide" by Dom Aldo Mongiano, the seventy-year-old bishop of Roraima, whose cathedral and house stands opposite the governor's palace in Boa Vista.

In September 1988 (one month after Jucá announced his plan), President Sarney published a government regulation that would have allowed the Yanomami about eight million hectares. This too was to be divided into nineteen areas, but all of them to be interconnected. This, in theory, would have allowed the Yanomami to hunt, to travel and to move between their regional communities.

Two months later, the government again changed its plan and published, through Funai, a new regulation dividing the Yanomami area into nineteen separated "islands" totalling 2.4 million hectares. Jucá was no longer president of Funai but the scheme was his. The plan "redefined" – by reducing – the "indigenous areas", thus circumventing the Article of the Constitution that prohibits mining in Indian areas except with the approval of Congress.

Romero Jucá has always been consistent in his support of the *garimpeiros* by calling for an "ordering" of the *garimpos* which, he asserted, would "attend to the Indians, attend to the *garimpeiros*, attend to the environment and to the economy of the state," he told a press conference in early January.

The governor of Roraima, Romero Jucá, dismissed the actions of Federal police two days before the mass meeting, saying, "They're trying to erect a Berlin Wall in the open forest. There cannot be racial segregation in the end of the 20th century in Amazonia. There's no way to separate White from Indian.

"Although this living together can be prejudicial to the non-acculturated groups, there's a necessity for the 50,000 men who survive by mineral extraction. We have to think not only of the situation of the Indians but also of the situation in our state and of our families," he said. Jucá blamed the government, Funai and Ibama (the Brazilian environmental protection agency) for failing the Yanomami by, "not even providing rice or an aspirin."

Jucá was determined and imaginative in his vision of a future

Brazil and he was a skilled political fighter. He already held victory in his pocket when he stood at midnight in front of the Palace of the Frontier to address the thousands of angry *garimpeiros* on the day the Federal Police had begun their operation.

He held a telex from the Minister of Justice, Saulo Ramos, in Brasília. Ramos gave President Sarney's approval to Jucá's own plan to resolve the situation. President Sarney, who appears like the Pontius Pilate of modern Brazil in his dealings with the Yanomami, was approving a plan put forward by Jucá and formulated by the *garimpeiros*' organizations "to promise to peacefully leave the Yanomami areas with a move by the workers to *garimpagem* areas farther to the north, suggested by [the *garimpeiros*] themselves," said the telex.

Justice Minister Saulo Ramos promised to send the head of the Federal Police to Boa Vista the next morning to "deal with the details of the accord with the representative organizations of the *garimpeiros* and to be in permanent contact with [Jucá] to secure, together, a rapid and full solution to the problem."

Saulo Ramos said of himself that he was, "of goodwill to everyone and love for Brazil, and that legality should prevail above the diversionary publicity with which, from outside the country, they (sic) try to divide or to confound us." The plan was totally in accord "with the effective protection of Indian life and health, as well as their lands, without neglecting the Constitutional right to work being exercised by the *garimpeiros*," declared the minister of Justice.

Anger became exhilaration when the demonstrators in the central *praça* realized what was being promised. Romero Jucá declared, "We're making a *garimpeiro* revolution. Roraima will be the example for the rest of Brazil as to how to order a *garimpo*. Let's work to organize the others not only in Amazonia but in the rest of Brazil. All can sleep tranquilly because the nightmare has been terminated," said the governor.

Romeu Tuma arrived in Boa Vista, as promised, the next morning. Five thousand people greeted the head of the Federal Police by shouting and waving placards saying, "We're *garimpeiros*, fathers of families but we're being treated as 'marginals'." The mood of the protestors began to change when Tuma told the crowd that the *garimpeiro* had to be respected as an individual. "We're trying to find a less traumatic solution for the workers and for the population of

Roraima," he said, to be greeted in turn with cheers of "Viva Romeu Tuma!" The demonstration bore the mark of having been planned and staged.

Romeu Tuma sat down in the Governor's palace to negotiate the details of the deal with Roraima's Attorney General, the chief of the governor's cabinet, and the directors of Funai, Ibama, the Federal Police, the Military Police (no connection to the Army) and the leaders of the *garimpeiro* unions. No Yanomami were invited.

The deal the men signed created three reserves for *garimpeiros* to carry on working and, in return, the *garimpeiros* agreed to peacefully leave the Yanomami islands within three months. Minister of Justice Saulo Ramos announced the settlement with the *garimpeiros* in Brasília. "We're defending the Indians. A problem that appeared insoluble will be definitely solved in three months. This is a way-out in the Brazilian fashion; with sugar and with effect," said the Minister. Tension in Boa Vista relaxed, though police had to stop some angry *garimpeiros* trying to storm the house of the bishop of Roraima and set fire to the lawn while he was meeting with Tuma.

The deal was immediately celebrated as either a victory for the *garimpeiros* or denounced as a sellout of the Yanomami by the federal government. What was the meat of the deal? The forest was being redefined on paper to take away from the Yanomami seventy per cent of the Yanomami land delineated by the federal judge. The *garimpeiros* got to stay inside the Yanomami area; two of the three *garimpeiro* reserves were to be inside the Yanomami area that the Federal judge had ordered the federal government to clear almost three months earlier. The third was partially inside the area. The three *garimpeiro* reserves covered a combined area of 665,000 hectares. In exchange for these, the *garimpeiros* agreed to leave the Yanomami areas – significantly, this latter word was in the plural, confirming the division of the Yanomami area into nineteen "islands". This also appeared to go against the federal judge's order from October.

"Jucá Won. Funai and Ibama Lost," read a headline in *O Globo*. "Sarney surrendered to General Custer and the Indian haters – it's a shameful retreat, a national disgrace," commented Senator Severo Gomes, one of the leading Brazilian politicians campaigning in favour of a Yanomami park. The authorities had watched the invasion "without moving a straw", he wrote in the newspaper *Folho de São Paulo* a few days later, "as if this disaster were part of some secret plan of the government."

The president of Funai condemned the agreement – though the agency had signed the deal – as the clamour of criticism rose in Brasília, Rio de Janeiro and São Paulo. The head of Funai in Boa Vista and the Funai coordinator with Operation Canaimé both resigned. The operation, "achieved a practical effect: before, the genocide of the Indians was illegal and, now, it's becoming legalized," said Funai coordinator Sidney Possuelo, who had worked among Indians for twenty-five years. "My exit is not the moment of personal glory or vanity. I do nothing more than my obligation. I'm paid to defend the Indian and nothing more," he said.

The deal was even denounced by officials of one of the minor *garimpeiros* unions, Codega (Commission for Support and Defense of *Garimpeiros* of the Amazon). The agreement was prejudicial to the *garimpeiros* and illegal, claimed the union. Two of its officers accused José Altino Machado of having "incited and financed" the invasion of the Yanomami area and said that he, in turn, was "financed by big mining companies wanting to take over the Indian land with the support of SADEN, (the Brazilian national defence council run by the military)."

The day after the agreement was announced, Romeu Tuma, Romero Jucá and José Altino Machado flew to Paapiú to pose for television and journalists' cameras, as a symbol in the forest of the peaceful exit of the *garimpeiros*.

The federal attorney who'd applied for the original court order to expel the *garimpeiros* reapplied to have Romeu Tuma, head of the Federal Police, jailed for disobeying a court order. "[His] job was to remove the *garimpeiros* not sit down and negotiate with them." The application was disallowed.

Flights taking fuel, food and equipment to the *garimpos* were back to normal just four days after the start of the operation to pull the *garimpeiros* out of the forest, according to *Estado de São Paulo*. The newspaper quoted a spokesman for the Federal police, João Martins, "The operation foresaw a shock, a confrontation. Now, there's a peaceful coexistence between police and *garimpeiros*."

Operation Canaimé was renamed Operation Selva Livre (a forest free for whom?) and the investigation of flights to and from *garimpos* continued at Boa Vista airport for a few more weeks as some *garimpeiros* moved to the three reserves. Police had to sign a form declaring they were flying to *garimpos* inside one of the three new *garimpeiro* reserves and not to one of the Indian Areas (the nineteen "islands"). It was another week before the Federal police closed the illegal runway at the Jockey Club of Boa Vista. Many other private landing strips, at ranches on the edge of the city, remained uncontrolled.

Charges of "genocide" were angrily rejected by the Minister of Justice, Saulo Ramos. "Our Indians exist because Brazil takes care of them," he said after a two-hour meeting with General Santa Cruz, the military commandant of the Amazon in Brazil. "Genocide is an invention of the Europeans, to internationalize the region known for its riches," he told journalists.

General Santa Cruz, an avuncular man whose candour was to shock me when we met a few months later, fully supported the accord with the *garimpeiros*, who were strategically important to the occupation of the Amazon. "The *garimpeiro* is not a bandit. He's a devoted Brazilian," he said. The general condemned, "the exaggerated interest and international hysteria to protect the Indian and the Amazon."

Many people in Brazil, Europe and North America rallied to support the Yanomami. The news media gave reports of the critical situation. Survival International began a protest vigil and published a booklet about the Yanomami. These protests were ineffective in themselves but together they extended public and political awareness. It was no small victory for them that, when the president-elect of Brazil, Fernando Collor de Mello, visited Europe in February to ask for financial help for Brazil, he met questions from political leaders (and from Prince Charles) and public demonstrations to support the Yanomami.

Lawyers at the Public Ministry in Brazil started proceedings to impeach President Sarney but this, and other political manoeuvres, were too late. Sarney's administration was in its last weeks. There was only time for the president to sign the decrees establishing the *garimpeiro* reserves. Their legality under the Constitution would have to be argued under the new president, after 15th March.

Thousands of *garimpeiros* did leave Paapiú and some of the areas around the other airstrips. But the mining and all its terrible effects continued at the more remote *garimpos* that lay outside the nineteen "islands" but inside the area closed by the federal court order. The Federal Police operation was suspended when the seasonal rain storms started in February. By then, perhaps 20,000 *garimpeiros* had left the Yanomami area to go into the areas of other Indians in Roraima or had gone home for Carnaval, or had gone feeling ever-hopeful to *garimpos* elsewhere in the Amazon.

Funai's emergency health programme for the Yanomami stopped in March when the money ran out. By then, a budget of five million dollars for the whole operation had gone. An estimated 2,000 Yanomami had died in two years, out of the population of 9,000 within Brazil.

6

To return to the Yanomami up the river Marauiá in April was, for me, both a welcome homecoming among friends and a journey of necessary escape. I was feeling raw. I could not separate the betrayal of the Yanomami from the appetites of our own factories and supermarkets for ever-more raw materials; constant growth is vital to keep society in good health, economics and politicians have told us. It's as if we've struck a deal with our souls to exchange ever-greater yearly offerings and human sacrifices in order to maintain the physical comforts of the majority of people. This has much in common with the Yanomami concept of spirits to be supplicated and monsters that eat people's souls, except that we use the demands of our dragon to justify the poisoning of the planet and the plundering of what belongs to other people. Responsibility for the destruction of the Yanomami lies firmly with the Brazilian military and sections of the government, but their war-cry of "Development!" is much the same as any industrialised society's creed of economic growth just to make statistics go up.

We defend the appetite of our dragon, yet we also want to believe ourselves generous, compassionate and fair; a definition of "civilised" behaviour perhaps. But there's an obvious contradiction between believing our own myths of European "civilization" and the subjugation, for example, of the peoples of the Americas since Christopher Columbus arrived in 1492. Pretending otherwise is the widespread hypocrisy in which I fully shared and from which I needed to escape.

The journey in April of 1990 was my third visit to Ironasiteri and I was arriving with a friend from England, though we'd met for the first time at Rio de Janeiro airport. We were on an assignment to report on the Yanomami for *The Sunday Times Colour Magazine*, This was in part a follow-up to the report called "Genocide" by writer Norman Lewis and photographer Donald McCullin, published in London just over twenty years earlier. They had revealed the extent and some of the methods used by the Indian Protection Service

(SPI) to exterminate Indians from lands wanted by ranchers, speculators and mining companies. A report from the Brazilian Ministry of the Interior had detailed how SPI officers had issued clothing impregnated with smallpox, given foods poisoned with arsenic, dropped sticks of dynamite from aeroplanes, injected smallpox instead of vaccine, massacred people with machine-guns and committed numerous other barbarous and sadistic acts.

Outrage within Brazil led to criminal charges against some of the SPI officers and to the replacement of the SPI by the National Indian Foundation, Funai. Publication of the facts in Britain led to the founding of Survival International by Robin Hanbury-Tennison, John Hemming, Norman Lewis and others.

Survival International's research, publicity, campaigns of petitions and letters by thousands of supporters, and the provision of medicines and money have helped tens of thousands of tribal peoples defend themselves. Our *Sunday Times* follow-up was to report the facts of the invasion by gold-miners and the deaths of the Yanomami. Was the Brazilian government now protecting the Indians or was there an unwritten policy of clearance by other means?

I was preoccupied all the way out to Brazil by an apprehension of who the magazine would send to take the photographs. We had a job to do, but I also felt a responsibility in introducing a stranger with a camera to friends. I worried that the photographer would be too pushy with the cameras, click-clicking people, trampling over mutual trust and ignoring their wishes, just to get pictures for the magazine back home. However, I knew that all would be well as soon as I met Chris Steele-Perkins in Rio airport. He was buoyant without being strident.

The flight north from Rio de Janeiro to Manaus was cancelled as we seemed to be the only passengers, so this gave us a twelve-hour delay before the night flight. We quickly established a comfortable collaboration over little cups of coffee in the airport and during the day's sightseeing in the city. Brazil was still in shock two weeks after President Collor's action to kill the country's 7,000 per cent inflation at a stroke and to control the government's massive spending deficit. All bank accounts with over $1,200 were frozen for eighteen months, 360,000 civil servants would be fired and many state companies would be privatized, the president promised on his first day in office. (It was the stark reality of Brazil that ninety per cent of the people held less than this balance or had no bank account at all.) The Collor Plan was greeted with disbelief and with applause at its boldness. "I think there's now light at the end of the tunnel in Brazil," commented a British banker, "but I think it's a train coming in the opposite direction."

Chris and I eventually flew north to Manaus; there to hurry round the shops buying food and gifts and to charter a boat to take the two of us up the Rio Negro, but it still took us nine days to reach Santa Isabel. We were rushing partly because haste is the normal pace of journalists and photographers, and partly because Domingos and I had agreed, during my last visit, to meet again in Santa Isabel during the first week in April. He and I planned to travel together up the Marauiá river and then to trek 250 miles through the forest from one Yanomami community to another. We wanted the more isolated *shabonos* to hear Davi's warnings about the dangers of the *garimpeiros* and the messages from Ironasiteri that were on the tapes I carried. We wanted to lead a group of *tuxauas* to travel to Davi's *shabono* on the Demini river. The journey would be an adventure and it seemed the only way to help independent communities to pull politically closer together in order to defend themselves.

Unfortunately, Chris and I arrived in Santa Isabel one week too late. Domingos had already been and returned home. We asked if we could hire a boat. A local Policia Militar (a civilian police force) took us to the police station to check over our passports and ask inconvenient questions about who we were and where we were going. The new mayor might have vouched for me (we'd met once) but he was said to be up the Marauiá with an army doctor vaccinating the Indians. Chris and I wondered what would happen when we met them there. The policeman let us go, with smiles and hand shakes, after exchanging twenty dollars for Brazilian money at a very poor rate. A local man offered his speedboat to take us up the Marauiá and, in addition to his fee, we bought 132 litres of petrol and seven tins of oil for the outboard motor. He was a big, round man with a smile and a good nose for an easy profit but the outboard motor broke down while we were still in sight of the town. We landed on a beach 400 yards upstream. I went in frustration to ask at a lone mud-brick house, in the midst of a cattle pasture, whether the owner might take us up the Marauiá in his canoe and slow motor. He agreed and promised to collect us after lunch. Then we drifted ignominiously back to Santa Isabel in the defunct motorboat.

Black clouds covered the sky from the east, bringing torrential rain for an hour while Chris and I sat in an empty floating store-shed, moored to the river bank, eating a huge lunch of boiled fish, rice and beans. It was so much food that three other men, in a large covered canoe moored alongside, ate from the bowls after us.

Our new guide arrived as the rain stopped and, after collecting his son at home, we motored happily up the Rio Negro towards the mouth of the Marauiá. The canoe was large enough to take four passengers in comfort, though without shelter from sun or rain. The large motor, with a long propeller shaft mounted on a swivel over the transom, powered us upstream against the fast current coming against us. The level of the river was higher than usual for early April making conditions better and worse; it's easier and safer to pass the long cataracts when the river's high, but travel would be miserable, if not impossible, on the Marauiá and in the forest if the season of torrential rainstorms was beginning a month early.

There were only the pigs at home when we reached a house below the waterfalls on the Marauiá where I'd stayed once with Renato and Valdira, who knew the Brazilian family living there. We drank sweet black coffee for supper and hung up our hammocks to stay the night, confident the absent owners would not object.

"This discourages vampire bats," I told Chris when I put an oil lamp to burn all night in the entrance way. He shrugged his shoulders with a laugh, "Oh I see," he said, but only half-believing my warning. He took our delays and upsets with laconic patience and humour, never allowing his own frustrations to frizzle into complaints.

So much water was pouring over the first waterfall, locally called "The Little Beast", that we didn't have to get out of the canoe at all. Our guide revved up the engine to force his way between boulders on the left side, through a channel like a mill-race. Storm water was pouring over the other four waterfalls and we had to work hard to drag the canoe and carry the motor and our sacks past these thunderous obstructions. "My brother's canoe capsized here," said our guide at the fifth waterfall, which was the smallest of the series. Two companions drowned, but his brother survived to walk home through the forest.

No-one came to the river bank as we approached Coatá, though people must have heard our motor, I thought as we came nearer the *shabono* where I'd stayed five months earlier. Why was no-one showing themselves? I stood up for a better view and was dismayed to see there were no canoes moored at the landing places. Coatá, we realised as soon as we entered the *shabono*, had been abandoned. Grass was growing through the grey sand of the arena. No-one had been here for a month, I guessed. We made coffee and dried clothes soaked in one of the day's rain showers.

Chris and I agreed to pay the guide more money to keep going. He said he'd never been farther up the river, so I understated the travelling time to the next *shabono*, at Apuí, because I didn't want him to refuse to go. He and his son agreed to go on and drank their coffee in silence.

Two hours later, we met Valdira and his wife Aoria on the river. We shook hands, made introductions with big smiles and lashed their canoe to ours to go upstream together. Valdira's first news was that his parents and younger brother had gone down to Santa Isabel to collect me, as agreed, the week before.

"They lost the shotgun at Piraíba [the fifth waterfall]," he reported.

"Lost? How did it happen?" I asked.

The force of water pouring over the fall had pulled the canoe from their hands, he said. "The canoe went over the waterfall. Everything sank in the water. Shotgun! Seven baskets of *farinha!*" Happily, the canoe had resurfaced on the other side of the river but everything else had been lost. "We didn't have anything. Nothing! Nothing! We couldn't go home so we went to Santa Isabel and our *patrão* [one of the shopkeepers] gave us four new hammocks [on credit]. We waited a week for you but you didn't come," said Valdira. So now the family were eating only fish, not bothering to hunt with bow and arrow, he said.

A dozen people waited on the big granite rock as we came up the river to Apuí, watching to see who was coming, pointing and waving when they recognised us. Piarina came first to embrace me tightly with her big arms. "Dennison!" she said. "Auntie!" I replied. Other women and youths embraced or shook hands. I introduced Chris. Renato hugged rightly. "This is my only true white friend," Renato said in Portuguese, one arm held up over my shoulder. I translated this phrase to Chris and left out the other compliments.

Our guide and his son decided to return downriver immediately though the sun was low in the sky. Perhaps they were afraid to stay the night with Indians. We watched them going swiftly downriver in the current then turned to take our sacks up the path to the *shabono*. "Bring them to my house," whispered Piarina, so that we should stay with her and Domingos. But Renato had already told some of the boys to take the sacks to his house so that is where we stayed. Domingos could not come to greet us, said Piarina, because he was busy with the *hekura* in a three-day shamanic exercise. Five youths and a German man, gaunt and blanched white, watched our arrival in silence. They were building a school a short distance up the river.

Apuí was more beautiful than on my first visit because the houses now formed an almost complete circle, 150 feet in diameter, with mango and peach palm trees in a central grassed area. Renato took me to every house, with children holding my hands, to greet every family by hugging or shaking hands. The warmth of their welcome needed no translation.

Gabriel, who had denounced me with such fury and cut short my last visit, hesitated only a moment to see my own reaction to him before we embraced, patting each other on the back. "My hammock has a big hole", he said with his usual laughter. "It caught fire when my wife was in it. She was not hurt but the hammock's useless," he said. Later, he brought a bead bracelet to tie on my wrist.

The distribution of items from our sacks took place next morning. We laid out everything on a piece of blue plastic in front of Renato's house; flashlights, hammocks, fishing line and hooks, parachute cord, barbed spearheads, batteries, needles, sewing cotton, shotgun powder, lead and detonators. Bars of soap and some of the clothes were missing, presumed stolen in Santa Isabel. Half the items were people's requests from my last visit and I handed these out myself, calling out each item so that everyone knew what each person was receiving. Inevitably, some people complained that they had been missed out. Most people were delighted with the colour prints of photographs of them I had taken the year before. Chris and I stayed out of the general division of the spoils; there were a few of most items but not enough for everyone to have one of each. With a total of sixty-five people in the *shabono*, there were too many people to be able to do that. Samuel and others ran with cord and fishing line across the shabono to measure out their shares.

The young German called Augusto watched from the side. "These gifts are good. But I'm sad you've brought them because now no-one will work on the school, if they don't need the things that we pay them," he said. The school was being built by a Frenchman called Henri Ramirez, who planned to train a dozen youths to be teachers and who would then return to their own communities.

"We couldn't come with nothing," I told Augusto. None of what we'd brought were gifts. Everything would have to be paid for, I explained. This is the custom among the Yanomami, though I let the community itself decide the prices. Chris and I would take payments in baskets, feathers, bows, arrows and blowing tubes when we left. Renato had requested a radio and Valdira a tape recorder in exchange for a traditional hammock and a carved stone axehead. I'd decided, after some hesitation, to bring both machines if these were what they wanted. The radio was useless because it didn't speak Yanomami but the tape recorder could serve to record messages for other *shabonos*.

Augusto did not like Renato. "He wants to be a *caboclo*" (Brazilian of mixed blood subsisting in a small house along one of the Amazon rivers by growing *açaí*, manioc and peach palms). "Renato's between the two cultures," insisted Augusto. Without doubt, Renato liked the Whiteman's tools and this made him eager to please Brazilians and to imitate them sometimes. Renato was always clear about being Yanomami in our conversations, but he also wanted to be respected by people he saw as being more powerful than himself. Certainly, Renato was eager to please the mayor of Santa Isabel when he walked unannounced into the *shabono* on our second afternoon.

The mayor and his entourage arrived in two speedboats. Two men fetched two styrofoam boxes into one of the homes out of the rain. The men told Renato to fetch tables (there were only two in Apuí left over from the missionary's attempt to run a school) on which to set the boxes. The mayor and his wife, a secretary, an army doctor and a guide were surprised to meet *gringos* (foreigners) in the *shabono*. "Will they expel us," I wondered. The army doctor, in jungle camouflage jacket, prepared his syringes and vaccines. The mayor said he wanted every adult to be thumb-printed to register as a voter. His secretary laid out the necessary forms, though no-one could read them nor knew what they were agreeing with their thumb-prints. Our position as outsiders was settled when the last member of the mayor's party walked in; he was councillor Paulo, with whom I'd stayed during the pneumonia on my last visit. He greeted me warmly, which gave us approved status. It was curious how the mayor and his party took over the *shabono*, telling Renato and the others what to do. Chris took out his camera.

The mayor explained, in the easy-going banter of the born politician, that he wanted everyone to register on Santa Isabel's electoral roll, not for them to vote for him, but because he could claim higher grants when there were more people enrolled. Renato nodded eagerly when the mayor said he'd give them a motor for their canoe in return for cooperating.

The army "doctor" revealed his true occupation (he was a dentist) when he checked the children's age by looking at their teeth before giving polio vaccine by drops in the mouth, followed by three injections for diphtheria, tetanus and whooping cough; BCG against tuberculosis; and measles. No wonder many of the children fled across the *shabono* or cried in fear when their mothers held them firmly as the needles went in. Vaccination was necessary but the work was done in haste. The mayor wanted to reach Santa Isabel that night, if they could.

They'd been far up the Marauiá enlisting 380 voters and vaccinating 183 children, though many others had escaped. The mayor had also taken a teacher up to the Yanomami community of Pohorowapihiweyteri. He promised Renato to send another to Ironasiteri. The mayor told me the teacher spoke Yanomami but this was untrue. He was a local lad who would want to return to Santa Isabel after a few months. The travellers hurried away down the river as soon as their work was done, leaving used hypodermic needles and syringes with which the children played. Augusto and I gathered them to burn.

Chris and I were keen to go further up the Marauiá, at least to Xamataweteri, where the Salesian mission was located, and up to Pohoro, if possible, to visit people who maintain little contact with the *nabe*. However, Chris was in a rush to get back to Britain, so the journey had to be without delay or not at all. Renato and Domingos agreed to take us upstream in the canoe I had left with them on the last visit.

Gabriel said he couldn't go to the mission because it was a long way and his backside hurt after so much sitting. His other reason was more serious. "I dream a lot of the journey," he said with a laugh that masked his serious apprehension that something bad would happen. Dreams are visits of *hekura*, or spirits, warning of danger or actually attacking the health and soul of the dreamer. Perhaps Gabriel already felt what we were soon to discover.

Geraldo, who was still serving as Renato's son-in-law, returned home at nightfall from fishing and hunting with a thoughtful face and empty hands. "Nothing," he said. One small catfish mixed with packet soup and *farinha* had to make supper for ten people. The season was obviously a bad time for food. "*Ohi ohi*," said Gabriel rubbing his tummy, meaning hungry. The river was too high and too fast to hook or spear fish. Animals did not come to the river bank but drank at pools of rainwater deeper inside the forest. Our hosts took the temporary shortage with fortitude, knowing the hunting and fishing would improve when the heavy rains stopped and the river level started to fall.

Renato, Domingos, Chris and I set out for Xamataweteri after sharing a big bowl of tapioca porridge for breakfast. The river was rising rapidly with the runoff of the recent rains, swelling up against the rock where the canoes were moored. The motor of the small canoe, left from my last visit, started first time and propelled us suddenly into the full force of the swollen river for the two-day journey towards the mountains. Tree trunks and bushes were the dangers to watch for in the swirling brown water; rocks and rapids were already safely submerged. Whirlpools pulled and pushed the bow of the canoe like a stubborn dog grasping and tugging a big stick in its mouth. The force of the water against us vibrated up through the propeller shaft making the engine and the rudder shake like a crazy tree branch in a gale. Both hands were not enough to grasp the rudder and hold it steadily on our course cutting across the river as we travelled up the inside of every bend. My knees, wedged under the rudder, gave the best support to reduce the shaking.

Nothing stirred on either side of the green walls of the forest. The river itself seemed to have swallowed the usually muddy banks beneath its flood, making the sensation for travellers of passing up a green canyon like a painted stage set. Only after several hours did a single pair of red and blue macaws cross the sky with their characteristic squawks.

Renato sat on the short bench in the bow of the canoe with his shotgun across his lap. He was claiming to be our hunter, though the only occasion he got what the Yanomami call in Portuguese a "duck" (like a cormorant) in his sights, the cartridge in his gun failed to go off when he pulled the trigger. Renato said it was a defective detonator from the batch Chris and I had brought. Domingos sat on the left side of the canoe on the second to last bench. He was silent and motionless almost all day in a state of personal calm yet fully awake. Chris and I each took turns for three hours grappling with the vibrating rudder to steer our way up the river. Renato said he couldn't take a turn because he was our hunter and might miss a bird or an animal for our cooking pot. Domingos claimed exemption because he was a *shaman* and said he didn't have the strength.

"Summon up the strength of spirits," I shouted at him above the roar or the motor, but he only giggled and repeated he didn't have the strength. Both men let Chris and I do the work all day. I resented their idleness for an hour or two but chuckled then at the lunacy of four men in a little canoe battling the river in spate. No doubt this work was beneath the dignity of *tuxauas*, especially if they could get us to do it for them. I suspected both men were afraid of the newfangled motor that was shaking so wildly. Their sons were the people eager to steer the canoe on all their journeys.

We discovered late in the morning that we'd brought no food with us except *farinha*. Domingos had brought none because he thought there was food in my sack. I had brought none because we'd already handed over all the rice, spaghetti and coffee we'd brought to both Domingos and Renato, as leaders of the two kinship groups in the *shabono*. We were left to enjoy *jibó*, if "enjoy" is the right word. *Jibó* is *farinha* mixed with water. It looks and tastes like sawdust in water, but the taste improves as you get hungrier. At most, we'd be two days without proper food but the demoralizing effect on Chris and I seemed out of all proportion to the minor gastronomic deprivation. Lack of food seemed to increase my appetite for meringues stuffed with cream, for whole barbecued chickens and big bowls of muesli heaped with raisins and bananas. I felt pathetic for letting my stomach be the barometer of my well-being.

We were coming up round the inside of a bend some time in the afternoon when the met the speedboat of the Frenchman Henri Ramirez. Eight young men were with him, coming down from two of the *shabonos* upriver to be students at his new school. We steered into the right bank of the river stopped the motor and grabbed overhanging bushes to hold ourselves against the current. Henri pulled alongside us and stared at Chris and I. He was a shockingly thin man, wearing a broad-brimmed straw hat to shade his dark eyes and pale skin. "Who are you? Where are you going?" he asked. I knew that he had official permission from Funai and from the local bishop to be on the river. We did not. "We're going to the mission," I explained, keeping silent about our hopes of going beyond there. Renato stood up to say Chris and I were friends of his and that everything was okay. "They're only going to the mission," he said. I hoped that this would not be true. Henri nodded slowly, like a headmaster being indulgent of his pupils. This man believes the Marauiá river is his private affair, I thought, as I watched him observing us. He speaks the language, he knows all about the Yanomami. His eyes seemed to be revealing his thinking; no other outsiders should be here. "Okay," he said, then put his idling engine into gear and turned the speedboat away from us to continue downstream. Renato signalled for us to start our motor again to go upstream.

Renato or Domingos pointed to the occasional sites of previous *shabonos* and camps along the river bank, now completely reclaimed by the forest. All communities are semi-nomadic, moving when their gardens are tired, when they need to hunt and gather in new areas of the forest or when a great *tuxaua* dies. Thus the Yanomami need to occupy a large area without actually being there all the time. The *hekura*, or spirits, are released when a person dies, making their old home dangerous. Domingos broke his silence abruptly to say that this was why they had abandoned their *shabono* at Irapajé. "Our father gave word for us to leave when he died. If not, his spirit would have destroyed us. So he forbade us," he said. Domingos was silent for a few more miles up the river, then suddenly began telling me about the deaths of five of his children. "It was the *pajé* who ordered [their deaths], not malaria. A single shot – ssoo! – of the *pajé's* arrow and my children died. When sickness happens, it kills people. No-one can become like God. We're only passengers of God.

"So today I have only two sons. No more are coming now. My wife Piarina took a medicine from the forest so she can't have more children. It's a type of red fruit. There's another that's green and looks like a child's penis. She drank and so no more children come," he said.

Domingos' father also died from a *pajé's* attack. Domingos knew the killer. He was one of the elders of the *shabono* where we were going. "People were jealous of him for discovering the Whiteman. They accused him of killing other men's children," said Domingos. "So they killed him. It was Pakatuba. He 'thought' my father, striking him with a [spiritual] arrow. I was already in the college in Santa Isabel. Dad visited me then he went upriver and he died. It was like that. Because of this, I don't like to visit; only from time to time," he said.

We refilled the four-and-a-half litre fuel tank three times the first day, more than twice the usual consumption when the river was low. Our progress was slow, despite keeping close to the river bank, where the current was least strong, so we travelled until almost nightfall before stopping to sleep. Our campsite for the night had a name as well as a piece of ground cleared of small bushes, two old campfires and a dilapidated thatched shelter wide enough for just two hammocks. Chris and I tied up plastic sheeting between four trees, earnestly hoping that it would not rain during the night. Another bowl of *jibé* was our supper for anyone who wanted it, before we climbed into our hammocks to welcome sleep.

Torrential rain started some time in the middle of the night. I was woken by the coldness of my legs on the soaked end of the hammock and by the noise of the thunder. Rainwater hitting the leaves of thousands of trees amplifies the tremendous din of a rainstorm in the forest. The total blackness of night exaggerates the loneliness of your warm body being soaked by the cold. "Be still and you will cease to shiver," your drowsy mind commands. That was only possible with at least some protection from the rain. Renato and Domingos doubled up their hammocks under the only dry square of thatch. Chris and I abandoned our hammocks and half-sat, half-crouched beneath one corner of the plastic sheet, listening to the boom and flash of the storm between our fitful sleeps.

The rain did not stop in the morning. I felt as miserable as I have ever felt on any journey anywhere in the world. My mettle was indeed puny. I tried cheering myself by dictating to the tape recorder just how thoroughly rotten I was feeling. Chris tried to keep smiling by imagining when the rain would stop. Renato and Domingos kept silent and motionless, apparently able to withdraw into an interior personal calm and coziness.

Rain pitter-pattered through the trees for a couple of hours before we reloaded the canoe to continue upstream. A mist of drizzle drifted over the river from the treetops, keeping us hunched over, silent and cold. We were alone in the world in our tiny canoe, with its roaring, shaking motor. No other life stirred, except the water swirling and rippling down the river through the forest.

We twice caught sight of the *serras* where the *hekuras* or spirits live – the volcanic mountains that divide the Amazon from the Orinoco river basin and, today, are the border between Brazil and Venezuela. One of these high, isolated peaks, Pico de Neblina, was the inspiration for Arthur Conan Doyle's *The Lost World.* Mist soon brought the sky down to the treetops again, bringing with it the cold rain to chill even our thinking. We didn't react at all when, at last, we did see half a dozen canoes moored to the grassy bank on the right side of the river. We continued motionless as if expecting the rain to suddenly cease now that we had arrived at the *shabono* of Xamataweteri.

Eighteen children and a handful of adults stood watching us from the bank, holding banana leaves over their heads to keep off the rain. Renato called out a greeting. Chris and I waved and smiled. The children smiled and laughed. A couple of youths recognized me from the journey up the river with them the year before. But we didn't get out of the canoe right away; good manners cautioned against entering the *shabono* unannounced. Eventually, we and our belongings were taken into the *shabono* to be warmly greeted by Ajinor, the community's leading *tuxaua.* Domingos, Chris and I sat facing a group of men sitting round the hearth. Renato stood to explain that Chris and I were friends. Men nodded and smiled. A large bunch of bananas and a bowl of crunchy tapioca were fetched for us. We were hungry, but we were thankful we didn't eat all the fruit because we suddenly realized that these were the only bananas in the community and that the hunting and fishing were as poor here as at Apuí. *Farinha,* tapioca and half a handful of catfish were the daily food while the river was in spate at the start of the rainy season.

Chris and I both felt immediately that the atmosphere was more relaxed here than in Ironasiteri. Our arrival had not caused strong reactions of either glee or concern. We put up our hammocks in

Ajinor's house, though mine was quickly taken away to be dried over a fire when a neighbour discovered that it was wet. Few women wore more than a small skirt. Many men were nude. Children played among themselves, some with small bows and arrows, or held our hands or sat one behind the other grooming each other's hair. Xamataweteri was a far larger *shabono* than Ironasiteri, housing about 180 people round a thatched "doughnut" 100 yards in diameter.

The priest from the mission marched into the *shabono* half an hour after our arrival, along with a young Italian couple who were setting up an infirmary in the mission building. Father Francisco Laudado looked like an Old Testament prophet, despite wearing a pair of striped pajamas. His grey beard draped down his chest like a bib and his hostile eyes and physical bulk confirmed the appearance of a man who knows he's in the right. "Where's your authorization to be here," he demanded. I explained we didn't have any written permission from Funai. "If you don't, then you must leave," he told us, without once speaking to either Ajinor or Renato. The other men in the group listened in silence. I explained the purpose of our visit, then foolishly spoke of my desire to take people from the Marauiá to meet Davi and others in the east. "Who will give permission for such a journey? Who will be responsible for the Yanomami?" Padre Francisco snorted at my suggestion that the Yanomami could look after themselves in a journey through the forest. "They're children," he replied in a stage whisper. "You don't have an authorization so you must leave immediately. I'll radio to Funai if you don't," he said and left the *shabono*.

"What a cantankerous old git!" remarked Chris.

I've always had an inordinate respect for authority – ever since being humiliated by a school prefect for a minor infraction of the rules – and felt less defiant, despite being a guest of Ajinor and Renato. "There's little food, the river's rising, it's raining hard and the priest's hostile. We'll have to leave tomorrow," I thought. However, my apprehensions were absorbed by the play of children around us and people's concern for a sick man farther round the *shabono*.

The Yanomami on the Marauiá river have a strange relationship to the missionaries. They want a mission near them to be able to obtain metal tools, beads and metal cooking pots but show no more than polite interest in the padre's Bible stories. No-one has ever "converted" to Christianity; Jesus, Mary and the saints have been incorporated into the Yanomami cosmos without denial of Oman and *hekura*. The priest is a necessary *nabe* contact but the Yanomami also resent his officious behaviour, being much too self-assertive for a polite guest.

Domingos told me how the padre had once expelled a party of men from Ironasiteri who'd come upstream several years before looking for gold with a Brazilian they knew from the Rio Negro. "It was before we knew not to want gold," explained Domingos. " 'What d'you want with gold?' the padre said. 'Look, Domingos, this gold is no good for you. If you go on, I'll communicate to Funai, to the police,' shouted the padre. This silenced us. The padre didn't allow us to discover gold. I told him, 'Look padre, you don't give the orders on this river Marauiá. We're the ones who order here. I was born on the *serra*, not in Apuí, and we want to go there for gold.'

" 'Where's the gold?' asked the padre.

" 'I don't know,' I replied.

" 'Why d'you want gold? If you discover gold, the *garimpeiros* will fall on you. There'll be no more padre here. Only *garimpeiros*. I'll have nothing to do with you. They'll take all your land. You'll have nothing. They'll throw you out!' said the padre.

" 'Look padre, I'm not going to lose anything. I only want to work a little. The people of Maturacá work to buy what they're needing. It's no different.' But the padre didn't agree. 'You're doing bad to allow *garimpeiros* to enter,' he said.

" 'Padre, you can't order things here,' I said.

" 'Go where you want. I don't tell any Yanomami what to do,' replied the padre.

" 'That's certain. You order in Italy where you were born. You can't prohibit anything here! It's we who are going to prohibit you,' I said to him." The Yanomami returned downriver, though perhaps none the wiser about what would happen if they did discover gold. Gold has no value in Yanomami society and it's one of the paradoxes of the situation that they need some contact with the *nabe* in order to realize the dangers from the *nabe* if gold were to be discovered.

The sick man laying in the hammock further round the *shabono* was called Geraldo. He'd not eaten for one month, saying his food had been poisoned and that a monster was eating his soul.

"What's wrong with him?" I asked, assuming it must be tuberculosis or another of the *nabe's* diseases.

"It's very hard to say. Many strange things happen here. Strangeness is regular for the Yanomami," said Franco.

Chris and I were the first Europeans from outside that Franco and his wife Angela had met for many weeks, so they were as eager to talk as we were listen to their news and insights. "What does the priest do all day?" I asked.

"Nothing," replied Franco, a tall, muscular thirty-three-year-old mountaineer. "He tries to push down everybody who comes here, to make no contact. He's an anthropologist; his idea is that these people must live like in old times, before contact with the Whiteman. Maybe this is good, but now it's hard because the wall he's put up is very thin," explained Franco.

Father Francisco and his brother Luis took over the empty mission in 1978, though Luis returned to teach in Manaus nine years later. From the start, the Salesian brothers from Italy were more interested in cataloguing than converting the Yanomami. Their inactivity has brought both good and bad results. No-one has been filled with Western notions of shame or greed. At the same time, no-one has learnt how to defend themselves from the *nabe*. For example, a Brazilian trader from Santa Isabel paid three kilos of sugar and some rice for two tons of *to-o* from Xamatawteri while the padre was away the year before. Exploitation is easy when people have no idea what to exchange for the trade goods they desire so avidly.

"What do you think of the padre?" I asked Ajinor when the group of men left his hearth.

"He's bad. He doesn't give, he doesn't exchange. He doesn't buy his food from here, no! We want to work but he doesn't give it. The first priest told us to take *to-o, sorva* and we earned a shotgun. The first thing I earned was this toasting pan [for toasting *farinha* and tapioca]. This padre says, 'I don't want to buy *farinha*, only one basket.' This is what he says," said Ajinor. The rate of exchange was three baskets of *farinha* for one hammock.

"It's expensive, or not?"

"He's wanting to rob."

"Have people gone from here to the Preto river to buy shotguns?" I asked.

"Six or seven men went. They're going to stay away many moons because the shotgun is very expensive. Twenty tons of *piassava* for one shotgun," said Ajinor. It was doubtful that he knew how much each shotgun would cost and instead was plucking a number from his imagination to express what he felt was the size of the expense, rather than a numerical accuracy. An equivalent among the *nabe* would be when someone who's numerically eighty years old says they feel thirty years old again. The usual price the Yanomami paid for a shotgun was eight tons of *piassava* for one shotgun. This represented paying 150,000 cruzeiros for a shotgun that cost 11,000 cruzeiros in Manaus. Was it any wonder the people wanted to learn to read, count and to speak Portuguese?

"What else do you want here?"

"Detonators and lead [for shotgun cartridges], knives and long trousers," said Ajinor.

"Why trousers?"

Ajinor laughed. "I want to wear clothes."

Isolation has not stopped the arrival of the Whiteman's diseases to Xamataweteri. Whooping cough killed most of the children in 1982, forcing the Laudado brothers to call for two doctors from Turin. According to Franco, they stayed only briefly gathering information for a book. A vaccination campaign by Funai in the mid-1980s, using a Brazilian air force helicopter to reach the *shabonos*, was only partially successful because many Yanomami fled or were away hunting on the day of injections. Thereafter, the priests preferred isolation to exploitation. Yet some contact with the Whiteman is inevitable for the Yanomami and I wondered whether they would not be better served by learning to cope with the challenges of the *nabe's* world rather than by being hidden away. A bamboo barrier keeps them ignorant of the *nabe's* vices and unable to defend themselves. The fight to guarantee the land of the Yanomami is not to create a museum but to recognise their land, to safeguard their lives and to guarantee them freedom of choice to decide their own futures.

Franco and his wife Angela, a trained nurse, were making the latest attempt at Xamataweteri to cope with the consequences of the inevitable contact with the *nabe.* They were being paid to set up an infirmary in the mission station equipped with solar panels to power a sterilizer and a refrigerator to keep vaccines and medicines cool. Five tons of equipment had been carried up the five waterfalls in thirty river trips. One-quarter of the three-year project's budget of $400,000, from the Italian Government, had been spent. The infirmary was ready but unused because the Yanomami, having been kept isolated, did not trust the infirmary's strange smell or appearance. Franco and Angela were due to leave shortly but there was no doctor or nurse yet arranged to replace them. Meanwhile the man called Geraldo was dying and they didn't know what to do.

"We've tried for one hour to put in a needle [to feed him intravenously] but his veins are too small," said Franco, while a small boy hugged his legs.

"What about taking him to the infirmary?" asked Chris, pausing between taking photographs.

"We can't. The family don't want him to go in the infirmary because, before we came, they took this man's brother to the mission. They gave him an injection and he died. So now the people think the injection is to kill the person. The people believe in me and my wife but it's very hard to recuperate this situation. It's stupid," said Franco.

Chris and I did not want to pry yet we did want to see Geraldo. Angela led us round the *shabono* to the section where dried palm fronds shaded the house from daylight. Geraldo lay in his hammock, with his wife and his mother holding his arms. Two dark, glazed eyes stared at us. I do not know how our eyes can reveal the secrets of our hearts, but I saw the deepest fear in Geraldo's eyes. Arms and legs lay uselessly against his emaciated body. He could no longer move without helping hands to lift his weight.

"He's looking down to the spirit when he's staring like this, looking down. The spirit's down there [in the ground]," explained Domingos in a voice trailing to a whisper. "Down there! Very deep!"

"Just like a city," added Renato, meaning an underworld of many spirits.

"He's afraid of the spirit. He can see the spirit," said Domingos.

"They think I believe it. It's the only way to try to give them the medicine. I try to give the Whiteman's medicine together with their medicine," said Franco in English, though I'm sure this duplicity was obvious to everyone.

A dozen men, kinsmen of the dying man, gathered beside us in Ajinor's home with an earnestness that excluded everyone else. Even the children kept away from the circle of men crouching on their haunches round three of the younger men in the middle of their circle. Each of them had fetched his own war club, some of them metal-tipped, a slender blowing tube and small container of *ebene*. The hallucinogenic snuff was in short supply, for it didn't grow in the forest round the community and had to be harvested in the forest below Santa Isabel on the Rio Negro. I remembered having met a few of the men from Xamataweteri, six months earlier, paddling upstream after their last unsuccessful expedition to gather the seeds of the *Virola* tree.

Three of the younger men sat in the middle of the circle waiting to help. None of the older men wore macaw or parrot feathers. None of them were painted with red *urucú* or the black lines of paint made from ash from the fire. They were preparing to fight. Silence was an agreement for united action; placing a little *ebene* in their tubes, distributing the powder by tapping the sides, they then turned the open ends to the young men, while holding the narrow end up to each nostril in turn. Blowing *ebene* up both nostrils requires strong and consistent breath, best delivered with bulging cheeks and force from the diaphragm. Each man coughed and slapped the back of his own neck to ease the pain from the blasts. Saliva and mucus drooled from mouth and nose, as unsightly side-effects of the snuff, but the drug is necessary to help the *shamans* in their work. Great *shamans* can see or feel the spirits unaided by the snuff but still it aids their vision. Even a dog can see the *hekura* if he takes *ebene*, according to Domingos.

A slow chant emerged from the circle as the *ebene* took effect after twenty minutes. Men began rocking from side to side on their haunches, slapping their thighs, letting chants rise from their throats. These chants came first as low murmurs, one from each man, hardly audible beyond their circle, but grew along with their rising physical energy. They sang for the *hekura* to fight with them, their voices strengthening into a unified cry, loud and urgent, matching their agitated bodies. Second vision opened to their bleary eyes, enabling them to see the spirits in the *shabono*.

Chanting continued while the men gathered their clubs and assembled in a line on the other side of the *shabono*. Pata-pata led them with his head down, knees half-bent and hands grasping the long club in front of him. Pata-pata, his name means great-great, was the oldest man of the community, the strongest *shaman* and the father-in-law of Domingos. He was the only man not to be wearing underpants or a pair of shorts; he wore the foreskin of his penis tucked under a thin cord tied round his waist. He led the men dancing in a line across the *shabono* towards the house where Geraldo lay dying in his hammock. The *shamans* came with loud approach, chanting and shouting, and stomping the ground with bare feet to frighten the monster. They paused in front of Geraldo's house to shriek and pound the ground with their clubs. Pata-pata led them forward, wielding his club to break open the barrier of palm fronds shading Geraldo's house from strong sunlight.

This was the main battle. They shouted insults at the monster devouring Geraldo's soul. They beat the ground inside his house trying to approach their companion slumped in his hammock. Men fell with cries of surprise and pain. Their companions carried them outside. Small arrows, fired by the bad spirits, were pulled from the backs of the wounded. Pata-pata fell back with his men to regroup outside the house after each failed attack. He ran alone once round the *shabono* while his men filled the community with chanting and shouts.

The *shamans* attacked seven times before they were able to push forward shouting and beating the ground to surround Geraldo. He lay slumped in his hammock with wide-open eyes. Pata-pata pressed his lips to the man's chest, trying to suck all the poisonous spirit from Geraldo's body. Then he spat it from his own mouth outside the house, where his men could kill it with their clubs or chase it from the community.

Many children watched their fathers from a safe distance. Two boys played with their miniature bows and arrows on the far side of the *shabono*. Few women watched the *shamans*. They lay in hammocks with their children or sat together weaving baskets or scooped tapioca back and forth in a wide toasting pan over a hot fire. Everyone scattered with screams when Pata-pata and the other men came abruptly rushing through the houses, apparently driving the monster out of the *shabono*.

Attack followed attack to dislodge the spirit and save the life of Geraldo until all the *ebene* was consumed. The men bathed in the river in the twilight, then lay in their hammocks warmed by the fires of orange flames leaping in the twilight. No-one knew if the cure would be successful.

Chris, Franco and I took photographs of the men's attack through long lenses, sitting with the children who were watching. Franco told us he'd waited three months before taking his first photograph. Soon afterwards, he'd arranged a slide show in the mission using solar panels to power the projector. "They loved to see themselves!" Franco said. His discretion, followed by sharing, had done much to remove people's suspicion that the machine stole part of their souls. Ajinor gave his own agreement to the cameras soon after we arrived, though this was no more than guidance. (Chris did not point the cameras at people who turned away.)

Photography reveals both a paradox and a truth about the Yanomami. Ironasiteri has far greater contact with Brazilians, yet the people distrust cameras and wish we would put them away. The people of Xamataweteri had probably never seen pictures of themselves before Franco showed them his photographs, yet they allowed outsiders to point cameras while their *shamans* were working and fighting with the *hekura*. This was rarely allowed in Ironasiteri. What has changed among the Yanomami with the increased contact with the *nabe*?

Franco told me about the very first contact between a Whiteman and the *shabono* farthest up the Marauiá, beyond Pohoro. Franco had made the first contact only a month before our arrival. Their reaction to Franco's arrival showed to me their trust of outsiders until proved otherwise. Their assumption was that Omam had created a Good World; not that mankind was debased or Fallen. The exception – when communities attack each other – proved the rule. Ironasiteri, with more contact, has learned to distrust even the *nabe* with whom they are familiar. They may trust me but do not like my camera. Trust of people in Xamatawerteri had not yet been eroded by failed promises and deceits. That was why they were unafraid of our cameras.

The first meeting with a Whiteman for the community near the headwaters of the Marauiá had come when Franco, Angela and their assistant had taken a brief holiday from the infirmary to go far up the Marauiá river near the mountains (and frontier with the Venezuela).

"We heard curassows [forest turkeys]. Mauricio [their assistant] went to hunt," said Franco. "But when he returned, he spread his hand out to show the size of human feet and said the curassow calls were people."

"No. It's impossible," I said. "The calls of the curassows continued for more than three hours while they watched us to see if we were angry or something like that. The first 'curassows' came out after three or four hours. Three children! 'Wait, wait,' they called [in Yamomami]. We stopped our boat. Angela was a little afraid because nobody had told us there were Yanomami up there," said Franco.

The party came back to Xamataweteri with their news. "Everybody want to go. Big talking!" Franco returned up river with one of the *shamans*, the priest and their assistant. "We called, 'Friend, friend,' in Yanomami, and more or less sixty people come out to us. That night, they make the rite for being friendly," said Franco. "They took my wrists to try to pluck out my body hairs." This was their first meeting with a Whiteman, though they already used a few metal knives and cooking pots traded with the other *shabonos*. It was also their first face-to-face encounter with the Yanomami of Xamataweteri. Two men went from Xamatawteri, to be welcomed with a feast establishing friendship between the two communities. Seven or eight people came down to visit the *shabono* of Xamataweteri.

"What did they know about the Whiteman?" I asked.

"They knew the myths. They'd been talking about us for many years," said Franco laughing loudly. His voice carried in the dark.

"Tell me about Pata-pata," I said, having heard about his expedition to Santa Isabel to rescue his daughter.

Franco laughed. "The padre convinced Pata-pata to allow the daughter – Piarina, Domingos' wife – to study in the college. In the mind of Pata-pata, who was still, well, *brabo* [wild], he thought the padre had taken his daughter and he wanted the padre to pay with a hammock and trade goods. Only the padre didn't want to pay.

"Pata-pata went down to Santa Isabel to look for his daughter. He was very intelligent. He went when the church was full on a Sunday. He went completely nude and painted all black. He went right inside the church with a knife. There he stood, in the aisle of the church, shouting at the padre Father Antonio Goes," said Franco, chuckling.

"All the nuns were crying because they think the Indians are still savages. Everyone was crying and afraid of Pata-pata. 'Where's my daughter?' Pata-pata cried at the priest, 'Where's my daughter?' Father Antonio Goes spoke very quietly to him. 'Don't do this,' he said to Pata-pata." Franco laughed again.

"Where's my daughter?" repeated Domingos with his usual giggling.

"Did Pata-pata take his daughter home?" I asked.

"The police didn't allow him," answered Renato.

Franco and Angela tried again in the twilight of the day to convince Geraldo's family to let him be moved to the infirmary but, they were more afraid of death as death came nearer, and would not allow him to be taken.

Renato signalled to Chris and me that it was time for us to give our gifts of fish hooks and line, glass beads, packets of tobacco, three machetes, five small knives, and powder, lead shot and detonators for their shotgun cartridges. We left Ajinor to share the items according to community politics but we soon learned we were in trouble about supplying detonators.

"The padre has forbidden these," said Franco, "because he thinks the people here are trading them to Ajuricaba and they have attacked another community who don't have shotguns. Five men have been killed," he said.

I could only plead innocence. "It was okay last year," I said feebly. "What will you use your shotgun for?" I asked one youth. "For hunting *xama* and *capybary*," he replied.

"The padre says you'll trade these to make war," I said.

The young man gave a caustic reply. "The padre gives nothing. He doesn't even want to buy our baskets."

I went to talk to Ajinor laying in his hammock. He dismissed my concern about upsetting the padre. "Let the priest be angry. He doesn't provide anything," said Ajinor.

I changed the subject. "When did you first see a Whiteman?" I asked.

"Myself? When I went to the [river] Padauari. It amazed me to see a Whiteman," Ajinor said chuckling. "It amazed me! I thought the Whiteman was wild. I thought the Whiteman was going to eat me. I became afraid."

"How old were you? This size?"

Ajinor pointed to his son, one of his four children. "This size," he said. The boy was about eight years old. Ajinor visited Manaus for the first time as a young man with a Brazilian trader after his mother died.

"You weren't afraid?"

"I wasn't. I found it very strange when I arrived. I wondered at it," he said with a laugh. "Later, I became accustomed."

I paused but Ajinor added nothing. "How did you explain a car and the city?"

"I didn't explain to anyone when I came back," he chuckled. We paused to let one of his two sons hear himself speaking on the tape recorder then I asked, "Some *garimpeiros* have arrived here?"

"Many came! With a boat," he said. Fifty or sixty *gamrimpeiros* had arrived in January that year, apparently invited by Ajinor himself. "I went to Manaus and I spoke with Funai, with the chief himself. 'Senhor Celmo, can you send two *garimpeiros* to me, just two, to teach us. We don't know how to excavate the earth. I want two *garimpeiros*,' I said to him. He said 'Okay! I'll send two *garimpeiros*.' But he sent a huge number of them."

"Did they teach?" I asked.

"Teach? Nothing! This padre stopped it. He called to Funai."

"How many days did they stay here?"

"One moon only," replied Ajinor.

"Did they find gold?"

"No. But also they didn't look. They didn't do anything," said Ajinor. Other people told me the *garimpeiros* prospected up the Marauiá then west to the Pico de Neblina.

"Let's talk a little more about the *garimpeiros*. Won't all the world arrive if the *garimpeiros* find gold here?" I asked.

"Now I've prohibited these *garimpeiros*. No more *garimpeiros*."

"If you find gold, the *garimpeiros* are going to arrive here, kill everyone and take the gold for themselves."

"They don't arrive any more. I've already forbidden them," said Ajinor.

"Why did you want *garimpeiros* here at all?" I asked.

"People from outside say gold is worth more for buying a shotgun. *Sorva* doesn't have a good price. *Farinha* is better, but not to buy a shotgun," he replied. One Yanomami community at Maturacá does occasionally prospect for gold when they want to buy something from the *nabe* but they harvest the gold only intermittently when it's wanted to exchange for a specific item.

"Did you send your son to the school in Apuí with Henri?"

"No, I will send but he's still small."

"What d'you want him to learn?"

"You learn Portuguese and numbers."

Angela invited Chris and me to the mission after dark. "Just come. Don't tell the padre," she'd said. We arrived as the padre was preparing to say Mass, for the day was Easter Sunday. "We'll come later," we said, anxious not to miss our chance of a meal. We went back to the hearth fires in the dark *shabono* to lie in our hammocks with boys and girls wanting to hear themselves singing on my tape recorder. No-one mentioned food and I doubt anyone ate more than tapioca porridge for supper that night. I knew we would be expected to leave next morning.

Angela was already serving dinner at the table when Chris and I tapped on the wooden door of the mission's kitchen. We willingly accepted bowls of rice with tinned fish and a few peas, followed by a creme caramel pudding from a packet. Packets of dried breads, a tin of chocolate drinking powder and a large cheese to be sliced – all imported from Italy – crowded the table between our bowls and the glasses of *graviola* juice, a pulpy white fruit with green skin. I was glad of the meal but not unaware of our gross selfishness in eating without sharing with our true hosts. Our gross selfishness showed in a single act what divides our culture from the Yanomami way of being human. Sharing food is one of their most important ways to show friendship.

We talked about what the padre called the afternoon "pantomime" with Geraldo. "His illness is fear but he doesn't believe us," said Angela. "You have to go with medicine and say, 'This medicine is for poison.' And he only looks at you. I don't know. It's very difficult."

"Is anything actually wrong with him, like tuberculosis?" asked Chris.

"I'd like to take him to the hospital in Santa Isabel, but I think he'd die travelling over the waterfalls," replied Angela. A pendulum clock on the wall chimed the hour.

"Another man came from Pororo in the same condition as Geraldo. We went down to Santa Isabel to the hospital but he died after ten days, because the hospital doesn't know how to care. A padre wanted to bury him and the Yanomami became very angry. So they took the body to Apuí; and cremated it and brought the bones here." said Angela.

I was keen to listen to the padre. What he said after the meal revealed a more sympathetic man grieving deeply for the deaths of the Yanomami. "Only international pressure is going to protect these people by securing their land for them. Nothing in Brazil will do that for them," he said.

Heavy rain during the night gave way to sunshine at daybreak. Warm light streamed into the *shabono* like rays from a halo hanging over the forest, but the joy of this bright new morning was broken by the chanting and cries of Geraldo's family.

"This man's dying," Renato said softly. Angela and Franco came to see Geraldo and left in silence, with tears in their eyes and holding each other's hands. Three *shamans* made a last attempt to drive out the evil spirit devouring their kinsman.

A single cry an hour later announced to everyone that their companion was dead. Shrieks took over from cries. Wailing replaced chanting. Quickly, the dead man's possessions were taken up by his mother, his wife, his father and his brothers, his kinspeople gathering round Geraldo laying in his hammock. Four women danced back and forth in front of him, holding in their hands the reels of his fishing line, his machete, his flashlight, his tube for blowing *ebene*. The pitch of their loud wailing rose and fell as their feet stepped lightly on and off the bare earth in the home.

Five men carrying axes advanced in a line across the *shabono*. They moved in rhythmic pace, yelling a cry and beating the ground with the flat side of their axes with every step of their slow march. They were going to gather firewood in the garden with which to build a funeral pyre in front of Geraldo's section of the *shabono*, Domingos explained in a whisper.

Boys and girls, all nephews, nieces and young cousins, were fetched to sit in silence around the dead man in his hammock. A recalcitrant dog was kicked away to make room. A woman knelt wailing and crying beside the hammock. Tears stung in her eyes. Her head leaned forward to his ears as if giving last-minute instructions to Geraldo's souls for their journeys to reach the resting places. Her sagging breasts rested on the edge of the fabric. Arms embraced the body.

I asked Ajinor, "What happens to the spirit when a person dies?" We talked of one "soul", though the Yanomami say humans have four.

"The spirit's very dangerous, you know. It goes to kill who killed him. And it does kill."

"Before the fire or after?"

"The spirit's already gone. It's no longer with him. Only the body stays and is burned."

"And if the spirit doesn't manage to kill who killed him?" I asked.

Ajinor shrugged his shoulders, "Then it doesn't kill. It goes to a place with other Yanomami there."

"What sort of place?"

"It's the same as here. But more food. Game! Fish! Everything! Men and women. And they make children too," he said.

"A place without illness?" I asked.

"Without illness. Without problems. Without insect bites, No *pium*!" he said laughing.

"Is the Whiteman there?"

"Everyone's there. Lots of whites, blacks and *morenos* [people of mixed race] as well," he said.

"Do they fight?"

"No."

"So why are there fights here?" I asked.

"There are no fights in this community," said Ajinor. "Only a little."

"Do very bad people go to the same place?"

"First to another place, then to the same place," he replied.

The dead man's brother led mourners into the sunlight to dance across the *shabono*. Each man and woman carried one possession in their hands, from underpants to feather ornament, which they held with arms outstretched as they turned round and round with slow steps or marched back and forth on the spot. Wailing, singing and loud cries filled the hot air with a full expression of grief and correct ritual.

The pyre was ready by mid-morning; built waist-high with split wood longer than the height of five men who did the work. Fire was brought from several hearths to ignite the centre of the pyre with a rush of thick grey smoke. Women still holding Geraldo's belongings gathered round the smoke. Men went to his home. Orange flames leaped high from the centre of the pyre. With one great cry, the men carried out Geraldo in his hammock, running to deposit him in the fire in a single uninterrupted act. Flames rose up quickly round his body. Thick grey smoke rose into the blue sky. Wailing and crying filled the air. Women and men fell to their knees facing the fire.

Geraldo's brother lay prostrate before his brother's cremation.

Chris, Franco and I took photographs from our distance, unable to hide our eagerness to click our cameras. We were intruders here and we knew it. Renato and Domingos also watched from Ajinor's home with tears in their eyes. No person spoke.

Flames and smoke engulfed the pyre with unexpected speed and heat, bringing to a climax the shrieks and hysterical tears of the people near the fire. Each stepped forward to throw Geraldo's belongings into the flames: feathers, bowl, machete, beads, flashlight. Everything must perish with the person. Angela told us about a dog that had been strangled and cremated with the body of the woman who had kept it.

All wailing, all mourning must be finished before the fire dies. Cremation must be a complete catharsis of grief, leaving the mourners exhausted. No-one will return to the pyre until the fire is out. Then Geraldo's bones will be separated from the ashes for a festival to be held after a week or two. Relatives and allies must be invited from communities for a party. Game must be hunted in the forest. Banana soup must be prepared to be mixed with crushed bones for the main guests to drink. And they will honour Geraldo by this. No-one will mention the dead man's name after the party. It will be as if he'd never lived.

In death is proof of the life of the community. A mother fingered through the hair of her children checking for lice. A young woman dried tapioca in a wide toasting pan over a fire. Another mother cleaned up her son's diarrhoea from the floor. A boy tied new feathers to his arrow. It was a short arrow with a short bow but he aimed into the sky and loosed it with the concentration of his elders. The arrow flew up, arched and plummeted to the ground just in front of him. The boy turned with a smile to receive the laughter of people watching him.

Renato and Domingos wanted to leave as soon as the mourners had walked away from the burning pyre. We waited only to speak to Ajinor, who lay in his hammock in tears, and to record messages in Yanomami to Davi from him and from Pata-pata. I too accepted that we had to leave. There was no food to feed us staying in the *shabono*. The river was already in flood at the start of the season of daily rainstorms. Chris was in a rush to return to England. Renato wanted to collect the new motor that the mayor of Santa Isabel had promised him. Father Francisco was threatening to call Funai on his radio. For all these reasons, the conditions were against the walk Domingos and I had planned to make through the forest to Davi.

Was it strange how my own enthusiasm for our journey had also waned? I was prepared for tough physical conditions and accepted the dangers as calculated risks. I still believed that meeting Davi and spreading his warning about gold miners were important to help the Yanomami defend themselves. But our objective was worthwhile only if it could be accomplished within the social structure of the Yanomami. No journey would help them if imposed by an outsider. Blunt, vainglorious ambition could destroy so much. I felt humbled by my ignorance after witnessing the *shamans'* fight to save Geraldo, and his death and cremation. I walked in silence round the *shabono* asking myself what harm I could be bringing to these people merely by desiring to be with them. I thought, "There's so much I might be taking from them yet so little I can give in return."

Renato and Domingos gathered bows and arrows and two baskets of *farinha* to take home with us. Ajinor and Pata-pata each recorded greetings to Davi inviting him to visit them soon. Franco and Angela said goodbye. Crowds of children played in the quiet water round our canoe or stood giggling on the river bank while we prepared to leave. The river was still rising, carrying away trees in its swirling brown waters. This promised a fast descent to Apuí. Children laughed and waved goodbye when I steered the canoe into the middle of the river. The canoe was caught abruptly by the current and moments later we were carried round the first bend away from the people of Xamataweteri. I kept the canoe moving through the fastest water, sweeping us downstream at least three times as fast as we'd travelled upstream. Blue and yellow macaws screeched overhead from time to time while we enjoyed the warmth of sunlight in the clear sky. Balls of cloud, white like cotton wool, promised no rain. Renato at the front, and myself steering, kept a lookout for floating trees and other debris being carried away by the river.

We were all eager to reach Apuí and did not stop, even when the sun sank behind the trees and a twilight gloom, and then darkness, settled over the river and forest. None of us wanted to sit in the canoe until dawn with our stomachs rumbling with hunger.

Nothing can be more exhilarating, or dangerous, than running a river in flood at night without being able to see where you're going. I steered down the centre of the river guessing, from patterns of black-black and black-grey, where we were between the bushes and trees stretching out from either bank. Renato shone his flashlight but its weak beam was more distracting than useful.

Sweeping round the bends terrified me. It was impossible to spot any turning until almost hitting one of the banks, as the river twisted to left or right. Renato twice cried warnings just in time for us to avoid ramming fallen trees that would have capsized the canoe.

Heavy rain began falling, adding a silver sheen to our miserable blackness. I couldn't see the river from the sky or the forest and was much too afraid to shiver in the cold. "This is madness!" I cried out. "We must stop!" I yelled at Chris.

"Wait ten minutes!" shouted Chris above the noise of falling rain and the motor.

"Probably our last!" I thought.

The rain eventually passed behind us and we emerged into blackness under a sky with stars. These cast a faint light onto the middle of the river by which I could navigate. Two hours later, we saw a light ahead of us. "Good evening! Good evening!" voices called in the black. This was Apuí and I steered into the river bank where a dozen people were waiting for us.

"If humans have nine lives, you've just used up one of them," I said to Chris, my voice shaking with relief. This was the third time I'd risked the wrath of the Marauiá river and survived.

"Providence," he jested with the happiness of the disbeliever.

Waking in Apuí next morning I was to become suddenly aware of the differences between this community and Xamataweteri. Renato was in front of his home yelling about the death of Geraldo, the cremation, our photographs, our gifts and the frightening return journey. No-one upriver would have stood in the arena shouting their news in this way. Noise – people arguing, children crying – was an obvious indicator of the greater tension in Ironasiteri. The atmosphere here was of contentment lost.

Huge pressures squeeze the Yanomami from the outside. Communities with greatest contact with the *nabe* feel them the most: goldminers in the east, and our warning of their arrival *en masse* in the west; epidemics of unknown diseases brought by spirits from the *nabe*; slow deaths overwhelming the power of the *pajés*; desire for trade goods to be obtained from men who cheat; ignorance of the

Whiteman's money and writing which give them so much power; frustration at the Whiteman's stinginess; anger over broken promises and distrust of change. It's important to keep separate the intertwined issues of land and contact with the *nabe*. Contact with the *nabe* is inevitable and brings great social upheaval but this is entirely separate from respecting the Yanomami claim to the land they have traditionally lived on. The Yanomami are quite able to cope with the changes brought by contact with us if the Whiteman respects their land.

And so much change! What cultural earthquake in the West could possibly let us experience change on the same scale as the sudden and simultaneous arrival of shotguns, malaria, helicopters, writing, land ownership and political autocracy among people who had never seen any metal object only one generation ago?

Yanomami reaction to change varies according to individual character and courage, and according to their spiritual and physical life. Yet there seems to be nothing people are not willing to investigate. My own tape recorder had once caused considerable anxiety but now young women wanted to hear themselves singing and the tapes were useful to send messages to other communities.

Even Gabriel asked me one morning to record him chanting to the *hekura*, though neither of us expected the reaction that followed. Recording the *pajés* had been banned before as dangerous because their own spirits as *shaman* would be vulnerable, but now Gabriel was more confident and he danced and sang for half an hour while I recorded him. Then he came to tell me how he'd nearly died.

"I took *ebene*. This tape recorder was turning round and round like this, and it caught me; my force as a *pajé*. The *hekura*. And I went inside," he reported.

"It pulled you?" I asked.

"Yes! The *pajé* [in me] called out, 'Oh brother-in-law this beast is squeezing and killing me. The beast is binding me round and round.' And my brother-in-law João took *ebene* and his *pajé* went right inside the tape recorder. And he secured me and pulled me," said Gabriel.

"João as *pajé* entered the tape recorder? He fought inside?" I asked.

"No. He didn't fight. The tape recorder was turning," Gabriel pointed to the spinning capstans, "and pulling my *pajé*, my singing inside. João went there and he secured me well in the middle and he wrenched me out. Pa! Pa!" exclaimed Gabriel. "That tape recorder's powerful. João's soul is strong. But I'm only a small *pajé*. A novice," he said. I did not dispute Gabriel's understanding of the tape recorder because I believed he'd grasped by intuition a metaphysical truth of the ingenious machine.

The one remaining chance to travel east with Yanomami leaders from the west to meet Davi, ended as soon as I proposed a new idea to Renato and Domingos. The plan was to reach Davi's *shabono* by returning down the Rio Negro to Manaus then to go first north by road, then, by some means, to travel westwards to reach the river Demini where Davi lived. Perhaps we could meet him in the city of Boa Vista, I pondered. But both Renato and Domingos had other priorities with which I was not willing to interfere.

Renato did not want to leave home because he was jealous of the two schools Henri and Simon (the Belgian) were building at Apuí and because Funai was rumoured to be coming to set up a post. Renato was irritable because he felt his leadership was being eroded. "Why two schools?" he asked me. The answer was that Simon's was to serve Ironasiteri, while Henri was to train teachers who could return to other communities. Parents wanted their children to learn numbers, written Yanomami, Portuguese and something about Brazilian society but, traditionally, learning has been by example from elders not by sitting in classes with an outsider.

Domingos did not want to leave home because he'd been invited to the festival at Xamataweteri to drink Geraldo's bones within a few weeks. Refusing to go would cause offence to these close allies.

Chris and I went after lunch to visit the young men building Henri's school 300 yards up the river from the *shabono*. Henri himself had gone to fetch more pupil teachers and had left Augusto, the young German, to supervise the feeding and behaviour of the five youths from other *shabonos* already waiting to begin classes.

Augusto's first name was Winfried but everyone found his family name easier to pronounce. He was a nurse by occupation and wanted to serve the Yanomami. This ambition was hard to realize because as yet he'd been refused permission to work by Funai. But he was a patient man, with a sardonic smile and a gentle manner that people liked. We sat in the sunshine, *piums* biting our necks, while Samuel, Henrique and others from Ironasiteri were busy splitting palm tree trunks to form the front wall of the school house.

"It's not easy staying here, is it?" I asked.

"No. It's really hard to prove that you're worth their confidence. Funai promised a lot but didn't arrive so the people [here] don't believe anymore," said Augusto. He talked of plans to train the teachers who could return to teach in their own communities in three years. This would not be straightforward.

"Their culture is beautiful but it's also very hard to change things. For example, take Chico. You know him? He's fifteen years old and already married. He's one of the most traditional. He studied with Henri [at the school] at Ajuricaba. He was the best schoolboy. 'The most intelligent,' says Henri. But he came here and said he was marrying this very young girl. Now he'll be a *pajé*. So he doesn't study in the school any more. You know, it's very hard to change the culture and, on the other side, to leave the culture without destroying it.

"Just our presence is destroying them. I'm changing something every hour I'm here. I have a lot of doubts," said Augusto.

"We fear to destroy the very presence that we have come to be with," I said, feeling more than ever as if I were contagious and that therefore I should leave.

Little of life is as it appears among the Yanomami. The young men were earning machetes and other trade goods for building the school but they were not expecting to keep these for themselves; their "wages" would be claimed by their older kinsmen.

Likewise, why had Chico dropped out of school? Was this just a capricious change of mind, as Augusto suggested? Answers to these questions confirmed both the strength of Chico's character and, I believe, revealed ways in which external pressures are dramatized within the community. There was no chance before leaving to ask Chico himself what had happened but I did learn from Domingos that Chico had met a *poré*, or supernatural being, in the forest.

The evening before leaving, Jacinto called me to the circle of five men outside Alippe's house waiting to record messages to Davi in the east. The men spoke in both Yanomami and Portuguese inviting Davi to visit the Marauiá.

"Davi excuse me," said Domingos. "You invited me there. [But], brother-in-law, it's not possible to go with Dennison on this next journey. We've lost our brother-in-law at the mission. We're invited to drink the banana soup. I'm going to dress for this festival and I cannot miss. They'll think badly of me if I miss."

"If I miss you, you too will think badly of me. Don't sit there saying, 'Domingos is a liar.' Wait. You'll see me and what sort of face I have. I'll come to you on the next journey when Dennison comes again. I want to know your land. I don't know when Dennsion will come again. Only he knows. He's almost becoming a Yanomami. He'll pull off his trousers next time he comes," said Domingos with his usual mischievous giggling.

Domingos and his family were still disappointed that Chris and I had not stayed with them, but Domingos called me to eat with them on our last night, and after supper he told me to fetch the tape recorder to record two messages. The first was a highly complimentary report to the people of my land telling them how much Domingos wanted Dennison and his friend to visit again. The second was a lesson to the newly-installed president of Brazil about political democracy.

"The government controls wherever there's a little city. But it can't govern the area of the Indian. It's we who govern on the Marauiá river [just] as the president governs over there. It's the same. We govern as he governs. I govern my land here. His [the president's] land is on the Rio Negro. This is what I can say now."

"I'm not saying that I govern in another *shabono*. Those inhabitants govern there. Each governs in their own *shabono*. I cannot order theirs. I govern only in mine. The government should act like this as well," explained Domingos.

The community gathered in the morning to give Chris and myself the presents in payment for the trade goods we had brought; small baskets for keeping fish hooks or sewing needles and cotton; large baskets for storing tapioca or our clothes at home; bows made of black wood of the peach palm and arrows with feather flights; majestic scarlet macaw tail feathers; vivid yellow feathers from the noisy *japiim* birds; black and white speckled *cuxubí* feathers; arm bands made of the iridescent blue scalp feathers of the *jacamí*; a headband made of the fine-haired tail of the squirrel monkey.

"*To-tihi-tawee*," we said (meaning beautiful, good) as each item was presented. We soon gained a heap of baskets and feathers that were quickly packed together safely for the journey down the river.

No-one knew when I might come again – not even myself – but I wrote in my notebook the requests from each household for specific goods I should bring next time for them. These shopping lists were never long, usually a machete and sewing thread and needles or a hammock for each family. Some offered to pay in advance but I said to wait.

Almost everyone assembled on the river bank to watch or to help load the two canoes. The big rock, on which we had landed just a week earlier, was now submerged under the thick brown flow of the Marauiá. The river was still rising, assuring us of a fast journey down to Santa Isabel beyond the five waterfalls. Renato, Domingos, Jacinto and several youths were coming with us to collect the motor the mayor had promised them, and then to go off hunting for a few days. Chris and I shook hands or embraced everyone who was to remain at home. Then we started the motor, waved again and were quickly carried away by the flood.

Two of the youths took turns steering the canoes, lashed side by side, allowing Renato and I to sit together. I asked him about the *poré* that Chico had met in the forest. Renato described him plainly, without excitement in his voice, so that I didn't realize at first that the *poré* was a supernatural creature.

"He arrived here two weeks ago. He's a real person! A true Yanomami," whispered Renato. "The *poré*, also called an *onka*, paints himself all black and whistles in the forest to lure the men to kill them and to steal their wives," said Renato.

"Chico was afraid. He grabbed his shotgun and ran. And the *poré* ran after him. Chico was in great danger. He fired to defend himself. Pah! Pah! And escaped to his companions, Jacinto and Alberto, on the river bank. Jacinto gathered a magic plant to counteract the poison cast by the *poré* but we know he's still there," said Renato. It had been this experience that had convinced Chico to switch from learning in school to training, with the old man Jacinto and others, to be a *shaman* to protect his wife, himself and the community.

The flood-level of water made passing the five water falls easier than ever before. We lowered the canoes on ropes through the terrific force of water over the fifth fall, then sailed over the next three with hardly a splash, and passed the first waterfall with the rope again.

It would be five months before I could return to Ironasiteri with renewed hope of travelling through the forest with Domingos to meet Davi. By then, all the forces that the Yanomami must fight would have encroached even deeper within their land. *Porés* would be actually approaching Ironasiteri. And, most shocking of all, Ironasiteri and Xamataweteri would be "at war" with one another.

7

We reached Santa Isabel late in the afternoon, in time to bathe in the river and hang our hammocks for the night under a rusting roof. The open-sided long shed was the only accommodation for out-of-town visitors. Some of the boys took one of the canoes to go fishing while Chris and I bought rice, coffee and sugar as treats for our evening meal. Renato and Domingos went to see the mayor about the promised motor.

I have visited Santa Isabel a dozen times in the past four years but have never much enjoyed the tawdry facilities of this outpost of "civilization" despite people's easy-going welcome. The long white mission school and church complex, built by the Salesian missionaries to impress newcomers, still dominates the town though their proselytizing zeal has diminished and today they serve only as parish priests. Diesel motors of the electricity-generating station roar for sixteen hours – in the middle of the town – to make power for televisions to watch the four daily soap operas from Rio de Janeiro, for lights and to pump a mains water system that leaks badly. Single-storey, tin-roofed buildings stand between stagnant ditches along the streets. Canned music blares from half a dozen bars. The first drinkers come at sunrise.

This town is not a self-sufficient pioneer community but a stump trying to heal itself after the deaths of the thousands of Indians who lived in the area. Today, self-generated activity is limited to football matches. Everything else – from building bricks to alcohol – comes from Manaus on barges. The town is not even self-sufficient in food. Protein often comes from tins. Supper may be a packet of biscuits. Few fruits or vegetables are grown. Processed juices in packets are preferred to picking the same fruits from trees.

No-one boasts of a town like Santa Isabel when politicians and military men in the Amazon speak of "progress" and the living frontier ("*frontier viva*" – one of the slogans of the Calha Norte project). What is "progress" when the town is wholly dependent on fashions and financial grants from 2,000 miles away? Santa Isabel's

5,000 inhabitants dangle at the end of the trail of Coca-Cola bottles, consumer toys and money. Wages (for teachers, nurses, etc) are paid in cash but there's no bank, so money must be spent quickly on tinned foods and cheap clothes before inflation reduces the paper money to pulp.

Like many other towns in the Amazon, Santa Isabel was founded as a one-hut outpost after Portuguese soldiers, slaving parties and missionaries came up the river to claim the land for Portugal 300 years ago. Pope Alexander VI had given Spain the whole of South America west of an imaginary line that runs through the mouth of the Amazon, while Portugal could occupy all heathen lands to the east. (This by the Treaty of Tordesillas in 1494.) However, the Portuguese also took control of the lands west of the Line. Bandeirantes – explorers, *garimpeiros* and slavers – explored the centre of the continent for more than a century and a half on expeditions of extraordinary courage and endurance, and of merciless savagery against the tribal peoples they encountered. These expeditions, and the mission posts, gave Portugal control of what is today Brazil. (Agreed between Spain and Portugal in the Treaty of Madrid in 1750.)

At least twenty-four tribes along the Rio Negro and its tributaries lost their land and their lives to the Portuguese. The Manau, under their leader Ajuricaba in 1723, were one of the valiant tribes who fought the invaders, but they too were defeated. The tribe is extinct.

Tens of thousands of Indians were taken from the Rio Negro before 1750, according to the 18th century Jesuit missionary Father João Daniel. Tribal land was taken by the government and tribal custom collapsed. Descendants of the survivors converted to the Church; they lived in family, not communal, houses; they married Europeans or Africans who came to gather rubber at the end of the 19th century. Today, they are Brazilians at the bottom of the social ladder and wholly marginal to the country's chaotic economic apparatus.

Defeat of the Indians was not a tragic byproduct of contact with the Whiteman but the exact aim of Portuguese policy to take over their land. Co-existence was not attempted. Today's tragedy for the Yanomami is that Brazil still hungers for their land, while the Yanomami expect contact as between respectful allies helping each other. The occupation of their forest is not inevitable unless the people of the self-styled "civilized society" are rapacious by nature.

Today, occupation of land is called "integration" by the military strategists who devised the Calha Norte project to colonize the northern Amazon with Brazilians. Santa Isabel has gained much from the project, including financial and equipment aid, as one of the region's outposts for "order and progress" – the motto of the Brazilian flag.

The Comara, a military unit of the Brazilian Air Force, has built a tarmac runway several miles behind the town and its bulldozers were still clearing a road west towards the Marauiá river. The trail will be opened as far as Apuí, according to Santa Isabel's thirty-year-old mayor, to make contact with the Indians easier. Five miles of the muddy gash through the forest have already been finished. Land on either side has been assigned to townspeople to clear for agriculture. The mayor says the land will certainly not be sold; but Brazilian law provides legal title to "squatters" after nine years.

Under the plan to divide the Yanomami land into nineteen "islands", the people of Ironasiteri would be confined to 35,450 hectares on the west side of the Marauiá river. The area looks large only on a map, but it would be too small for the community to be self-sufficient by hunting and gardening because the soils are poor and the game in the forest is far from abundant. The Yanomami method of shifting agriculture is well-adapted to ecological conditions of their forest. The Rio Negro and its surrounding forest has been called the River of Hunger ever since the first Europeans sailed up it in the 17th century. The river and its tributaries flow off an ancient geological formation, the Brazilian Shield, that was leached of nutrients long ago. The water carries few nutrients to support insects, fish and birds and mammals. There's almost no commercial fishing on the Rio Negro, despite a market of a million people in Manaus, because there are no large shoals of fish.

The forest north of the Rio Negro grows from the infertile soils that cover the ancient geological formation. The trees are stunted compared to the huge trees along the Solimões river (the name of the Amazon flowing thick with nutritious silts from the geologically-new Andes mountains). The forest of the Yanomami is crowded with light-hungry, short trees. The air is quiet. Every visitor is surprised by the absence of animals and birds. The land is an impoverished forest, from which the Yanomami have learned to sustain themselves by moving their *shabonos* every few years. Ironasiteri for example, have moved their *shabonos* and gardens to at least six different locations along the Marauiá river in the last thirty-five years. They need a large area of forest to feed themselves and would have to beg food from the *nabe* if their forest were to be taken from them. It is perhaps startling to consider that the population in the whole Amazon is only about double what it was 500 years ago, yet eighty per cent of the food for its six million people today must come from outside the region.

The mayor of Santa Isabel, José Ribamar Fontes Beleza, known as Zezinho, is an affable, energetic man with many plans to improve his municipality. "I've thirty-seven communities, including many in the indigenous area. The 600 Indians on the Marauiá belong to Santa Isabel.

"My service with them is education and health. I've already sent a teacher to teach Portuguese and Yanomami because I think it's just for them to continue with their language," said the mayor. He told me the teacher spoke Yanomami but this was untrue. Zezinho is probably genuine in his concern "to carry the Indian forward" but his best efforts are drawing the Yanomami of the Marauiá river into the culture of his town and weakening their control over a future that is being decided for them elsewhere. "I think the Indian has to be civilized, in my opinion," he said, glancing up from signing papers in his office. I asked him about the enrollment of 380 Yanomami as voters, some of them under sixteen years old, which Chris and I had witnessed at Ironasiteri.

"No! Look, I don't consider them electors. I took a census to enable me to help them financially. Funai doesn't help," he said. The municipality as a whole gets more government grants the more people enrolled.

"Our area is very rich in minerals but unfortunately there are the laws and Funai and the army. For me, I would give support to anyone who brings development to the municipality. Unfortunately no-one has come. They're blocked before they arrive. The area is rich but what can we do?" asked Zezinho.

Renato, Domingos and the others were delighted with the motor Zezinho gave them for enrolling as voters, but how much do they understand of the *nabe*'s political, legal and military appetites to claim their land? I lay in my hammock listening to the rain in the night wondering what the chances were that the new president of Brazil would treat the Yanomami according to Brazilian law.

Chris and I called to Manaus for a plane to come to fly us back to the big city. The journey would save perhaps a week of waiting for a boat, but I was ambivalent about such extravagance when there wasn't money to bring a tuberculosis team to the Marauiá nor to fly Renato, Domingos and Ajinor to try to meet Davi. Such is our world, I muttered to myself as the Cessna accelerated across the river to take off in front of the town. The plane belonged to the Federal Police; the pilot was taking a day's sick leave to earn $5,000 in cash for the three-hour ride to Manaus (six hours up and back for the pilot).

In Manaus, Chris and I discovered we didn't have enough money to pay the pilot. It was late Friday afternoon. "*Calma, calma*," I kept repeating to the pilot. "We'll sort out something." Chris flew to London that night promising to telex the money on Monday morning. I gave the pilot my passport until the money arrived. The pilot accepted grudgingly. Happily, I have two passports, so I was still able to fly north to Boa Vista for the weekend.

The last time I'd been there, people had rushed at the airport to get a taxi and I'd dashed into the city to take the last room in the hotel. This time I was one of only four guests and half the hotel was closed. Next door, the shop that had bought and sold gold was for rent. Restaurants were empty.

By one of those happy coincidences, and thanks to taking the plane from Santa Isabel, I arrived in Boa Vista just in time to meet Davi Kopenawa Yanomami on his way home to the Demini river. We talked in the CCPY office (Commission for the Creation of the Yanomami Park) located in a street of houses.

Rain poured all morning while Davi and I talked and his three children enjoyed a pillow fight round the sofa where we were sitting. I gave Davi the tape with the messages from Ironasiteri and Xamataweteri and explained why they couldn't come. "I'm thinking a lot about them. They don't know the whole situation. They know the situation of the Yanomami but not with the Whites," said Davi.

"Can you visit them?" I asked.

"I'd like to visit my relatives to explain what's happening [but] it's difficult. I have work in my own community and invitations come from Brasília and from outside," he said. "It would be good to go when I'm on holiday next March." He explained he was starting a health project for his area and he wanted to stay home. This was to be a pioneer project among the Yanomami, devised by Davi and partly funded by Funai and the Overseas Development Agency of the British Government (when the paperwork was signed many months later). Davi's project was different because he based the area to be served on the regional allies of his community. Previous health projects by Funai or the missionaries had been planned according to the *nabe's* logic. Davi's project would first serve the traditional regional allies round his *shabono* and later extend to other regional groups of allies. The objective was to provide long-term health care against the diseases the *garimpeiros* had brought. But Davi was cautious about the project. "First, you have to organize; to think how it will function. You have to have enough nurses and doctors to stay inside the reserve, not just to visit and then go home. You have to make a garden with bananas and sweet manioc for the patients to eat," he said.

"How was your visit to Europe?" I asked. Davi patted his stomach, calling it "Europe tummy". "They treated us very well." Davi was returning home from a visit to Europe with Ailton Krenak, leader of the São Paulo-based Union of Indigenous Nations who went to receive the Onassis Award.

"The only prize I want to receive is our land demarcated; a signed paper stamped by the President of Brazil," commented Davi. He was sombre and tired and didn't smile at all. He wore no feathers nor paint today, only red shorts and a green and white t-shirt tight round his waist.

"Is the pull-out of *garimpeiros* only for show?" I asked.

"It's only to speak beautifully. To cheat you all. You think he [the president] is doing good work with the Indians. But he's not. He's deceiving everyone. *Garimpeiros* pay him not to do anything. *Garimpeiros* are continuing to work. They have come now to the high Catrimani river.

"I've heard President Collor is going to dynamite the clandestine airstrips. To throw a bomb to each. I don't think it's good. He will scare the game, scare the relatives and the smoke will bring epidemics and poison. It's just his idea. He's never asked us, 'Yanomami, what do you think?' He doesn't consult us," said Davi.

"The Kayapó [on the Xingu river in the eastern Amazon] have *garimpos* inside their area and they earn ten per cent of the value of the gold. The *garimpeiros* pay them. Do you think this would be good here or not?" I asked cautiously.

Davi fell silent for a long time. "I don't know what to say. I know what I think, but we would have to think a great deal about what to do. Speak with people who know how to think well, who know how this would turn out. If it would be good or not. I myself fear this. I don't need *garimpeiros* working in my community. I want them to stay far away," he said.

How many *garimpeiros* were still working four months after the Federal Police arrived to withdraw them from the Yanomami area? How much was due to economic recession as a result of the new president's dramatic economic measures and how much due to the work of the Federal Police? The best assessment of the effectiveness of the operations came, perhaps inadvertently, from President Collor who flew north to visit the army base at Surucucus and a couple of Yanomami communities, within two weeks of taking office. He posed with his wife in jungle camouflage uniforms for the cover of one of Brazil's top magazines.

"There's space for everyone in Amazonia. We have to respect our Indian brothers but also the Brazilians who take from the earth a little food with which to kill their hunger," he said in Boa Vista in the morning.

"Dynamite the airstrips and do it quickly!" Collor ordered the Federal Police in the afternoon, after seeing the airstrips, polluted rivers and decimated *shabonos*. It was an admission of the failure of the first operation under Sarney's government and the confirmation that the *garimpeiros* were still mining gold and tin ore.

Thousands of *garimpeiros* had left the area – airlifted by the Federal Police – but many were returning with fresh supplies after the celebrations of Carnaval. My own estimate was that six or seven thousand men were still working and the principal airstrips – such as the one at José Altino Machado's tin ore mine – still operating.

José Altino Machado dismissed what he called "pyrotechnics with dynamite". "We can repair an airstrip in less than ten hours. But we can also reach areas through the forest," said José Altino, who was about to stand as a candidate for senator in the first elections in the history of Roraima. Like the governor Romero Jucá, he was calling for the area to be "administered" by the government and warned against the dangers of leaving the Indians without support if the *garimpeiros* were taken out.

"What's the government doing now?" I asked him.

"It's a spectacle for you to publish. The world's going to publish the migration of the *garimpeiros* with the police behind, with the army, with the bombs. But three or four months or a year from now everything will return as it was," said José Altino.

The operation to dynamite the airstrips was a fiasco. Only seventy-five airstrips were targetted – out of 156 known to exist – and only thirteen of the targets were actually blown up. But the explosions looked effective on television.

I returned to the CCPY office in the evening, after Davi had left for his *shabono*, to talk to Carlos Zacquini, CCPY coordinator in Boa Vista. He's a gaunt Italian who speaks quietly but with an absolute conviction. Carlos was one of the remarkable people drawn to help the Yanomami after personal contact with them; he visited a community on the Catrimani river for a month in 1965 at the age of twenty-eight and stayed. He was banned from the region in 1987 when possible witnesses to the goldrush were expelled by the Army.

"What do you most admire in the Yanomami?" I asked.

"You notice with them a larger liberty and a sincerity that disarms even those who, sometimes, initially don't have a sympathy for them. Their generosity is extraordinary. It's a society that shocks us. It's a society that has functioned well without traumas; a society that has demonstrated a happiness, a desire to live peacefully even with the wars among them. I know of several wars where they tried to kill others for various motives but, in reality, these wars killed a lot less than one epidemic.

"What leaves you worried, and with the wish to do something, is to see them so unprotected, so innocent, in a certain form, and fragile facing our society. To see them thus pressurized produces a feeling of revulsion, something unacceptable in those who know them. We're not asking for a favour for the Indians. We're asking only that the law of Brazil should be respected," said Carlos.

"Change is necessary for them to survive. They have to adapt, but this needs a long time. It's not possible to change a way of thinking from one day to another. We have to remember that they didn't have a single piece of metal until the middle of this century. Our European society has arrived after thousands of years.

"I've worked closely with the Yanomami for twenty-two years. Now, I have the wish to leave. I've seen people who were full of mental and physical health become skeletons. You don't even know if they have life inside. They walk but don't know why they walk. They manage to smile to me because they know me but with a sad smile," he said. Carlos cries when he visits sick Yanomami.

"Has this changed your faith in God?"

"No. Maybe my faith has not been so great but my faith in God continues. My thinking about certain institutions and about our society has changed.

"It's a perverse society here, dominated by a few. Those who respect the law are dead," he said. Yet he acknowledged the difficulties of even honest contact between the Yanomami and the *nabe*.

"In reality, there doesn't exist a model to follow to leave the Indians in the best possible way. It doesn't exist, but we have to reflect that everything done in the past to the Indians has brought misery or exterminated them. We have to look again. We must stop a while to think. At least this!" said Carlos, who was to return to Italy a few months later.

I returned to Manaus after a few days to receive the money wired by Chris for the pilot, and stopped briefly to meet Simon LeFevre, the man from Belgium starting a school at Apuí. He was bivouacked in a little house he'd bought in Manaus with money sent by supporters in Belgium to be a base for himself and the Yanomami on visits to the city. Building work on the house had stopped with every room taken over by beams and supports holding up the roof: "Collor's economic plan!" exclaimed Simon with a laugh. "The dollar fell and I can't buy materials to finish. I've had to send to Belgium twice for more money," he said, mixing *caipirinhas* (*cachaça*, sugar and lime juice) on a sideboard in the middle of the floor. Packing boxes of school supplies, tools and trade goods (including a big box of beads!) filled one room.

Simon had been an architect before coming to the Amazon for a visit, meeting the Yanomami and deciding to stay with them.

"What do you think of Apuí?" I asked.

"It's lost much of its culture. There're already many problems. But you know, deep down the culture stays. It's important to save the community for them to stay together. Save the community and the culture will stay. Renato is always criticizing the Indians up the river, saying they're wild, backwards, but deep down he's still like them because they all have close family contacts," he said.

"How long do you intend to stay on the Marauiá?" I asked.

"To the end of my life," replied Simon.

"No desire to return to Belgium?"

"What will I do there? It's completely lost in Europe. I've planted my coconut tree here," he said.

I looked puzzled.

"I've chosen where to hang my hammock," he said smiling. We toasted to success for his school with several more *caipirinhas*.

Simon sailed to Santa Isabel with his supplies and tools within a few days. I flew south to Brasília to meet French anthropologist Bruce Albert who had just returned from two weeks as an interpreter with a medical team at Paapiú, one of the airstrips cleared of *garimpeiros*.

A dozen doctors, from government and non-government organizations all over Brazil, had been treating Yanomami in a series of flying visits into the area for four months. Lack of transport restricted access but the health situation was improving, Albert reported. Malaria infection was down at Paapiú from ninety per cent of the people to forty-five per cent. "But still, you know, the *tuxaua* of a community near Jeremias died two days ago of a malaria coma with four attacks of *falciparum* malaria," he said. Both *vivax* and *falciparum* (attacking the brain) malarias were still epidemic. "Imagine! A baby of seven months who has caught seven successive malarias. Now she has a mixture of *falciparum* and *vivax* and we sent her to the hospital in Boa Vista. She looks like a little dead thing, yellow," said Albert. "Medical books say that children don't catch malaria before six months of age, because of the immunity given by the mother's milk, but this doesn't work. It's a first infestation in the area so there's no immunity transmitted by the mothers," he said.

Health teams were only able to reach about one-quarter of the communities because of the lack of aeroplanes and a helicopter. "FAB (the Brazilian Air Force) promised Funai, they promised us twenty times but the helicopter never arrived!" said Albert shrugging his shoulders.

It was one of the commonplace perversions of the situation that the medical teams were using the *garimpeiros'* aeroplanes to get into the area; Funai's own planes were out of action for repairs. *Garimpeiro* planes were allowed to fly inside the Yanomami area using permits issued by Funai for them to remove mining equipment and personnel. Corruption was rife; the permits passed from pilot to pilot regardless of the aeroplane prefix, pilot's name or the date. Albert confirmed frequent flights to four mining sites near the medical team.

One day, the medical team asked the pilot of a plane that had brought out two laboratory technicians, to take two mothers with two sick children back with him to Boa Vista, Albert told me. "No. I can't," the pilot said. "I'm going to get cassiterite [tin ore] from the airstrip of Altino [Machado]. I'm only passing by here to get there." Funai pretended that they'd chartered the plane but the pilot said, "No, this flight is courtesy of José Altino, so why are the Indians angry with me?"

"Another time an aeroplane of Altino [Machado] descended full of cassiterite. The following day the same plane returned carrying the Federal Police. This is so irresponsible. It's a crazy business," said Albert. Carrying friends and enemies in the same planes was certain to bring confusion and trouble as the Yanomami were determined to stop *garimpeiros* re-taking the airstrip at Paapiú. "I know a youth there whose father was shot by the *garimpeiros*. His wife died of malaria. This twenty-year-old is alone with his two-year-old daughter. He has a tremendous hatred of the *garimpeiros*. He's always the first to run onto the runway armed with bow and arrows every time a plane comes. I'm sure he's going to end up shooting someone," says Albert.

Yanomami men rolled oil drums to block the runway one day when one of Altino Machado's planes landed. "Everybody was tense against the *garimpeiros*. They started gathering round the plane armed with axes and bows and arrows. It was a day when the Indians drink *caxiri*, made of manioc, only now they put in *cachaça* from the *garimpeiros*, so they were very drunk. Funai had not advised that the plane was coming," said Albert. One of the men fired an arrow at the plane but missed. The pilot was trembling.

"I went into the middle of them, because my work is as an interpreter, to explain that the two passengers were not *garimpeiros* but medical technicians from SUCAM [government agency responsible for fighting malaria]," said Albert. The incident was defused but the hatred, fear and confusion remained.

"What do the Yanomami think of the diseases?"

"They told me in Paapiú that all the epidemics are spread by the smoke. When they don't have direct contact with the Whites they interpret the epidemics as witchcraft by other enemy groups who threw magical plants in the fire to spread a pathological smoke. When they have closer contact with the Whites, they attribute witchcraft to the Whites. The Whites throw manufactured articles into the fire. Now, with the *garimpos*, there's a new interpretation. They attribute these malaria epidemics to the smoke of the motors of the machines. They say the machine is '*makinari wakeshi*' that is, the smoke of the machines, the pumps, spreading everywhere and poisoning the region."

"This is to kill all of them?"

"Yes. They see that they are ending; all the old people have died. The majority of sick people are children. In the four *shabonos* [where Albert was working], I think there were only eight children under one year old. A child of seven years died on the day we left," he said.

"How are the people managing to cremate all their dead?" I asked. Bruce Albert explained that the funeral custom among Yanomami in the east is not to cremate but to wrap a corpse in palm leaves and hang it in the trees to decompose. The bones are recovered afterwards to be burned and crushed for the usual funeral festival.

"What happens to people who die in Boa Vista?" I asked.

"Their bodies are not returned," explained Albert. "This is a scandal for which Funai is not forgiven. The most horrible thing that two enemies could do, in the traditional universe of the Yanomami, is to throw bodies in the river to prevent their families recovering the bones to be able to make the ritual etc.

"Maybe Funai don't know the importance. One Funai doctor told me, 'We have to bury them because we are going to catch diseases.' It's an explanation totally mixed with ignorance," said Albert.

"What happens if the Yanomami can't drink the bones?" I asked.

"It's a cosmological scandal. It's unbearable. It's not cutting the connection with the living people. So the dead keep coming back in dreams, bringing more illnesses. The whole of their funeral ritual is in order to definitively cut the dead from the world of the living.

"In a war, if an enemy dies in your house, you begin the funeral service for them and later your enemy will send an ambassador, one of the oldest men or a widow, who can move between the two communities, to recover the bones. They may be your enemies but they are people; civilized. So there's this courtesy. Throwing away the bones is a situation almost impossible to imagine. It's at the limit of aggressiveness," said Albert.

"What is gold to the Yanomami?"

"My interpretation is that [traditionally] gold was nothing; just something in the river. It had no use or interest. Davi says Omam, the Creator of the Yanomami, put all the metals under the earth because they are dangerous substances for humanity. He put them all in a cold place under the earth. And the Whites, who don't know anything about anything, who are ignorant people, are taking all these out into the heat of the sun. This creates dangerous connections. Gold is an extremely dangerous substance that has to stay underground, where Omam put it. Omam knew it was a poison for mankind. Gold is seen as a poison [being] brought to the surface of the earth to cause craziness in the Whites through its poisonous magnetism," said Albert.

"In Brazil of today, how can the government not touch the mineral riches?" I asked.

"That's not the question. There are so many riches in other places that don't have the ecological and social costs. If we talk of cassiterite, there are huge reserves of tin ore in Brazil that could be used before this. It doesn't benefit Brazil, only Altino Machado. The tin ore goes into the parallel [black] market of tin ore; it doesn't pay taxes, it damages the jobs of the official companies because it increases supply at a lower price.

"And gold comes from other places in Brazil. The country doesn't benefit from this activity. The government spends more public money to send doctors, police and aeroplanes of FAB. Taking these riches actually costs the country much more in social, financial and ecological terms," said Bruce Albert.

The summer was months of waiting for news while the new Collor government settled. I returned home to write the commissioned story for *The Sunday Times Colour Magazine*, to be used beside Chris Steele-Perkins' photographs of Ironasiteri and Xamataweteri in the late summer.

Brazil's new Environment Secretary, Dr. José Lutzenberger, a respected ecologist, repeated yet again on the telephone to me that President Collor was serious about tackling the illegal burning of the Amazon forest and about protecting the Yanomami. Many people in Brazil wondered how long such an honest or naive man could last in the snake pit of Brazilian politics. The good doctor was exhausted by his commitments and thankfully candid about the political difficulties within his country. "We need your pressure from the outside, the more pressure you put on the better," he told me.

International support for the Yanomami was gathering pace since Davi's visit to Europe last winter. But what good would come of sacks of letters, lines of signatures on petitions, fund-raising, news reports or even Survival International's campaign and weekly vigil outside the Brazilian Embassy in London? It was difficult to keep faith in the face of so much greed and violence everywhere else in the world. Were the Yanomami just another "flavour of the month", as a television researcher told me? My own answer to these doubts was prompted by a student at a lecture who asked me what good letters and petitions would do. "Will the Yanomami still be alive in twenty years time?" she asked.

"I can give you two answers," I replied. "Some Yanomami will certainly be alive, despite what's being done to them. Secondly, to me, there are only two sides in this issue. Are you someone who knows what's happening and does nothing, or someone who tries to help the Yanomami? To my mind, we have only this choice." I remembered meeting Mother Theresa one misty morning in Calcutta and her answer when asked if her work made any difference to an ocean of suffering. "Our work may only be a drop in the ocean, but I think the ocean would miss the drop," she said.

Simon LeFevre arrived briefly in Lisbon in June on his way to study tropical nursing in Belgium for a few months. He arrived hobbling on crutches with his left leg in plaster, and with just enough time between planes for a few sandwiches and coffees. The tale of his misadventure emphasized comically the difficulties of doing anything in the Amazon – even government efforts to withdraw the *garimpeiros*.

Simon had reached Santa Isabel from Manaus with all the tools and materials to build his school in Apuí. In Santa Isabel, Simon met ten Yanomami from Pohoro, the community beyond Xamataweteri, who'd come in a big canoe on their two-yearly shopping trip with forty baskets of *farinha* to exchange for hammocks, ammunition and other trade goods.

"Let's go up together," they said to me because I had a big motor and they didn't want to paddle their canoe against the river's current. Simon loaded his chests of tools and strapped forty sheets of aluminium sheeting for the roof under the benches of the great canoe.

"We passed the first, second and third waterfalls safely," said Simon. They were above the fourth waterfall, called Tucuman, when the accident happened. "We'd unloaded the canoe, carried everything above the fall, dragged up the canoe and reloaded at the top," said Simon. Two of the Yanomami fell into the water as they were drawing away from the rocks. "I turned the motor so as not to run over them with the propeller. The canoe rushed into the middle of the river. The current caught us and we were washed – canoe and all – over the waterfall. I thought I was finished. But I came to the surface," said Simon. The two Yanomami also swept over the fall were saved but the canoe sank under the weight of the trade goods, forty aluminium sheets and the outboard motor. "I found one plastic bottle, well closed and later the Yanomami found two small canoes. It's thanks to God if I'm still alive. And I didn't even hit a rock," said Simon. His leg was broken later.

"The Yanomami were crying. They'd lost everything and they were angry with me at first. One young man was furious but I stopped that. 'I've lost too. Everyone has lost,' I told them." Simon laughed. "I went up with two Yanomami to Apuí paddling the two little canoes while the others waited," said Simon.

He was back in Santa Isabel a few days later in Henri's boat to replace, on credit at the stores arranged by mayor Zezinho, all the trade goods the Yanomami from Pohoro had lost. Zezinho lent his official boat to transport everything to the first waterfall, from where the Yanomami could collect their goods. Simon's misfortune happened as they were about to leave Santa Isabel. "It was stupid! I wanted to secure a pole in the middle of the street for a tractor to pass over. But the pole passed over my leg as the tractor passed over it. So it was all over with me! I couldn't go to Apuí." It was a week before he reached Manaus to have his leg set in plaster and then fly to Europe where he wanted to take a course in tropical nursing. Simon laughed and tugged at his ginger beard in frustration.

"How's the Henri school for teachers?" I asked.

Simon chuckled. "Half the twenty students had gone home when I arrived. A married man wanted to return to his wife. Henri sent home the youths from Pukima [far up the Marauiá] because they never took part in the lessons, only eating food. It was too much too quickly. They didn't know what a school was. Three from Ajuricaba didn't want to stay any more," said Simon. They were far from home; away from the regional allies of which Davi had spoken. "Ajuricaba doesn't know the Marauiá people. They're another group so there's a coldness between them," said Simon. Their alliances for marriage, for example, are with the communities of Maiá, Maturacá and Pohoro. "They don't fight but it doesn't create a climate of cooperation," said Simon.

Simon reported that Padre Francisco had left the mission at Xamataweteri with the local bishop and had left instead a sympathetic but inexperienced lay brother called Tomas. Franco and Angela had gone away, said Simon. The bishop gave a ride downriver to a young Yanomami man and a young married woman, though no-one had realized at the time that they were lovers eloping. Their flight was to have many local consequences.

Welcome news of fresh action to take the *garimpeiros* out of the Yanomami area came one Sunday in August when I telephoned Claudia Andujar.

"With the military co-operating?" I asked, because action without their helicopters and planes would be no action.

"Yes, they're going to use the armed forces."

"You sound more optimistic?"

"Look, I think it's now or never. It will depend on the international pressure. We just have to keep it up," said Claudia.

The news redoubled my determination to make the 250-mile walk with Domingos and others to meet Davi and the Yanomami in the east. I decided to go back to Ironasiteri in September when the hunting would be good after the rainy season.

Too many promises had been made and broken to allow much faith that the Brazilian government would indeed withdraw all the *garimpeiros* from the Yanomami area. But there was always hope of President Collor acting with integrity or that domestic and international pressure might make protecting the Yanomami politically worthwhile. Calculating these odds and studying the centuries of double-dealing towards Indians was making me more and more aware of my own political naivety. What I'd taken as the "public interest" was again and again being revealed as bald self-interest. Yet I was still to be shocked by what the military commander of the (Brazilian) Amazon, General Santa Cruz, told me in Manaus when I returned in September.

General Santa Cruz spoke gently like an uncle instructing his nephew. At first, he had declined to be interviewed because, he told me, his words had been misrepresented by journalists. But I asked a friend of his to intervene on my behalf and thus found myself being shown into his office, which was big enough to practice a round of golf.

"What are the military preoccupations here in the Amazon?" I asked.

The general led me to the big map on an easel; his command of 15,000 men stretched over 3,600,000 square kilometres in six Brazilian states. He drew his pointer along Brazil's 9,600 kilometres frontier with seven Amazon neighbours; Bolivia, Peru, Colombia, Venezuela, Guyana, Surinam and French Guiana. One of the main justifications of the Calha Norte project had been to protect Brazil's northern border.

"Thanks to God, we don't have frontier problems. Our relations with all the countries is the best possible," he said, adding that he'd been a guest the previous week of the chief of the Venezuelan army. "We have an excellent relationship with all of them, including Colombia, where the problems are great today because of the drugs trade," he said.

The general pointed to his military units dotted across the map to explain what he called the "special mission" of his men in the Amazon, "to support the colonization of the area. It's a work that started in the 16th century when the Portuguese arrived; to occupy the area and support the populations there. To help the development of the area. To occupy the territory. And indirectly we help control the drugs trade in the area.

"We occupy the space and give our collaboration, our support, to the people in these very difficult areas. Help with health, education, transport, roads; all the ways of support to help fix populations in these lands.

"We also participate in a very big way with the indigenous populations, which should not be our mission, but the Indians look to us for this because there wouldn't be anything in these areas if there wasn't the army. We do this work with a certain passion and enthusiasm. This work of the units should be known by Brazil and by the world because it's heroic work they're doing there.

"The government created the Calha Norte project exactly to fill the emptiness in the northern moat. Here for example, there is nothing," said General Santa Cruz, waving his pointer on the forest where the Yanomami live.

"Will mineral exploration be the foundation for development in this area?" I asked.

"The economy of the Amazon is very diversified. The area has a very big potential, and what we have to see, in my understanding, is a rational exploration," he said. The whole Amazon needed to be zoned according to the suitable types of development. "We have here in Roraima, an exclusively mineral vocation for strategic minerals. Roraima has many riches: tin ore, diamonds, gold, silver, and strategic minerals like titanium, molybdenum and uranium.

"There are other areas [of the Amazon] that are no good for anything, because of the soil, so they can be reserves," he said. Ecologists were creating a philosophy that, "the Amazon is untouchable, not even to cut one branch, but it can't be like this", said the general.

"I understand rationally the problem of the Indian. It's worrying. But I'm much more worried about the [Brazilian] *caboclo*. There aren't 200,000 Indians in all Brazil, including Raoni who lives in Europe and all these acculturated ones, and including the children. Brazil has given the Indians about 800,000 square kilometres in 467 reserves. That's 400 hectares for each Indian. They're the greatest *latifundarios* [big landowners] in this country," said the general with a laugh.

"And for what? For them to live their natural life, etc. Very beautiful, very poetic. I think care should be taken to bring the Indians into civilization; because in reality, contact is inevitable. The economic frontiers are being displaced and the Indian doesn't want the indigenous habits any more after he's had contact with civilization; after he eats food from a tin, he doesn't want to go down to the river to catch a fish, he wants to open a tin and eat. After he's been with a civilized woman he doesn't want an Indian woman again. After he knows the pop drinks, he doesn't want to drink fruit juices any more. This is inevitable.

"I'm not saying it's right or wrong, but it's inevitable. So you have to treat them to prepare these groups to receive civilization in the best way possible and turn them into citizens useful to the country. Because in reality, what is the Indian today? He's someone who lives by begging for something. He doesn't produce anything," said the general. I checked my tape recorder was running, hardly able to believe that a Brazilian general would speak so openly, knowing he was being recorded. I was so amazed that I repeated what he'd said to be sure I was understanding him correctly.

General Santa Cruz continued, "The Indian doesn't produce food, he doesn't have medicines, he doesn't have culture, so he lives on the favours of the groups that support him – the Church, the missions, the military and the *garimpeiros*, who so many people criticize but who, in reality, help the Indians a lot with food, medicines, etc.

"On the other side, we have the Amazon *caboclo*, who lives in precarious conditions, who works planting his garden to produce *farinha* or fishing to sell his fish. He lives in incredible misery and no-one worries about this group of a million people.

"I think these things have to be studied with a cold head, without passion, with feet on the ground, looking for a rational solution that won't hinder the advance of development. This problem will be solved more easily in the proportion to which civilization advances. It's a challenge. The distances are very great. The illnesses in the area frighten so many people. But these problems will not be resolved by discussion in Brasília nor commissions in Cinelandia [Rio de Janeiro]. You have to roll up your sleeves and come here to work. And very few people do this. But we do. We fulfill our part. My companies are all in position and I provide the best assistance possible to all these populations living there," said the general.

"Do you know José Altino Machado?"

"He's an interesting man. He's a man dedicated to the *garimpo*. He comes here frequently to speak with us. We have a very good relationship with him. He's an intelligent man, a worker, expert."

"Hard too. He knows what he wants," I said.

"He knows what he wants. Very expert," said the general chuckling.

"The government of President Sarney and the new government have already made two or three operations to pull out the *garimpeiros* in Roraima. Was this only for the English to see?" [Brazilian idiom meaning a charade, a spectacle.]

General Santa Cruz chuckled again. "You've entered a dangerous area. There exist very big pressures with this problem. Theoretically, the *garimpeiros* are invading the area reserved for the Indians and they are violating the Indians. According to the Constitution and the law, the *garimpeiros* should be withdrawn.

"It's a very difficult operation, with the distance, difficulty of access, various reasons. The government of President Sarney had a meeting here to discuss this subject and we defended the *garimpeiro*. I believe the *garimpeiros* are Brazilians also, who work hard looking to gain something. Sometimes they are not orientated nor controlled. But don't imagine that they are bandits, as some want to say," he said. The general supported the three reserves for the *garimpeiros*, though the federal court had struck these down as illegal.

"In March, it was all considered to be solved. Then there was news of the return of the *garimpeiros* to the old camps. So the order came [from President Collor] to dynamite the airstrips to hinder this return.

"This dynamiting wouldn't solve anything, in my opinion. But the order came and we did this. It was the Army, not the Federal Police, who destroyed the airstrips selected by the Funai," he said. Dynamiting was no solution because there were too many airstrips. "If you don't have effective control, the *garimpeiro* is going to go there and reopen airstrips. He's going to return because the Indians want him to return," he said.

Men would always be attracted by strong concentrations of gold, diamonds, tin ore. "There's no force that can stop this," said the general. Meanwhile the church wanted, "to transform nineteen indigenous reserves [the 'islands' separated by national forest] into a single reserve two-thirds of the state of Roraima and a little piece of Amazonas, and put all these mineral riches in a prohibited area. Do you think we can do this? Can we have the luxury of maintaining the gold buried? My question is, 'Why is the church interested in doing this campaign?' "

"Do you think there's something behind it?" I asked.

"Honestly, I think there is. Because, coincidentally, these missions are located generally where there's a very strong concentration of minerals. So these things leave me in doubt about objectives."

"Last question. What is your vision for the next century in the Amazon?"

The general paused. "Perhaps I exaggerate a little [but] the future of Brazil is in the Amazon. Brazil is orientated to the south but it has to make a half-turn and throw all its forces into Amazonia in search of a rational development of such a rich area. My vision, my dream for the next century is that this should be realized."

8

September or October are good months to be travelling in the northern Amazon. The days of constant rain or thunderous storms have cleared. A few lacy clouds give shade. The level of the Rio Negro is falling, exposing beaches of white sand, and giving the river boats easier passage against the currents. I was keen to get out of Manaus as soon as possible while conditions for travelling were so favourable. "Third time lucky," I told Brazilian friends with whom I was staying and who knew about my intended journey through the forest from the Marauiá to the Demini river. This time we would surely make the walk to visit Davi's *shabono*! Confidence was like adrenalin pushing me to go shopping as quick as I could; it took just two days to fill two sacks and a cardboard box, big enough for a washing machine, with trade goods and foods bought hastily in the market and from street stalls.

Traffic up the Rio Negro from Manaus has increased greatly since I first searched at the port of São Raimundo in Manaus for any craft heading up the river. At that time, in late 1986, only one boat ascended regularly and only as far as Barcelos thirty hours away. You had to hitch a ride on a boat to go any farther. Today, boats taking passengers and cargo make frequent, if irregular, departures all the way up the Rio Negro to São Gabriel de Cachoeira (Saint Gabriel of the Waterfall, one of the most beautiful places in the Amazon). Cement and other building materials, and foodstuffs and beer are the main items carried to supply the military and commercial personnel active under the military's Calha Norte project.

I joined a double-decker passenger and cargo boat that promised to get me to Santa Isabel within four days, though we delayed three hours to take extra cargo – boxes of pan scrubs and crates of Coca-Cola. The Rio Negro is twenty-five miles wide in stretches but strewn with green islands like *canapés* on a plate. Every afternoon was hot and calm. The water flowed as flat as a black lacquered board and the trees stood so still that we seemed to abandon reality and be sailing for hours through a painting. My confidence in the journey to the

Demini river and the river's mood of contemplation lasted all the way until Santa Isabel.

The boat reached the town after lunch on the fourth day, just behind a black rainstorm moving to the east. I received the first bad news as soon as I shook hands with one of the shopkeepers who knew me. The jovial, pot-bellied man told me the Indians were "at war" on the Marauiá. The second news was that the town had no gasoline and hadn't had any for more than a month. The third news was that Funai had opened a post up the Marauiá and that I would be prohibited from going up the river.

News of fighting among the Yanomami was the saddest shock because it made them even more vulnerable to the land grab already underway. They needed to pull together, not apart, it seemed to me as an outsider.

The opening of the Funai post was welcome news, even if I were to be excluded, and its arrival was proof of the effectiveness of public pressure both inside Brazil and abroad. The Brazilian couple who ran the post had been relocated from another Indian area on the Solimões river. The new post would give the people some protection from the *garimpeiros* and, more immediately important, act as a health post to treat the *nabe*'s diseases such as tuberculosis.

Jacinto was in hospital with a broken arm and his son Henrique and his family were here in Santa Isabel with him. I went to see them camped out in a thatched shelter in a field behind the mission buildings and we talked briefly about what had happened.

Henrique took me early in the morning to meet the Funai couple at their official residence. Their new bungalow stood next to the town office facing the football pitch. Three rabbits and a monkey shared the house with their two children, who were looked after by a local woman when the parents were away.

We drank small cups of coffee and chatted for half an hour about the fall of the river, the price of food and the health of the Yanomami. It was clear they cared for the Indians as much as their own children and said that the people criticizing Funai didn't know how difficult it was to help Indians. "They don't take their tablets regularly as they should," explained the wife. I agreed and nodded, though I also wondered how many people understood why mothers themselves often took the pills given to cure their child's fever. (They were following the custom of the *shaman* who takes the drugs before healing a patient.)

"Do you have permission from Funai to go there?" asked the husband.

"I'm invited by the Yanomami," I said.

The man chuckled as if I'd told him the Pope was on the telephone. "You know you cannot go there," he said.

I didn't reply. The couple knew I'd been invited by Ironasiteri and they told me how Jacinto had smiled when told I'd come back. "We're not going to grab you by the arm," said the wife but their displeasure was obvious. I didn't know what to say because I knew the Funai couple were absolutely right to want to prohibit outsiders, yet as Domingos told me later, "Don't worry Dennison, you came before Funai." I suggested that I'd stay only one week with Ironasiteri and that the Yanomami should then bring me back to Santa Isabel. I would get to visit and continue my interviews, if not the journey; the Yanomami would receive the trade goods I'd brought and the Funai couple would be doing their job by excluding me. It was important that Ironasiteri retain the favour of the Funai couple because they were promising to call in a health team to treat tuberculosis in all the *shabonos* up the river.

Jacinto lay in his hammock in one of the small wards of the hospital with his left arm in a sling. His wife Emma was with him and an older woman from Xamataweteri sat in another hammock. Jacinto was weak but still with enough energy to ask me for his tobacco; the packet from my pocket was our way of greeting. Neither of us could speak more than a few words of each other's language so we expressed our friendship by such gifts and gestures. Jacinto held my hand when I knelt on the floor beside him to ask how he was feeling. He smiled and leaned forwards to show off three long cuts on the top of his head but his quick movement of head and eyes had deserted him. He was confused and exhausted as if he'd collapsed inwards like a man dying. Jacinto had refused water and said he was dying when he'd arrived at hospital. "Live! Live!" the Funai couple had screamed in his face. His eyes were still glazed three days later, but he flashed with sparks of his old temper at any mention of Xamataweteri. Perhaps his desire for retribution could keep Jacinto alive until his physical body recovered.

The hospital doctor suspected Jacinto's left arm was fractured, maybe also one finger and that his shoulder was dislocated, and wanted to send him to the small hospital at Barcelos, 155 miles down the Rio Negro. This trip was, in truth, part of a joint deception by the doctor, the Funai couple and myself. We told Jacinto truthfully that there was a camera in Barcelos to look into his arm. "The doctor'll see where it's broken and then he can heal it," we said. We did not tell Jacinto that he would be away at least one month – enough time, we hoped, for his anger against Xamataweteri to cool. The old man and his wrinkled and smiling wife agreed to go to Barcelos. Henrique asked if I could give Jacinto a pair of trousers and his wife Emma a dress to wear to go down river.

The Funai couple said that a special team would be arriving to treat the many cases of tuberculosis in all the *shabonos* on the Marauiá. This was excellent news, though the medical team had been promised so many times before that no-one raised their hopes too high. It did mean, however, that I could not ask Domingos, or anyone else, to leave the *shabono* while there was even a chance of them being treated for tuberculosis. The opportunity to be properly treated for this slow killer was obviously more important than our journey to meet Davi.

No new supply of gasoline was expected in Santa Isabel for at least a week, but several of the passengers who had come with me from Manaus had brought barrels of fuel with them and were willing to sell some at a premium. I bought sixty litres from the owner of the boat I'd arrived on and put my sacks and big box in Henrique's motor canoe beside Anna, Henrique's wife, with their baby daughter, and their young daughter and pet parrot, who travelled with the family.

Henrique delayed leaving the town until mid-afternoon to look for lead (for shotgun cartridges). "It's difficult," he told me, though I knew the supply had been stopped by traders and others to prevent the Yanomami making war on each other with shotguns. Henrique was angry and felt that Xamataweteri needed to be punished and he was doubly angry that outsiders – *nabe* who didn't understand – were telling him how to settle his own affairs.

We reached just inside the mouth of the Marauiá river by sunset and stopped to camp at a thatched house that I called Senhor Filipe's because this elderly Brazilian lived there while tapping rubber in the forest before the rainy season each year.

Our supper that night was one packet of onion soup because we had not had time to fish during the day. Anna said she'd tasted onion soup before and that it was all right mixed with rice. We didn't have rice so I boiled a watery mix over the fire. Henrique mixed his portion with *farinha* and tasted it gingerly. He smiled broadly when he saw me watching. "What d'you think?" I asked. He laughed. "We're friends," I said holding his hand, "you don't have to like it. It's like that."

He laughed. "Awful!" he cried and threw the soup into the bushes. He made himself a pot of coffee. I found a packet of crackers. Plenty of female mosquitoes came out hunting blood when we got into our hammocks side by side under the roof. I passed out a small bottle of insect repellent and smeared the noxious liquid over myself and round the backs of my ears; the drone of just one mosquito can disturb me for hours. Henrique and Anna didn't really believe the repellent could work and rubbed themselves only to show their willingness before settling, Anna nestled with the baby, to try to sleep. The other daughter slept in her own hammock. The parrot perched with eyes closed on one of the cross beams of the shelter.

The Marauiá was still brimful, with only ripples warning of the submerged granite rocks, but the water was already four feet below last April's torrent. That deluge had cleaned both banks of fallen trees so that both sides now looked like lofty hedges protecting secret gardens. New leaves of bright lime or dark red were unfurling at the tips of every branch. The first green fruits were hanging from the stems of the *açaí* palms. Purple flowers, hanging like draped decoration, were open for bees and wasps to pollinate. Flocks of parrots cried across the brown water. Here is spring, if there are such seasons in the Amazon amid incessant birth and death, germination and decay.

We passed the five waterfalls without much difficulty, though sometimes we were up to our necks pulling the canoe through water swirling between the rocks. Anna spotted a bee hive in a tree at the second waterfall and called to Henrique to knock it down with a pole. The grey, *papier-mâché*-like ball fell with a hollow thud on the rock, releasing hundreds of small stingless bees to tickle on our arms and necks. Henrique quickly broke open the hive to reveal lots of honey, white larvae and black bees walking lugubriously over the wax combs. The honey was deliciously sweet and the little white grubs tasted of nothing in particular and slightly acidic. We scoffed the lot in a few minutes.

Henrique collected leaves of the cabbage-like river weeds from the rocks at the third waterfall, called Irapajé, with which to fish. I've seen Valdira pull fish the size of dinner plates with this unlikely bait. We stopped half a dozen times between the falls for Henrique and Anna to twirl and throw their lines. Henrique quickly plucked catfish still chattering from the shallows along the river bank. Anna caught fewer, partly because she was also nursing the baby and being helped by their other daughter.

Children lined up on the bank as we approached Coatá late in the afternoon. Most of the men were still with their *pajés* but those who were not, and most of the women, came running from the *shabono* to see who was arriving and to laugh and wave as we cut the motor to glide between the moored canoes.

"Hello! Hello!" I cried to friends and familiar faces, calling, laughing, waiting on the bank to shake hands or to embrace with eager hugs that lifted me off the ground with their welcome. Everyone looked chubby round the waist; this was proof of better hunting and good eating. "Meat! Fish!" I exclaimed, pinching Chico's flabby belly. He giggled as we hugged. The canoe was quickly unloaded and my sacks and the big cardboard box carried up to Renato's house, while Henrique carried home his hammocks and bag of *farinha*.

Only Domingos, Piarina and their sons Mateus and Valdira, and Valdira's wife Aoria, were missing from Coatá. They were staying at Apuí, I was told. "He wanted it like that," replied Renato when I asked if there'd been a quarrel. Renato said he would send a message for Domingos to come and everyone agreed that his share of coffee and sugar from my sack should be kept aside.

Martins brought half a roast *paca* (a small rodent) to eat as soon as my hammock was hung again in Renato's home. Chico said there was plenty of fish now but that hunting animals was still not too good. Renato fetched a ripe banana almost one foot in length and a bowl of tapioca still warm from the toasting pan where Robi, his son, was working.

Pots and pans! Yes, lots of fishing line and hooks. And needles. Wait and see! I answered the group crowding the low stool while I chewed *paca* meat. "Chris is in his house. He has sent pictures," I said and pulled from my sack a packet of the photographs Chris Steele-Perkins had taken on our visit last April.

"Have you a message from Davi?" was the next question. "Then put him on," I was told. Half a dozen men and several grandmothers settled in a circle round this small black tape recorder to listen to Davi for half an hour. Davi started by thanking them for their invitation to visit the Marauiá and asked apology for not coming straight-away. He also wanted to reassure them that the shamanic work in his community was not directed against them. "We go up with the *pajés* but it's not to kill you all," said Davi. "We're all friends. *Shorima* – real friends. We can all help. And you have to help me," he told them in Yanomami.

Renato briefly summarized the rest of Davi's message by saying, "He spoke about the *garimpeiros*, not to help them, not to want their things and clothes because they are poisoned, diseased. And he spoke about the fight of the *pajés* to defend the children and to defend us. And for us to help him."

Renato immediately gave me his own reply for Davi; "Davi, I'm replying from here, the tribe of Ironasiteri. I'm like you. I don't want the *garimpeiro* because I know they bring sickness. Don't worry. I'm not afraid of the *pajé*, it's not to kill you when we use the *ebene*.

"We are also asking help with the *poré*. You said you had *poré* also. The same thing. Long ago, there were no *poré* but now Ironasiteri is never free of them. Davi, are you seeing *poré*? Do you know where they live? I don't know why they've appeared. We would know if he was a real Yanomami," said Renato.

I asked Renato if he was prepared to defend the Yanomami's land.

"I can defend if there are many Yanomami who understand and are in accord with me. If it's one person – just me – no-one's going to believe me. I want to make a list with the names and the leaders of all the Yanomami to show them that this land already has an owner and is ours," he answered.

"We have to defend the land of the Yanomami. A Whiteman cannot do this."

"Is the Whiteman going to take all the land or not?"

"The Whiteman cannot!"

"He cannot, but do you think he will?"

"This is the business, isn't it?" Renato answered. "The Whiteman already has his land. It's over there. And I'm living here."

Henrique came to eat with Renato that night, having shown himself *waiteri* – valiant – in the war with Xamataweteri. I wanted to know what had happened but it was not yet the appropriate time. "What happened with the school?" I asked instead.

"Henri went downriver. Simon went to his land. No-one's giving lessons," replied Renato.

"Why does Funai have to help the Yanomami?" I asked him several times.

Renato didn't answer this question in the direct way I expected, but told me Funai had given twenty machetes to the communities on the Marauiá river when they'd first come but now only wanted to exchange these items. Renato was not the best person to answer the question because his hunger for trade goods was so much greater than other peoples'; yet I think even he could not understand the question. It was too scandalous to imagine that Funai would not share the unlimited boxes of machetes, toasting pans and cooking pots that came on a boat from the Whiteman's factories. Omam gave the forest to the Yanomami and gave factories to the *nabe*. The Yanomami need to receive a share of the Whiteman's bounty, just as the *nabe* visitors receive a share of fruits and meat from the forest. The rightness of giving and receiving is so obvious, so accepted that all people are demeaned if they must seek to justify this hospitality.

Sharing food among kinspeople in the *shabono* is as unremarkable as the expectation of embracing. The act of sharing is more important than what is being shared, though families sometimes argue about receiving their full share of game, honey or palm fruits; grievances only emphasized the strength of the expectations. Sharing confirms relationships. Brothers-in-laws, for example, may share meals with each other's families as often as they eat in their own homes. Gabriel came every day to eat with his sister Francesca and Renato, and we often ate with his family.

Gabriel usually came for coffee as soon as he saw Louisa, Renato's daughter, squeezing the cloth filter over the coffee pot. Coffee was a luxury my visit provided.

"Sleep well?" I asked Gabriel on my second morning, more as a greeting than a question.

Gabriel nodded his head from side to side. "Uum," he murmured. I'd heard him like this before. "What is it?" I asked, guessing he wanted to share his thoughts.

"I was sleeping here at night and I was dreaming," he stared. "I went out and a Whiteman appeared. He was the owner of gold himself! Alive. I was just standing. He had a saint – Our Lady – standing like a doll on top of a stone.

" 'Do you know what this is?' asked the Whiteman.

" 'It's a doll, Our Lady,' I said.

" 'It is.' And he had a stone. 'Do you know this?'

" 'No. I don't know,' I said.

" 'Come here. Do you want to see?' " The owner of gold lifted up the doll to open the rock and gold came out, "shining like the sun itself," according to Gabriel. "The *pajé* took out two hot, gold stones. 'No-one knows this,' he said. 'This is how it is. You won't find but I know where the gold is,' he said. And he closed the rock and put the doll on top again. Aah!" exclaimed Gabriel.

" 'You can return,' said the owner of gold. So I returned home and Jacinto appeared. 'Oh brother-in-law,' I said, 'they're making gold there. The man showed me.'

" 'Leave it there,' Jacinto said. 'Watch out. When you see gold, it's bad. I am a *pajé*. I know. Don't go to see a stone like this again. If you do, he's going to give a shock,' he said.

" 'There's an owner,' I said, but Jacinto spoke to me, 'Don't look at the stone. It'll hurt you if you do.'

"So I was afraid. And I returned and arrived in my house with my family. My family was there. And I woke up, 'Amazing, I dreamed gold,' I said. 'A man showed me gold.' This is what I thought. 'One day I shall take my wife and we shall go there.' "

"Who is the owner?" I asked Gabriel.

"I think he's a type of *hekura pajé*. A teaching *pajé*. It's to him I'll pray to know where there's gold," he said.

"What d'you think of what Jacinto said? Did he speak correctly or doesn't he know?" My question slipped between the common confusion between two states of being – the person we see and the person as *pajé*.

Gabriel replied, "Jacinto doesn't know. It was the dream that spoke but he doesn't know he spoke."

"One day we're going to discover gold. I dreamed this. One day, when we're working hard gathering *to-o*, Jesus or Our Lady is going to show it to us. This is my thinking," said Gabriel.

He went home when the coffee pot was empty. Renato helped several children and me to bring out the big cardboard box and the two sacks of trade goods I'd brought from Manaus. We set everything down on a sheet just outside the pole on the ground that prevented rain water running into the house. The big cardboard box created the most curiosity though it contained only half a dozen big aluminium pans which several people had requested in April. I took out the list I'd made of people's requests at the end of the last visit and counted off the items for each family. Only clothes were missing, except one pair of trousers for a young man who had asked for nothing else. Prices in Brazil were now so high, even for a tourist with dollars, that I couldn't afford to buy everything and had decided to leave out the skirts and trousers. There were plenty of extra items for those who'd forgotten to ask and for the girls and youths who wanted to receive at least beads, fish hooks or tobacco.

We distributed first what was on the list for each family, leaving the extra smaller items such as tobacco, fish hooks and needles to be divided by Renato and the other leading men of the *shabono*, sitting in the front row within arm's reach of everything.

I have not written often in this account about the women and the girls of Ironasiteri though they live, of course, side by side with the men and the boys. The omission is due to my own place in the community; for it is not the custom for a male visitor to mix with other men's wives. The women themselves discouraged me by saying little if I asked a question and by looking round for a male relative to come to be with them if I sat with them.

The work and the responsibilities of each family in the *shabono* were divided between the men and women, though it seemed to me that the women were doing the heavier work; fetching heavy baskets of manioc and firewood every day. Two anthropologists have written about wife beating and rape, but I've neither seen nor heard evidence of this during my own four visits. The men always acted publicly for the family but, as in any marriage, he was a foolish husband who acted against his wife's advice.

Girls learned cooking, gardening and child-rearing by imitating and working with their mothers and female relatives, just as the boys learned the tasks expected of them with their fathers and male relatives.

Boys and girls generally played separately and the girls had one particular game that they always played away from the boys, who wore catapults round their necks or fired miniature bows and arrows. The girls' special game was to catch stingless bees and then to tie lengths of cotton thread round the bees' abdomens. It's a delicate task requiring patience and nimble fingers. The knot must be tied without squeezing any bee's tummy but must not be so loose that the thread slips off. Harming a bee spoils the fun because the purpose of the game is to let the bees fly away with the lengths of thread dangling from their middles. The bees buzz off into sunshine but they cannot escape by flying either too high or too fast. The girls chase the bees back and forth, ready to grab the threads like dogs' leads whenever a bee might be thinking to fly up and up on the currents of warm air. The red cotton threads float in the air like gossamer while the girls laugh and let the bees crawl tickling up their arms or chests.

Francesca, Renato, Louisa, the young son José, the baby Sabbá and myself went down the river in the middle of the morning to gather *to-o* in the forest on the other side. We wandered through the shade but there were few strands of the vine dangling from the trees, and no noises of wild pig or other game close by. The children were told to wait while their parents walked ahead together and their small figures were soon lost in the thick of undergrowth, sunlight and shade. I stayed with Louisa, José and Sabbá in a warm spotlight of sunshine that discouraged mosquitoes. Renato and Francesca probably wanted to be alone in the forest to make love. There's no privacy at all in the *shabono* and it's usual for a husband and wife to go together for a day's hunting when they want to be alone together.

The children and I played cub fights with green stems that broke over our heads or tickled each other all over until we were reduced to hysterical giggling. Baby Sabbá sat on a big leaf, like a king on his throne, thoroughly happy in the forest with his sister and brother and looking round when we heard cooing or shrieks from unseen birds or animals beside us.

"Do you have a woman?" Louisa asked after a long time.

"No," I replied. "If I had a woman I would have to stay home and not be able to travel."

"Yes," she nodded and smiled, though she was not deceived. She knew the real reasons why I was not married. "Do you know how to fish?" she asked.

"No," I confessed. "Nor to hunt."

Louisa was silent. "Can you build a house?"

"No," I replied.

Louisa nodded and watched me in silence. Perhaps she was

thinking, "No wonder he isn't married. No woman would have him." The greatest mystery was to know how someone who couldn't fish, hunt, build a house, who could hardly paddle a canoe or handle an axe, who didn't know how to plant bananas or peach palms or even defend himself with a war club could possess so many machines and tools.

Francesca and Renato returned from their excursion after a few hours carrying the roots of a few plants to be transplanted at home. We travelled back to the *shabono* for a fish lunch with Gabriel. Soon afterwards we heard the drone of a motor boat coming up the river and ran out to find the Funai couple tying up their aluminium canoe. They wanted to reach Apuí quickly and only paused to hand over a new motor still in its box. This was for the whole community, though Renato signed his name on the receipt, in exchange for the old wreck with which everyone had been grinding their manioc to make *farinha*.

"He's leaving soon," Renato said about my continued presence, though I'd only just arrived. The Funai couple checked round the *shabono* to see if anyone was ill, then set off again in their motor boat and disappeared up the river with the dreadful drone of their motor lingering behind them.

There is a lull in the activities of the *shabono* in the afternoon when the day's main tasks are done or people have settled to doing them. People snooze in their hammocks, or sit upright weaving a few more strands to the basket in their lap or toast *farinha* or tapioca in the big flat pan over leaping flames. This was the appropriate time to settle with someone in their hammock, to sway with them back and forth with the languor of a hot afternoon and to ask about the war with Xamataweteri. I recorded many people's accounts of what happened but, for the sake of clarity, have combined them here into a single story. Of course, this account is totally partial; I have not yet had the opportunity to go to Xamataweteri to record their version of events.

Amildo was the protaganist of the story, though he looked an unlikely lad for the part. He was the youngest of Jacinto's three sons, short in height and quiet. He looked too young to have run off with a married woman after living a year in the *shabono* beside the mission. But this is what the war had been all about. Amildo had eloped with a young woman by getting a fast ride in the Funai couple's motor boat with the bishop, who'd been visiting to take padre Francisco down from the mission. They'd gone some distance but then left the party to go on alone in his small canoe. Domingos and Piarina were at Apuí when they arrived but the young couple didn't stay long. "Piarina called the woman a dog," said Amildo. "She wanted to frighten me. I didn't speak," he said. Piarina was related to the husband left behind.

"Why did she want to leave her husband?" I asked.

"Her husband didn't do anything. He fished but didn't catch anything. He didn't work. He didn't make *farinha*. He didn't want to. She wanted to stay with me, so we ran away," said Amildo in a low, flat voice. "Dad welcomed us. Then her brother came down to take her back to Xamataweteri. Dad said she was staying.

" 'No. My sister's not living here. I've come to fetch her,' said her brother.

" 'You've a girl there who was born here. [Geraldo's daughter who has lived with his mother-in-law since his wife died.] Bring her here and there'll be no fight. You can take your sister,' Jacinto told the youth standing in front of him.

" 'I'll bring no-one!' the brother replied.

" 'Then your sister'll stay here,' said Jacinto.

" 'I'm not going back,' the woman told her brother. 'I want to live here. My first husband didn't work. He didn't make a garden. He didn't hunt; there was no food for us. He didn't buy hammocks, nor a pot, nothing. He only slept and didn't do anything. I suffered a lot. I want to stay here with Amildo,' she said.

The brother paddled home alone. The journey would take him at least three days, even though the level of the river was falling and the flow of water was calm. Perhaps he thought about his own chances of marriage if his sister was allowed to run away with that boy Amildo.

If she did not stay with her rightful husband then the mutual obligations for marriage between the families would be undone. Would he ever be able to marry – given that there were more women than men in the community – if the husband's family were no longer obliged to betroth their daughters to himself or to his brothers?

And what consideration could his Xamataweteri show Ironasiteri when they gave us no help in the last elopement, three years ago? he may have thought to himself. Our three men, armed with bows and arrows, had chased after another youth running away downriver with a married woman with a child. That old man Jacinto and Renato did nothing to stop them escaping to the Rio Negro, nor give help to fetch back the women and to kill the youth. We can't remember them now! It's a long way to paddle up to Xamataweteri. Perhaps this is how the brother argued with himself as he paddled home, keeping close to the river bank where the current was slackest.

What did Ajinor and Pata-pata say when the hot-blooded brother arrived back from Ironasiteri without his sister? They would have listened with everyone else in the *shabono* to his report of what Jacinto had said. And probably after supper they'd sit round his hearth to talk more about resolving the crisis with their neighbours. Perhaps Ajinor tried to calm those people who were still angry that Ironasiteri had not helped three years ago. That episode was finished; Ajinor's listeners would know that the husband was dead, though, of course, his name could not be spoken. There was nothing to be gained by fighting with Renato nor by involving Domingos, who was related through his wife to the husband's family. The quarrel was with old man Jacinto and his son Amildo, who were clearly in the wrong. The best solution was also the proper one – the sister must come back to her husband. As *tuxaua*, Ajinor could lead only by comment and suggestion until their discussion gained a consensus. This might take many days. Everyone would have their say and no-one would be forced to take part in whatever action was decided.

Whatever the form of their discussion, Xamataweteri sent invitations to the communities of Pohoro and Pukima farther up the Marauiá river for them to join in a war-raid against Ironasiteri. It was two weeks after the brother's return that the combined war-parties set out to attack Ironasiteri.

By coincidence, Martins was out fishing for *pacu* on the night the war-parties approached their destination. "I pulled into the bank to wait for the fish. Then I heard coughing. I stopped still, but I thought it was Alberto and Cassiano returning from Apuí. 'Who's that?' I called. A canoe passed in front of me so I whistled and turned on my flashlight. And they called to me. So I went out.

"There was a canoe full of people painted black. And they took hold of my canoe.

" 'Brother-in-law,' they called me, 'how is it with you?'

" 'Fine,' I said.

" 'How are the people there [Ironasiteri]?'

" 'Fine.'

" 'What do they say about us?'

" 'Nothing. It's fine,' I said. 'Why are you here? To make war?' I said.

" 'No-one's here to make war,' they said. Then Ajinor arrived, quietly paddling the motor canoe. Then another canoe arrived and another. Full of people all painted black, all armed with clubs or shotguns. I think there were five canoes.

" 'No-one'll fight with you or Renato. We're wanting to fight only the old man and his sons. This is what we came to do,' they said.

I waited. " 'Good,' I said, 'Are you going to let go of my canoe? I came to kill fish.'

" 'Everyone has to stay here. You can't leave.'

" 'I can! This is my canoe. I bought it. That's your canoe. You came from upriver. I'm not holding your canoe. You can't hold mine,' I said.

" 'Stay here. We'll talk early tomorrow. No-one's going to do anything against you,' they said.

" 'I'm going to the other side [of the river] to kill *iwa* [alligator]. The night's full with their eyes,' I said. My flashlight was shining on their pairs of eyes.

" 'All right. Come back soon,' they said.

"So I went off. I could hear the *tuxaua* Ajinor angry with them; 'You should have secured his canoe,' he said. 'Why did you let him go? He's going to tell the people.' So they started searching for me with their flashlights. Two canoes went downstream to wait by the bank to shoot me. It was the middle of the night. The moon had set and it was black black. So I paddled down the middle of the river. Very quietly. And I passed two canoes and so arrived home. Chico was also returning from fishing. 'Good Chico,' I said, 'people have come to make war here. Tell João.' "

Martins woke Renato and passed a warning to every family. Amildo and the woman slipped out of the *shabono* for her to hide in the forest. The men retrieved their war clubs from among paddles and garden hoes at the back of their homes and took down shotguns hanging from the rafters to be ready and to wait in their hammocks. The attack would come at dawn while the mist still hung over the river. Meanwhile, the thirty men from Pohoro and Pukima crept silently through the gardens to surround the *shabono* with their shotguns loaded.

"Which of you is valiant?" cried a youth breaking into the *shabono* at first light. "Answer me! Get out of your hammocks and come here! Let's fight," he cried from the centre of the arena. This was the brother. Twenty men, smeared black with war-paint and armed with black clubs and some with shotguns, entered behind him to join the fight. The husband was among them but the father had not come.

"Pah! No talk! It's better to fight right now! Let's fight," shouted the attackers. Ajinor was there standing. "You want to shoot me," he cried to Martins whose home was near the entrance. "He grabbed my shotgun and he pulled me and I pulled him" said Martins. " 'Oh my son, you can't fight these people from the mission,' cried my old aunt. 'It's not for you to fight, only that old man. Only Jacinto,' " she cried. So I stopped and Ajinor stopped.

"I don't want to fight," Renato told the attackers, knowing the community was surrounded by the men from Pukima and Pohoro armed with shotguns. "Don't say that you'll get me. If I wanted to fight I'd take an axe to break your heads. You'd not leave my house," boasted Renato loudly.

"No-one is helping Jacinto. No-one should interfere," said Renato. "But if you shoot him, then we also have shotguns. If you're going to fight, it's better only with clubs. For no-one else to die," he said.

Amildo and Henrique stood shoulder to shoulder with their father Jacinto, facing the attackers in front of their home. The other sons stood ready with their clubs. The rest of Ironasiteri watched from their hammocks around the *shabono*.

"They wanted to receive first. So dad and I struck first," explained Henrique in his version of how the attack happened.

"You'll have to explain to me how it is, because when the Whiteman fight he just hits and hits," I said.

"We have another way," replied Henrique. "Whoever wants to fight first with the club – toh! – hits the other man on the head. And again. Toh! Toh! Toh! Dad hit them and they struck in exchange, everyone attacking and hitting – toh! toh!"

"How many times?"

"Dad received five hits. They received two hits each. Dad fell first. And they broke his arm."

"Where can you hit when you fight?"

"Only on the head. Not on the body. It's prohibited. To break an arm is prohibited. Dad's very angry because of this," said Henrique laughing. "He wants to fight more because they broke his arm. He doesn't want to leave it like this. Dad's very hard." Henrique and Alberto fetched the clubs made of hard black palm to show how they'd used them.

"Lots of blood. Blood," said Henrique's wife, the first words she'd spoken.

"I hit them first. There was blood. My old man hit a lot. They surrounded us with the old man in the middle. Toh! Toh! And so his arm was broken," explained Henrique.

"And you?" I asked.

"I was struck here on the head," he said, drawing apart his hair. "I hit five heads. A lot of blood! Someone hit my arm and my arm was very heavy. I forgot my arm. I wanted to pick up my club but I couldn't. My arm was weak. So I fetched my shotgun to break heads with it.

"The old man Jacinto said to them, 'You can't hit on my arm! I'm old but I'm not weak. I'll fight you. I've fought many more club [fights] than you. Now you've hit my arm and for this I can't pick up my club.' So the old man stopped. 'You've broken my arm, but you'll get it again when my arm's better. One day you'll receive.' Then he stopped," said Henrique.

The joust ended. "The attackers went down to the port where the woman they'd come to rescue was standing, having been found in the forest. 'I've taken a lot of blows on the head coming to get you,' shouted the brother to his sister. 'My head hurts greatly because of you, so you're going to get the club as well,' he shouted. Toh! And he struck her on the head with his club. Done! 'You caused this war,' he shouted at her but he didn't hit again," said Henrique.

"They put her in a canoe and all of them were ready to leave. Paulo, my brother, and Amildo were outside on this bank waiting to shoot.

" 'Let's go, let's go,' the attackers were shouting. I think they already knew there was danger. They paddled straight to the other side of the river and were pulling and pulling the cord to start their outboard motor.

"Paulo fired his shotgun – pah! pah! pah! – and they all went into the water. Then they all climbed onto the bank. One of them had been shot and he was crying – 'Aah! Aah!' – but it was only lead in the shoulder. I don't think the shot was sure. We'd have hit them if they'd been in the middle of the river.

"All the women and children ran into the forest," said Martins. The attackers escaped up the river and the people of Ironasiteri fled down the river to the safety of the waterfalls. "We passed two days down river, eating fish on the Tucuman waterfall. We were there when Funai came up. They asked what happened. 'Nothing. People from the mission attacked us. Look at the old man, he's all chewed up,' Renato told the couple from Funai. 'He was all chewed up so his son fired his shotgun. I don't know if he [the man shot] died or not.' "

Ironasiteri returned to Coatá when the Funai couple went down to the hospital at Santa Isabel with Jacinto and several of his family, including Henrique and his wife. Jacinto was still eager to revenge the insult of his broken arm when I'd visited him in the hospital.

"Have you seen many fights?" I asked Martins.

"This was the first time. Long ago they fought and made war. People from the mission attacked when we lived at Irapajé when I was little. But I've never killed a person," he replied.

"What's going to happen now?" I asked Henrique and Amildo .

"I don't know," said Henrique. "But if dad dies we shall make war." Henrique denied making an alliance with the people from Maiá against Xamataweteri. "It was just to tell them what happened," he said.

"Dad's asking for the girl from there. If they don't hand back that girl, then they'll have to pay. They'll fight with clubs. When they want to pass here. When they want *ebene*, if they come, we'll fall on top of them. It's like this. To be able to pass they have to hand back the girl who was born here. If they do, then the old man will not say anything more to them," said Henrique.

Most of the talk round the hearth that night was a mixture of bravado and hurt pride to have been overwhelmed by superior forces from several *shabonos*.

Where did the hostilities – the "war" as everyone called the fight or the "joust" as the fighting sounded to me – leave relations between Ironasiteri and Xamataweteri? The communities are too close as neighbours and families for them to maintain hostilities once their cuts and bruises were healed, but even as an outsider, I could feel the outrage that accepted custom had been broken when Jacinto's arm was broken. Gabriel echoed Henrique's plan to close the river to stop Xamataweteri going out to gather more *ebene* seeds from trees on the Rio Negro. Renato, as usual, did most of the talking while the others nodded or enjoyed sucking on their *brixeiras*, the roll of tobacco in the front of their mouths.

"Did you return to the Xamataweteri to drink the bones in April?" I asked.

"Only Domingos went there. I didn't go there. I went with all my family but the motor conked out. It broke. The canoe was loaded, the river was full so we returned home. Only Domingos went in the other motor canoe.

"I don't want to go there any more. They can come here but I'm not going there. They've dirtied the land by fighting here. I don't want any more fighting because of this woman. I'm not angry, but just that I don't like it. I'm valiant. If you kill my son, it'll be bad for you. If you hit me for no reason, it will be bad. But otherwise I'm calm. I don't want to kill someone. The account with Xamataweteri is closed," said Renato.

We crept away in silence to our hammocks to sleep. I lay crossways in mine, wrapped with a cotton sheet against the chill that would come in the middle of the night. Perhaps it was only my own conceit to worry that the internal wrangle would make it harder for the Yanomami to win friends among the *nabe*.

Alberto, Jacinto's youngest son, was the eldest of the boys who came with me to the river each morning when I went to wash and brush my teeth. Sometimes we were alone; other times several women would be working in the water with fine-meshed fishing nets catching whitebait-sized fish that shimmered in shoals in the water. Alberto was a lad at the beginning of his spiritual training and his father and other men were saying he would be a powerful *shaman*. Yet the *hekura* were already with him and this was acknowledged by Jacinto and other experienced *shamans*. He would crouch beside me, our toes almost in the water, while I brushed white lather on my face and rinsed the razor in the tepid river to shave. He never spoke while I shaved, but waited beside the boys to take his turn with my toothpaste and toothbrush. Half a dozen people were now using a toothbrush – a necessary adjunct to even their infrequent sugar eating. (Brazilians in the Amazon have awful teeth, when they have any at all. Dental care is non-existent or expensive and aching teeth are pulled out, not patched with a filling.) The Yanomami have excellent teeth, probably because of the absence of sugar in their diet and the juice of the tobacco always in their mouths.

However, it was not concern for his teeth that brought Alberto to the river bank with me so early each morning. He came with me because he was crazy to receive a personal gift from me. It was a ritual between us that we knew would end happily and by which to start our day while mist still hung over the forest at sunrise.

We walked back from the river a few mornings after my arrival to find Domingos swaying in my hammock, having come in the night with Valdira, his eldest son, from Apuí. Both greeted me warmly and gave me feather decorations and baskets they'd brought with them to exchange for the items I'd brought them. Valdira had also brought three small packets wrapped in leaves to give to Renato. The exchange was done while I was eating tapioca at Gabriel's home, but I saw Renato quickly put away the packets in a basket hanging from the rafters at the back of his home. I knew it was best to await the opportunity to ask directly about these.

Domingos took a share of *ebene* seeds from Renato and sat for a time to talk, before shaking hands and returning home to Apuí in the afternoon. The *shabono*, with sixty-five people, was often a noisy place where you always seemed to be sharing whatever your neighbours were doing, but this only emphasized its infrequent silences. I was shocked one afternoon, during one of these silences to hear the faint rumble of a motor. "Tractor," said Renato. The rumble in the afternoon breeze was the noise of bulldozers building the road westwards towards the Marauiá river from Santa Isabel. Renato welcomed the road because the five waterfalls broke his canoes, but he was being tragically naive when he imagined that his community would be able to control who came to the Marauiá river. He did not speak for most people in Ironasiteri – who were against the road – but even he was clear the road should not be used to claim the land for the *nabe*.

"We shan't allow hunters to come. The Brazilians can come to buy fruits, if they have a car," said Renato. "There's no danger. I've spoken to the mayor and he says there's no danger. 'It's for you,' he says. The Whiteman can come to visit but not to live here."

"Who's going to control it?"

"I think Funai will put someone else here."

"Do you trust them?"

"I don't know," replied Renato.

We sat silently for several minutes, then I changed the subject.

"What did Valdira bring today?" I asked, having seen Valdira handing three packets to Renato in the morning. Each packet was the size of a large sandwich, well wrapped in broad leaves.

"Ah! The footprints!" replied Gabriel. Immediately, I knew he was taking me through one of those portals to the *shaman*'s labyrinth. "*Poré* takes the footprint with a sort of knife and wraps it in a leaf. He took four of our footprints pressed in the earth. And he goes home to their land, where they live, and he arrives and says to one of his relatives, 'I brought four footprints in order to kill.' "

"How do they kill?" I asked.

"They mix the footprint, the earth, with their poison and already the man with the footprint falls down. He's already attacked. A Yanomami knows, 'This is a *poré* that's ordering from where they live.' "

"How did Valdira get the footprints?"

"From Cassiano – my nephew, the son of João. He's one of the friends of the *poré*; Chico, Cassiano, Alberto and Samuel. He went to fetch," whispered Gabriel.

"He met the *poré*. He says he's meeting him a lot, on the *serra*," said Gabriel.

"It's dangerous?" I whispered.

"Very dangerous."

"Why does he want to meet?"

"Because he's already poisoned. That's why he's a friend with the *poré*. When Chico met the *poré*, he ran for three days and nights."

"Who is the *poré*?" I asked. "Is he a Yanomami who doesn't live with other Yanomami? Who walks alone?"

"I don't know. They have a *shabono*. Cassiano asked the *poré*, 'Where do you live?' "

" 'I live there! on the Marauiá river. I live behind the mountain,' the *poré* told him. No-one sees them, only someone who's 'poisoned' can see them. Other *poré*'s live in a hole inside the mountains! Living in the dark. I don't think *poré* is a person but an enchanted spirit. That's what I believe, but the young men say he's a person. You know, he walks on his toes," said Renato.

"Cassiano went into the forest and the *poré* said he was sorry for Jacinto because he was beaten up, with a broken arm and with so much pain. So the *poré* gave Jacinto's footprint back to Cassiano," Renato told me.

"How does the *poré* attack?"

"It's like an arrow with poison. The man dies quickly," said Renato, blowing a stream of air through his lips. "Jacinto has the footprint of the *poré*. Yes! It's with him. He has to hand it back," said Renato.

"Yes? How did he get it?" I asked, my eyebrows still standing in surprise.

"He was in the forest, gathering *ebene*. Jacinto arrived home and remembered that he'd dropped a shotgun cartridge, so he returned to where he'd gathered the bark of the *ebene*. And Jacinto found his footprint had been taken. So he looked for the footprint of the *poré*. And he took it quickly, wrapped up, and returned home," he said.

"What does the footprint of the *poré* look like?" I asked, enthralled by the complexity of the story.

"It looks like the footprint of a pig or an *xama*; an animal. That's how it appears," replied Renato.

"What does the *poré* look like?"

"The *poré*'s something enchanted. He's like a spirit, a vision. And all black. And tall or short just like us. They don't appear to us, only to the people with the remedy they give to be able to see them. Only them! You won't see if you go. And they kill," said Renato.

Alberto tried to persuade me several times to lend him my camera to take a photograph of the *poré*. "Let me take the machine into the forest. I can see him. You can't," he would explain, but I declined.

Gabriel told me there were three types of *poré*, each with a different tail. "Five *porés* have come this year. They're coming all the time," he said.

"Do they kill women as well as men?"

"They say they kill beautiful women. They tried to kill Jacinto because his 'aura' is very big. They don't like this, so they want to kill him," explained Gabriel.

Further stories of the *poré* were told to me by Renato, Alberto, Chico, Gabriel and others over several days, like sagas to be retold act by act during many sittings. I am too much of a sceptic to believe stories of the Wizard of Oz or Jack and the Beanstalk without meeting them myself but I do not doubt the truth of the experiences Chico and the others were trying to explain to me. I can say only that their truth is not my own.

Every person in the world uses the reference points of his or her own culture to interpret change, new objects or threats that may come from outside. Each culture has its own mythology comprised of self-evident truths which may be unintelligible to outsiders. We try to understand new situations in terms of our existing pictures of the world; our beliefs literally make sense of the place where we live and think. They tell us where we are. And we are nowhere if we lose these peculiar ways of understanding our world. For example, the Yanomami cosmos does not make sense without the forest they live in.

The Yanomami are more aware of what I may call the spiritual dimension of the cosmos than people of the Industrial Society, though their stories may be strange to our imaginations. They live directly with nature and side by side with the supernatural. There is no meal until someone catches and kills a fish. Illness comes from spiritual imbalance, visitation or dream. Every event in the temporal world has its balance in the spiritual world. The arrival of the *poré* in the forest round Ironasiteri mirrors the trauma of people who know their existence is threatened by outsiders, the *nabe*.

I woke one night, near the end of my stay, to find Renato dancing in the middle of the arena. The moonlight cast his lone figure as a grey shadow turning and jumping and waving his arms with shouts and cries. He became ever more agitated, throwing his arms and snatching flaming logs from the fire as he danced, to hurl them across the arena. Orange sparks flew like shrapnel in the night. I lay watching for as long as he was fighting, fascinated and frightened by the force of whatever vision impelled him. "What were you doing during the night?" I asked him at sunrise, when the chanting of *pajés* was already in the air.

"I was dreaming," he replied. "The *pajé* [spirit] of a man from Arakem came here, trying to attract me to kill me. But I got up and defended myself and I threw him on the fire. 'Aaah!' he cried, because I had him on the flames. His spirit's still here, hidden here," he said in whisper. "The rain was him."

"How do you mean?" I asked.

"He came behind the rain to arrive unseen. The rain fell in front and he came behind. The rain's water, isn't it? We see water falling, but it's not water. The water is people."

"How's that?"

"Water is people. Yanomami."

"Water is people?" I was baffled.

"Yes. Yanomami. That's to say; the rain is water. Everyone sees water. But it's not [just] rain it's [also] the spirit of the *pajé*. This was in the dream I had. Everything appears in dreams. I don't dream like a Whiteman. It's another type of dreaming," he said.

"Can you see the future in your dreams?"

"The future's born in our dreams. We see our enemies, even from far away. For example, [awake] you see a friend from Arakem. I can go there to visit his house. He's a true friend. But his *pajé* spirit is not a friend. Dennison, you see nothing of the *pajé*. It comes only in dreams and that's why we sing with *ebene*. We can see everything when the *ebene* ascends. The singing is the music of the *pajé*.

"The sky comes down when we take *ebene* and stays low. And Jesus Christ comes out. Everyone comes out. All the saints appear. All the dead appear, everyone. We're learning. At first they didn't appear. Today this is what we're studying. It's like the Bible, though I don't know if the Bible is true," he said.

"Do you ever dream of the Whiteman?" I asked.

"Yes. A Whiteman appears! All soldiers making war! All the cars appear in the street. The whole city appears. We see only the *shabono* here and, where we take a bath, we see only water. It's water on top. And it's an enchanted city below the water," said Renato relishing his story. He listed all the people, machines and all the animals to be seen when a man takes the hallucinogenic snuff.

More evidence of the supernatural presence came in the early afternoon when Joãozinho (João's son) was carried into the *shabono* amid much shouting and commotion. I was with Francesca at the time, drinking a bowl of boiled palm fruits. "What is it?" I asked without thinking the commotion might be something serious.

Renato did not reply for several minutes and, when he did answer, his voice was flat, "Joãozinho [little John] is dying," he said.

Four young men, Joãozinho's peers, fetched their tubes and *ebene* from their homes to enable them to see the *hekura* or whatever it was killing their kinsman. Other people built a large fire and four men lifted Joãzinho into a hammock beside the blazing heat.

Renato, Alippe and Henrique took the snuff and emerged as a trio chanting and slapping their sides. A low wail, a moan or a groan, emerged from amongst the people beside Joãozinho. I sat alone in my hammock watching in silence. The trio rushed suddenly from the arena into the group beside the hammock, shouting, crying and making short jumps into the air. They tried lifting Joãozinho from his hammock to shake free the *hekura* that was attacking him, to get it out of him through his arms and legs, to get it away, to knock it outside, to eject it from the *shabono*.

Francesca came back briefly with tears in her eyes to fetch her new baby to join the group. The trio ended their "thinking" of Joãozinho after more than an hour. People dispersed to their homes. Conversation resumed. I asked Gabriel what had happened. They'd been in the forest gathering *to-o* together when Gabriel found an armadillo hole and stopped to smoke out the creature. Joãozinho kept working until Gabriel arrived carrying the dead animal. "He was wrapping up his bundle of *to-o* and then he felt – tah! – in his foot. Tah! – up to his left knee. Tah! – the top of his leg," said Gabriel. I could explain away this attack as a snake bite but was well aware of Gabriel's sense of foreboding: "They were rubbing his footprint with poison," said Gabriel. "They're trying to end us all," he said, speaking of the work of the *poré*.

Joãozinho did not die. He lay immobile until nightfall, then asked his young wife for something to eat. This was proof that the *hekura* had been expelled from the community.

Gabriel's wife served the boiled armadillo that night. It was easy to relish such a feast of meat after those long days eating only *farinha* and water and feeling *o-hi oh-i*. I was given chunks of the white meat and pieces of the animal's backplates and, though I chewed and chewed, I cannot remember the taste of the meat.

Renato blamed the attack on Joãozinho not on the *poré* but with people from Xamataweteri who, he said, had stolen their footprints during the recent attack. "They mix poison and stab them with a bone – hah! – just like Joãozinho," he said. Domingos would have to go to Xamataweteri soon to ask them to give back the stolen footprints, said Renato. He was confident the footprints would be returned.

Perhaps this could be the diplomatic opening for reconciliation to end the dispute. Both communities were acting on their own priorities and I admired each for defending what was right, according to their own principles. At the same time, as an outsider, I could not be unaware of the forces of the *nabe* waiting to exploit just such internal disputes. I believed Davi when he said the Yanomami communities must speak together and must be united to defend their children and their land. My own regret was our failure after more than one year to link the communities of the Marauiá river to the Yanomami in the east, including Davi's *shabono* on the Demini river. I had planned (never actually set out) three times with Domingos to make the journey through the forest to take Davi's warning to the more remote communities and his invitation for them to visit him. Sickness, death, war and the weather had each broken the momentum of our plans. These were neither excuses nor apologies, for I had always assumed that the journey would only be worthwhile if it could be accomplished within the social priorities of the Yanomami. I'd never wanted to impose such a journey (by offering a payment of trade goods no-one could refuse). I still believed that linking the communities of east and west could benefit the Yanomami, but only when the people wanted it for themselves. I was certainly disappointed by our failure to make the planned journey but did not feel defeated. The failure was proof, in one sense, of the vitality of the community that they were not abandoning their own social priorities with families and neighbouring *shabonos*.

I myself have learned so much from the people of Ironasiteri about being a human being that I regard my time with them as a personal success. What is most important to the Yanomami, and what I have learned from them, is the paramount importance of being in active relationship with the people and the place surrounding them. It would be inconceivable to Domingos or Francesca, for example, that the *nabe* can live in a building without ever knowing their neighbours. The Yanomami do not always like their neighbours, but they're never indifferent even to the people they dislike. They are sometimes afraid of the creatures in the forest but they cannot walk there with their eyes closed, as the *nabe* often do.

It's a cliché to write that people live in the "here and now" but time among the Yanomami is indivisible from their awareness of where they're standing. The Yanomami are strongly aware of the future and of the past – they look forward to visiting relatives and attending festivals and Ironasiteri can remember the names of every Whiteman who has ever visited them. Yet their concept of time is very different to the Whiteman's expectation of tomorrow or memory of yesterday. The difference between the concepts is best explained with two illustrations.

The Whiteman's view of time is like riding a train across the prairie. Look behind, and all your yesterdays are still travelling with you. Look ahead, and you're already part of all your tomorrows.

To enter the Yanomami concept of time, imagine standing like Tom Thumb on a can of Coca-Cola on its side. The can represents time and slowly rotates. Present time is the top of the can where you're standing. The past is the part of the can that's falling away behind you. The future is the part of the can that is yet to come to your feet. You're aware of both past and future, yet you stand completely in the present. This different concept of time and place is one of the reasons why the Yanomami find it so difficult to be concerned about rumours of a future the *nabe* are constructing for them.

I myself dreamed the future of Ironasiteri during my last night in the *shabono*; what will surely happen unless the Yanomami receive legal title to their land, as the Brazilian Constitution promises: I saw the road come to the silty water of the Marauiá river and the mayor with the military engineers, the town councillors and the town's traders driving in jeeps along the dirt road through the forest. I saw the *tuxauas*, Domingos and Renato, and the old man Jacinto, and Francesca and Piarina and the other women riding in the back of an open truck to the special lunch in Santa Isabel.

In my dream, the community decided to stay at Coatá after the end of the season for gathering *to-o* because Apuí was far from the road. Four aluminium motor boats were brought from Santa Isabel when the river was low and their owners took Renato, Gabriel, Martins and others as hunting guides and went speeding up the river. They brought beer and *cachaça* for everyone; they divided their kills when the hunt was successful, though they always took the lion's share. The hunting was good for two years and many people came out to the Marauiá. Settlers built houses and made gardens. A rancher came to clear the forest and he offered work to half the men of the *shabono*. This was good at first because now everyone needed money to buy food. "The wild pigs and *xama* and monkeys have all fled the forest. The *iwa* have gone from the river," the younger men complained each day when they returned empty-handed.

Tins of food were expensive at the small store built by a Brazilian at the end of the road; there was never enough food for anyone to eat well. They had to go farther and farther to find *sorva, to-o* and rubber to sell at the store, now that the settlers were also taking these from the forest. Neither the men nor the women had enough energy to clear new openings in the forest as the yields from their old gardens declined. Families started to buy *farinha* from the store. The children were sickly and feeble and the breasts of the nursing mothers were dry.

Renato and other men started working as daily labourers for the ranch along the road. A truck came, when there was work, to take them away before sunrise and to bring them home at sunset. But what they received for working did not buy enough food for their families, while the ranch owner lived in a big house with plenty of meat on the table.

Garimpeiros came out regularly from Santa Isabel to search far up the Marauiá for gold. One day a rumour said they'd found it and every man in Santa Isabel rushed up the river to look for the gold that makes the *nabe* crazy. Gabriel, Chico and some of the other men went with them and worked hard to bring a little home to the *shabono*, but the prices in the store were higher than ever and the yellow powder was soon gone.

Jacinto and his wife Emma died in an epidemic when everyone had diarrhoea that came out like rice water. Jacinto took *ebene* and danced to expel the *hekura* killing his wife and his sons' children. But Emma lay immobile in her hammock and died. The effort of dancing exhausted Jacinto and he died soon afterwards.

Invitations were sent far up the Marauiá river for people to come to the festival to drink their bones. Many people came to honour Jacinto and Emma and their anger was great.

"Let us expel the *garimpeiros* and all the settlers from our land," cried Henrique. "Let us close the road and tell the Whiteman not to come here any more," he said. So the people of all the *shabonos* on the Marauiá river asked the priest in Santa Isabel to ask the president of Brazil to take his people from their land because they had brought misery and hunger.

However, the president replied that the land was no longer their land and that they must leave the *shabono* because it had been sold to a mining company. The Yanomami were angry when they heard this, but they didn't believe the land of their ancestors could be taken from them. Then one day, big yellow machines and loud men in jeeps came along the road from Santa Isabel to destroy the forest beside the *shabono.*

"Where can we flee?" asked Henrique, "there's no game left in the forest." So the people moved to Santa Isabel where the women could wash dishes in people's houses and the men could dig in the gardens. And the *nabe* in the town saw the misery of the Yanomami and the *nabe* consoled themselves by telling one another that their own theft of the Yanomami forest had been inevitable.

I woke early in the morning in the *shabono* shocked by my dreaming, though there was nothing in the vision that has not occurred many times already wherever people are without guarantee of their ancestral land. Rain was falling steadily and people stayed in their hammocks until it was fully daylight and the rain slackened to drizzle. I was glad of the chance to lie longer in my hammock not wanting my last morning in the *shabono* to begin. Renato had already delayed our departure one day because of a lack of meat for the journey down to Santa Isabel. Smoke rose lazily from the hearth where a pot of water was heating to make coffee.

The drizzle had stopped by the time we'd eaten breakfast, and people gathered in Renato's home to bring me the baskets with which to pay for the trade goods I'd brought them. I'd specifically asked only for baskets, not wanting more feathers or bows and arrows, and there was soon a stack of baskets where my hammock had hung. Some baskets were small, for keeping fish hooks, others had flat bottoms and had been made by the men. Two of the baskets were the size of kettle drums and Henrique and Alberto quickly packed all the baskets and tied them together with a length of split *to-o.*

I walked slowly right round the *shabono* to embrace and say goodbye to every family. "When will you come again?" people asked. I promised to return but could give them no month nor year. Renato, Daniel (his son) and Alberto loaded the canoe and we set off swiftly down the river waving our arms and calling farewells before settling to the journey and the silence, except for the running of the motor.

We passed the waterfalls safely and reached Santa Isabel late in the afternoon. The mayor had had a new thatched shelter built in front of the river, where visitors could stay, and we hung our hammocks there and bathed in the river before nightfall.

I was invited to a wedding that night – the first church wedding in the small town in ten years, I was told. The bride was a nurse in the town's hospital, the bridegroom was one of the men building the road through the forest to the Marauiá river. I knew the bride's father from my previous visits, when I'd sat in his garden and listened to stories of the days when the town was called Tapuraquara and was no more than six houses built of sticks and dried mud. Senhor Marcelino, now an old man but still with a sparkle in his eyes and a vigorous sense of humour, was a pioneer gardener who'd adapted his methods to the nature of the forest. He grew his fruit trees in long cuttings through the forest, not in cleared squares, so that fruit trees were protected from predators by the abundance of bug-eating insects in the forest on either side. He was successful but unacknowledged and no-one came to listen to his practical advice. He offered beer, Coke and cake for the guests at his daughter's wedding, but I was unused to staying up more than a couple of hours beyond nightfall and went back to my hammock after the toast to the bride and groom. Later, two drunk youths fought with knives and stabbed each other at the party, we heard in the morning. One of them was in the hospital.

Renato, Daniel and Alberto didn't comment on the fight, though their silence was uncharacteristic and revealed their surprise at the futile violence. Truly, the *nabe* were strange people, as unpredictable and as greedy as wild pigs, from whom it's best to escape by climbing a tree. Yet the Yanomami cannot escape contact with the *nabe*, even if they want to. And they believe that we have much to learn about being civilized, about living fully as human beings. They want to teach us to respect ourselves and other people and the animals and the many spirits with whom we share the universe. What they want in exchange is to live in peace in the forest of their ancestors.

A trader's boat left Santa Isabel for Manaus the next morning and I was able to join twenty other passengers hanging their hammocks across baskets of *farinha* stacked on the deck. I was now like the Yanomami in not wanting our farewell to be long. What could I say in thanks or hopes for the future? My throat was dry and I couldn't speak when Renato, Daniel and Alberto each embraced me in silence. They waved from the river bank as the boat pulled out into the open water of the wide Rio Negro, then turned away.

I'd hoped to visit Jacinto and his wife Emma, still in the hospital in Barcelos, but we reached the town at three in the morning on the second night and it was impossible. We stopped only long enough to unload the forty baskets of *farinha* from the deck, to leave them stacked against the wall of the public market at the top of the river bank. The *farinha* had been bought by the mayor of Santa Isabel from Yanomami from the river Cauaborí, on one of their occasional shopping expeditions from their *shabono*, but no-one in his town will eat *farinha* prepared by Indians, believing it's unclean, so he sends what he buys downriver to Barcelos for the mayor of that town to supply to his employees and to the hospital. Nothing could better illustrate the Whiteman's long-standing prejudices of the people we call Indians.

Epilogue

"Do you think that land as rich in mineral resources (as the Yanomami area) can stay intact?" asked Jarbas Passarinho, the Brazilian Minister of Justice and former army officer, to journalists in Brazília in September 1991.

The straight answer is – yes. Many Brazilians are arguing that there are no reasons for the government to allow mining, logging or ranching. Protecting the land of the Yanomami does not depend on economics, but even the arguments put forward by the pro-mining lobby do not make economic or political good sense. Neither Brazil nor the Yanomami would gain anything from a land grab organized to benefit a few individuals and companies.

Whole regions of the Amazon have already been devastated by ranching financed by tax incentives, logging without replanting trees and huge mining projects exporting iron or other minerals at give-away prices. Twenty years of "development", spending billions of dollars have provided sustainable livelihoods for no more than a few thousand families in a region the size of western Europe.

Multinational and Brazilian mining companies are waiting, some with permit already in hand, to get into the Yanomami area. Geological surveys have revealed deposits of uranium, silver, emeralds, niobium, molybdenum, a huge deposit of cassiterite (tin-ore) and, of course, gold in the form of powder as fine as flour. But there are no economic or social imperatives to start mining in the Yanomami area. An abundance of these minerals, and many others, are already available from other sites in the Amazon where tribes no longer live.

The Yanomami themselves, in two or three generations' time, may eventually want to exploit the mineral resources and receive royalties (as the Kayapó do now in the eastern Amazon). This must be for them to decide in the future.

Military and industrial leaders in favour of immediate mining and logging are today trying to portray protecting an area for the Yanomami as a threat to Brazil's nationhood. It is claimed that

Venezuela might invade if Brazil's northern border is not colonized by Brazilian settlers. This is nonsense. The military commander of the Amazon told me that relations with all Brazil's neighbours are excellent and that none pose any threat to Brazilian sovereignty.

The Yanomami are asking only that the Whiteman lives by the promises already proclaimed to them; that their land will be safeguarded for them and that they will be allowed to decide their own futures. The threat to the Brazilian sovereignty comes from the small group attempting to subvert the law and the Brazilian Constitution for their own profit. For example, it was discovered in July that the Brazilian Army has been secretly building a road through the Neblina National Park towards the Yanomami *shabono* of Maturacá along Brazil's northern border. The covert operation was an attempted *fait accompli* in support of the military's wish to build a 6,929 kilometres highway west to east along the country's northern border. The road would give access for mining, logging and colonization projects throughout the forests already occupied by the Yanomami and many other tribes.

Public awareness and support for the Yanomami, both inside Brazil and internationally, continues to be an effective safeguard against their annihilation. President Fernando Collor has spoken several times in favour of a Yanomami park. In June, he appointed Sidney Possuelo as president of Funai, replacing his earlier choice of a retired air force officer. Possuelo has worked with various tribes for over twenty-five years and resigned as Funai coordinator in Roraima after denouncing, as "legalized genocide", President Sarney's creation of *garimpeiro* reserves inside the Yanomami area. Government departments were given until late October 1991 to comment on Funai proposals, made in July, for a Yanomami park of 9,419,108 hectares as a single protected area.

Meanwhile, Brazil's high inflation rate and deepening economic woes have decreased President Collor's political leverage against the military and pro-mining interests eager to get into the Yanomami territory.

However, there is good news from the Marauiá river. The war-skirmish between Ironasiteri and Xamataweteri has been settled amicably. Relations between the two *shabonos* are back to peaceful co-existence, according to a message from Simon LeFevre, sent out via Daniel De Vos of KWIA in Belgium. This probably means that

Jacinto's broken arm has healed satisfactorily. I have received no report about Domingos, Renato, Chico, Jacinto or other friends of Ironasiteri; no news is probably good news. Direct communication to the Marauiá river is impossible. Even telephoning over a satellite link to Santa Isabel on the Rio Negro produces no more than futile shouting and wholly distorted voices.

Davi Kopenawa Yanomami's health scheme to protect the *shabonos* in his area from the Whiteman's diseases has begun successfully. Davi's plan is to eventually establish clinics throughout the Yanomami area to serve all the groups of regional allies. His pioneer clinic is equipped with vaccines and first aid for measles, chickenpox, influenza, pneumonia and malaria. These are kept cool, in the tropical heat, by a refrigerator powered by solar panels. This is another example of how industrial technology can be used to serve tribal societies, not to destroy them.

The official health programme, under the Brazilian Ministry of Health, continues its painstaking treatments in the eastern area most infected during the illegal invasion. The rates of infection of malaria and other diseases are falling. Renewed health means people have more energy for gardening, hunting and fishing. New-born babies are more likely to survive. Health and prosperity may never return as they were enjoyed prior to the invasion, but the Yanomami population is no longer in decline. Their situation will go on improving if the forest where they live is protected from logging, mining or ranching. The success of the government's health programme, aided by many Brazilian volunteer groups, is proof that the destruction of this tribe is not inevitable.

Now, more than ever, the future of the Yanomami depends on the good will of people they have never met. Are we still the savages the Yanomami and all other tribal peoples have experienced us to be – arrogant with our power, ignorant of the deeper values that make us human beings and greedy beyond imagination? Can we, members of the industrialized societies, show them that we are civilized – or at least that we honour our commitments, value lasting relationships and desire cooperation with all inhabitants of this planet?

Dennison Berwick, Lake Kashagawigamog, Canada, *November 1991*

Note to the Reader

As this book was going to press, it was announced on November 15th 1991 that in spite of strong opposition from Brazil's military chiefs, President Collor had decreed the demarcation of a reserve for the Yanomami, covering the full 9.4 million hectares occupied by the tribe. This follows a similar announcement by President Carlos Andres Perez recognizing a reserve of 8.3 million hectares for the Yanomami inside Venezuela's national border. Recognition of the Yanomami lands provides the necessary legal status for protection of the areas from colonization. Mining projects might still be allowed in Brazil, but only with the authorization of the full Brazilian Congress.

Glossary

AÇAÍ Hard black berries the size of peas; fruit of the pencil thin palm tree *Euterpe precatoria mart.*

AGOUTI South American rodent about the size of a rabbit (*Dasy procta*).

APUÍ Place on the river Marauiá where the main village of the community of Ironasiteri is currently located. The name is also used on the Rio Negro for various types of epiphytes that drop roots from their host trees to the forest soil to grow to envelop their hosts. Often called strangler figs.

ARAXÓ Peach palm, with spine-covered trunk (*Guilielma* sp.). The fruit is shaped like a spinning top with orange flesh and is boiled before being eaten. Tastes like a roast chestnut or a dry sweet potato. Called *pupunha* by Brazilians.

1ARMADILLO From the Spanish *armado* meaning armed man. Called *o-po* by the Yanomami. (Member of the Dasypodidae family.)

CABOCLO Brazilian name for a person of mixed Negro, Indian or European race and living along a river in the interior of the Amazon. Often used as a derogatory term by townspeople meaning country bumpkin.

CACHAÇA The most popular Brazilian liquor, made by distilling unfermented sugar-cane juice.

CALHA NORTE PROJETO Instigated by the President of Brazil and the National Security Council on 19th June 1985 but kept secret for three years because politically sensitive. A project to colonize with Brazilians in a 150 kilometre-wide corridor along the 6,500 kilometre northern border of Brazil with Colombia, Venezuela, Guyana, Surinam and French Guiana. *Calha* means moat or ditch. About 50,000 Indians live in the area that would be opened for mining, logging and other industrial development.

CAPYBARA World's largest rodent. It looks like a guinea pig grown to the size of a sheep (*Hydrochoerus hydrochaeris*).

CAXIRI Manioc beer traditionally made by chewing and fermenting with women's saliva. Today, often made with *cachaça.*

CCPY Comissão pela Criação do Parque Yanomami founded in 1978 by Brazilians to campaign for a park for the Yanomami.

CUSTIRIM Fruit of the palm tree of the genus *Oenocarpus*. A hard, black fruit, called *bacabá* by Brazilians.

EBENE (*Virola theidora*) Hallucinogenic snuff made by the Yanomami from the reddish bark resin of several *Virola* trees.

FARINHA Manioc flour, made by grating, washing and drying the manioc tuber (also known as *cassava*). It looks like sawdust and has an equally bland flavour but adds texture to foods and is an important source of carbohydrate throughout the Amazon. May also be '*farinha de trigo*' meaning wheat flour.

FUNAI (Fundação National do Indio) the National Indian Foundation of Brazil, set up in 1968 after its predecessor, the Indian Protection Service, was revealed to be massacring Indians.

GARIMPEIRO Prospector seeking gold, diamonds, tin ore or other minerals. They have traditionally worked alone, but often today are either employed by mine owners or work in small groups as cooperatives.

GARIMPO Place where *garimpeiros* work and live.

HABRUA Drink made from a palm fruit; called *patuá* by Brazilians.

HEKURA Humanoid spirits of the Yanomami who may either help them cure sickness or may spread illness.

IGARAPÉ A smaller river or stream, literally *igara* (canoe) *pé* (path) in the Tupi Indian language.

IRONASITERI Community of 65 people living on the river Marauiá, who live sometimes at Apuí or at Coatá during the season for gathering *to-o*.

IWA Cayman, a type of alligator (*Order Crocodilia*).

MANIOC Tall plant grown for its starchy root (*Manihot esculenta*) and used to make *farinha, caxiri* and tapioca.

NABE Non-Yanomami people. It originally meant all people but, after neighbouring tribes disappeared, enslaved by the Portuguese and Spanish or killed by their diseases, the word has come to mean the Whiteman.

NORESHI Part of a person's soul; also an animal living in the forest that corresponds to that soul, like a shadow.

OMAM Creator God of the Yanomami.

OPERATION CANAIMÉ First operation by the Brazilian

Federal Police in January 1990 to withdraw the *garimpeiros* from the land of the Yanomami area. The operation collapsed on the third day when the government gave in to demands by *garimpeiro* leaders and the government of Roraima to establish reserves for the *garimpeiros* within the Yanomami area. *Cainamé* is the name given by the Macuxí and the Wapixana (not the Yanomami) to any enemy that kills, whether it comes as a human, an animal, a spirit or a disease.

PAJÉ State of being a *shaman*. A trained Yanomami becomes himself-as-*pajé* by taking hallucinogenic snuff that enhances his vision of the spirits or *hekura*.

PARURÍ Forest turkey or curassow, called a *mutum* in Brazil. Prized for its curly black scalp feathers which are worn as armbands.

PIASSAVA Palm (*Leopoldina piassaba wallace*) growing along some tributaries of the Rio Negro. Produces a thick mane of fibres from its fronds which reach to the ground. The fibres are gathered and exported for making brooms and brushes.

PIUM Tiny black fly with a massive bite (Simuliidae family). They congregate in sunlit places, such as riverbanks and garden clearings and can be carriers of onchocerciasis (river blindness).

PLANTAIN Similar to a banana but shorter and sweeter. One of the staple foods of the Yanomami, eaten fresh or baked or made into soup.

PORÉ Yanomami humanoid spirit painted black from head to toe who attracts men by whistling in order to kill them. Also called *onka*.

SHAMAN Witchdoctor and healer. The word comes from the Tungoso-Manchurian word "*saman*" meaning "he who knows".

SHABONO Circular communal village of the Yanomami in which each family shares a part. The design may also be with a small or a broad opening in the middle, giving the appearance from the air of a doughnut. Also called a *yano*.

SHORIMA Yanomami term meaning friend, good people, brother-in-law.

SORVA White resin collected from the Sapodilla tree and one of the raw materials for making chewing gum.

TO-O Lengths of the vine are gathered by the Yanomami to make baskets or to exchange with Brazilian traders for knives, metal cooking pots and other trade goods.

TUXAUA Leader among the Yanomami, usually hereditary. He leads and advises but has no authority to coerce anyone. He must gain a consensus in order to put his ideas into action.

URIHI Yanomami word for land or place, implying the land where a person belongs, the land that nurtures a person.

URUCÚ Plant (*Bixa orellana*) cultivated throughout the Amazon for its scarlet oily seeds, used by Brazilians to colour food and by Indians to paint their bodies and as a medicine. Also called *bixa*, *achiote* and, in English, annatto. Used in industrial processes to colour cheese, butter and margarine.

XAMA Tapir, (*Tapirus terrestris*) a mammal with a pig-like snout; called *anta* by Brazilians.

XAMATAWETERI Commuity of 180 people living where Rapi-rapi stream enters the Marauiá river. The Salesian mission stands beside the *shabono*.

WHITEMAN Collective noun to mean the European people or culture, or developments from them. Equivalent to Spanish *blanco* and Portuguese "*homen branco*".

YANOMAMI Name means "the folk" or "human being", consisting of four loose cultural and linguistic groups, the Yanomami, the Yanomam, the Yanam and Sanima. *Waika* is a derogatory term meaning the people living "over there".

Chronology of Political Events

1787 Existence of the Yanomami noted by Portuguese traveller Gama Lobo d'Almada, a member of the Portuguese Border Commission. No further reported contacts with the Yanomami until the 1950s.

1950s Many Yanomami see the Whiteman for the first time when Border Commission surveys frontier between Brazil and Venezuela.

1954 First Roman Catholic mission founded among the Yanomami at Maturacá by Salesians on Rio Cauaburí.

1961 First Protestant missionaries arrive among Yanomami when Missões Evangelicas de Amazônia (MEVA) start on the Rio Mucajaí.

25th July 1961 Parima Forest Reserve created by decree 51.042 (covering main area of the Yanomami).

1973 9.5 million hectares covering the Yanomami area are recognized for the Yanomami by decree of the Brazilian Minister of Interior.

1973–76 Brazilian military builds Perimetral Norte BR210 road through the Yanomami area for 225 kilometres, from BR174 to just inside Amazon border. Epidemics of measles kill many people and devastate Yanomami communities. Road subsequently abandoned.

1975 Project Radam-Brasil conducts mineral survey of the Amazon, setting off invasion by 500 *garimpeiros* for tin ore at Mount Surucucus inside Yanomami area.

1977 Funai survey finds 8,400 Yanomami living in 203 communities.

1977 Funai proposes to divide Yanomami land into 21 islands or pockets. This "Yanomami Archipelago" plan is eventually rejected.

1978 Commission for the Creation of the Yanomami Park founded by Brazilians.

5th June 1979 Yanomami in the west included in public lands when Park of Pico de Neblina created by decree 83.550.

1980 Invasion of 2,000 *garimpeiros* for gold on Alto Rio Uraricoera, at Furo de Santa Rosa.

9th March 1982 Ministerial decree GM/025 assigns area of seven million hectares for the Yanomami.

1985 Organization of American States recommends a park be established for the Yanomami.

8th January 1985 Funai sets aside 9,411,108 hectares as the Yanomami area (Instruction 1817/E). "Of the area, 33.5 per cent is mountainous and an area of permanent protection" according to Brazilian Forestry Code; further 44.5 per cent is land unsuitable for agriculture and cattle-ranching, according to Radam-Brasil.

13th February 1985 José Altino Machado leads an invasion (by *garimpeiros*) of Mount Surucucus inside the Yanomami area.

19th June 1985 Calha Norte project approved by the President under the National Security Council , but kept secret because politically sensitive. About 50,000 Indians live in the affected area, which covers 20 per cent of Brazil. (See also Glossary, p.225)

15th March 1986 First Yanomami Assembly, a three-day meeting attended by *tuxauas* and representatives from 14 communities. Senator Severo Gomes and government officials also attended.

May 1986–September 1988 Romero Jucá Filho is President of Funai. Later appointed Governor of Roraima by President Sarney.

1986–1987 Airstrips built by Brazilian military under the Calha Norte project at Surucucus, Erico, Auaris, Maturacá, Paapiú, Uaicaás, Apiaú and Lower Mucajaí, all within the Yanomami area.

14th January 1987 President Sarney agrees to create a continuous Yanomami park by decree. General Bayma Denys, General Secretary of the National Security Council, says that there will be no demarcation of Indian reserves within 150 kilometres of border.

June 1987 President of Funai signs agreement allowing mining in Indian areas if a royalty is paid. Blocked by Minister of Mines and Energy until after the new Constitution.

August 1987 Large-scale invasion by *garimpeiros* of Yanomami area starts, using airstrips built by the Brazilian military and missionaries.

August 1987 Four Yanomami killed by *garimpeiros*. One *garimpeiro* killed by the Yanomami. Newspaper stories of "massacre" by Yanomami is used as a pretext to expel doctors, nurses, anthropologists, missionaries and any other witnesses from the Yanomami area by the orders of Funai and the National Security Council (later called SADEN, Secretariat for National Defense Assessment).

24th April 1988 Davi Kopenawa Yanomami, head of the Funai post at his *shabono* on Demini river, wins United Nations Global 500 Award for "exemplary work in the defense of a healthy environment and quality of life".

19th August 1988 Funai president Romero Jucá Filho makes known plan to divide Yanomami land between 19 islands, (totalling 2,435,215 hectares), and two national forests open for development by logging and tourism (the planned area is 13 per cent smaller than the area previously recognized by Funai).

13th September 1988 Interministerial Directive 169 creates Yanomami archipelago of 19 islands.

5th October 1988 Brazil's new Constitution promulgated. Article 231 guarantees Indians their traditional lands and charges government to defend them.

18th November 1988 Interministerial decree 250 repeats the division of Yanomami land into 19 islands.

January 1989 Report to President Sarney details the violence, corruption of public officials, pollution and illegal mining within the Yanomami area. Report from Minister of Justice Paulo Brossard who then leaves the government.

17th February 1989 Presidential decrees 97,512 to 97,530 designating 19 Yanomami areas published in Diário Oficial.

2nd March 1989 Presidential decrees 97,456 to 97,545 designating two national forests published in Diário Oficial.

19th April 1989 President Sarney promises to withdraw *garimpeiros* from the Yanomami area. Promise given during interview with Davi Yanomami after he had addressed the National Congress of Brazil.

5th May 1989 National Guard of Venezuela expels about 3,000 Brazilian *garimpeiros* who have invaded the Yanomami area in Venezuela.

12th May 1989 Brazil and Venezuela sign measures to avoid repeat invasion of Brazilian *garimpeiros* into Yanomami area in Venezuela.

June 1989 Governor of Roraima, Romero Jucá Filho, former

President of Funai, announces Meridiano 62 project, to establish *garimpeiro* reserves inside National Forest of Roraima, inside Yanomami area. Scheme shelved.

August 1989 Two multinationals (Brascan and Anglo-American) along with at least 30 Brazilian companies, and over 300 additional applications, apply for exploratory mining permits on Yanomami lands to the National Department of Mining Production (DNPM).

11th September 1989 350 Indian leaders of 76 tribes and 14 Indian organizations hold a four-day demonstration in support of the Yanomami in Brasília. 500 Indians, of 9 tribes, demonstrate in Boa Vista, Roraima.

20th October 1989 Federal Court judge Novély Vilanova da Silva Reis issues a provisional order (no. 244/89) upholding the zoning of the Yanomami area of 9,419,108 hectares and orders the *garimpeiros* to be removed.

November 1989 Levels of mercury in Yanomami above WHO acceptable limits; revealed by tests on 18 people carried out by the Faculty of Medicine, University of Kumamoto, Japan.

26th November 1989 Reports of new invasion by 10,000 Brazilian *garimpeiros* at headwaters of the Orinoco in Venezuela, in 43 mining camps and 20 airstrips.

27th November 1989 President of Funai declares situation of the Yanomami "hopeless" and reopens the area to doctors and non-government workers expelled in 1987.

4th December 1989 Davi Kopenawa Yanomami speaks out about the situation at House of Commons, London, England.

5th December 1989 Federal court judge João Baptista Coelha Aguiar orders Brazilian Air Force to destroy clandestine airstrips. No deadline. Nothing happens.

7th–8th December 1989 Guardia Nacional of Venezuela dismantles Brazilian *garimpeiro* camps inside Venezuela. Twenty-five motor pumps destroyed.

12th December 1989 President Sarney and Minister of Justice Saulo Ramos sign Decree 98.502 approving removal of *garimpeiros* from Yanomami area.

15th December 1989 Venezuelan President, Carlos Andrés Pérez, declares Brazilian *garimpeiros* are causing "incredible damage in the headwaters of the Orinoco river". Promises law to regulate the activity.

18th December 1989 First democratic elections in Brazil since the military dictatorship began in 1964. Fernando Collor de Mello wins on the second ballot.

2nd January 1990 Yanomami health programme officially begins; one aeroplane takes off with supplies, another 2 have mechanical problems. Funai planes don't appear.

7th January 1990 Official start to Operation Canaimé to withdraw *garimpeiros* from the Yanomami area. Minister of Justice reaffirms no force will be used.

8th January 1990 Seventy-seven Federal Police agents and 11 inspectors block the airport in Boa Vista affecting the operations of 350 aircraft and 30 helicopters.

10th January 1990 *Garimpeiros*, federal and state government agree to set up 3 reserves for *garimpeiros* and to mine only these areas. Two of the reserves are wholly inside the Yanomami area.

25th January 1990 President Sarney signs decree 98.890 establishing first *garimpeiro* reserve, Uraricaá/Santa Rosa of 100,000 hectares. Other areas are Uraricoeria of 125,000 hectares; and Catrimani/Couto de Magalhães of 280,000 hectares.

26th January 1990 Flights start to resupply *garimpos* inside Yanomami area after judge Giorgeio Lopes Leite in Boa Vista overrules federal order on a technicality.

30th January 1990 Flights stopped again when the Roraima judge's order is cancelled by the president of Tribunal Regional Federal (TRF).

15th February 1990 Decrees 98.959 and 98.960 to establish Catrimani-Couto de Magalhães and Uraricoera reserves signed by Sarney.

15th March 1990 Fernando Collor de Mello becomes the President of Brazil.

19th April 1990 Federal judge Novely dismisses as unconstitutional President Sarney's decrees establishing three *garimpeiro* reserves.

April 1990 Health teams enter the Yanomami region, after being evicted at the start of the invasion in 1987.

2nd–15th May 1990 A total of 75 of the 156 clandestine airstrips in the Yanomami area are targetted to be destroyed, on the orders of President Collor, but only 13 are actually dynamitted.

September 1990 Eviction of *garimpeiros* resumes.

November 1990 Yanomami Health Project created by the Brazilian Health Ministry.

February 1991 Only an estimated 2,000 of the 45,000 illegal *garimpeiros* are still in the Yanomami area.

30th June 1991 New president of Funai appointed by President Collor. Sidney Possuelo, with 25 years' experience working with many tribes, had previously resigned from Funai after denouncing as "legalized genocide" the creation of *garimpeiro* reserves inside the Yanomami area.

July 1991 Discovery that the Brazilian Army has been building – in secret – a road into the Yanomami area through the Neblina National Park to the *shabono* of Maturacá.

19th July 1991 Federal police began the third operation to remove 8,000 *garimpeiros* still working inside the Yanomami area.

25th July 1991 Official publication of Resolution 02/91 by Funai to demarcate 9,419,108 hectares as a single protected area for the Yanomami.

26th July 1991 Authorization to prospect inside the Yanomami area issued by the National Department of Mineral Production in Brasília to Mineração Guaralema. Permit revoked after strong protests from Funai and the Nucleus for Indigenous Rights, a Brazilian law group.

25th August 1991 Deadline set by Brazilian president for government departments to comment on the size of the Yanomami area to be recognized.

September 1991 New Bill before Brazilian Congress authorizing a new 6,929 kilometres road to be built along Brazil's northern border. The road would open up all the areas occupied by the Yanomami and by other tribes to Brazilian miners, loggers and ranchers.

September 1991 Treasury Department in Brasília sets aside $2.7 million to pay for demarcation of the Yanomami area, if or when approved.

26th September 1991 Funai says only 700 *garimpeiros* are still working inside the Yanomami area.

15th November 1991 President Collor marked out a reserve for the Yanomami covering 9.4 million hectares in Roraima and Amazonas states.

Bibliography

The Yanomami Indian Park, A Call for Action, Anthropology Resource Centre, USA, 1981.

Becher, Hans, *Poré/Perimbó*, Kommissionsverlag Munstermann-Druck KG, Hannover, 1974.

Berkhofer, Robert Jr., *The White Man's Indian,* Vintage Books, New York, 1978.

Berwick, Dennison, *Amazon*, Hutchinson, London. 1990.

Biocca, Ettore, Yanomami: *The Narrative of a White Girl Kidnapped by Amazonian Indians,* E. P. Dutton, New York, 1970.

Blackburn, Julia, *The White Men, The first response of aboriginal peoples to the white man,* Orbis Publishing, London, 1979.

Bodley, John W., *Tribal Survival in the Amazon Campa Case,* IWGI, Document no 5, Copenhagen.

Bodley, John H., *Victims of Progress,* Mayfield Pub., Palo Alto, California, 1982.

Chagnon, Napoleon A., *Studying the Yanomamo,* Holt, Rinehart and Winston, New York, 1974.

Chagnon, Napolean A., *Yanomamo The Fierce People* Holt, Rinehart and Winston, New York, 1983.

Cocco, Luis, *Iyëwei-teri quince anos entre los yanomamos,* Libreira Editorial Salesiana SA, Apartado Postal 369, Caracas 1010-A, Venezuela, 1987.

Constituição, República Federativa do Brasil, 1988, Centro Gráfico do Senado Federal, Brasília.

Davis, Shelton H., *Victims of the Miracle Development Against the Indians of Brazil,* Cambridge University Press, 1980.

Driver, David Miller, *The Indian in Brazilian Literature,* Hispanic Institute in the United States, New York, 1942.

Dufty, David G, *Seeing It Their Way,* Reed Education for the Intercultural, Sydney, Australia.

Hall, Edward T., *Beyond Culture,* Anchor Press, New York, 1977.

Harner, David, *A Guide to Power and Healing, The Way of the Shaman,* Bantam Books, New York, 1980.

Hemming, John, *Red Gold*, Papermac, London 1987. 1st edition with detailed notes publ. Macmillan, London, 1978.
Hemming, John, *Amazon Frontier, The Defeat of the Brazilian Indians*, Macmillan, London, 1987.
Kumu U. P., *Antes o Mundo Não Existia*, São Paulo, 1980.
Levi-Strauss, Claude, *The Raw and the Cooked*, Harper & Row, New York, 1969.
Lizot, Jacques, *The Yanomami in the Face of Ethnocide*, International Work Group for Indigenous Affairs, Copenhagen, 1976.
Lizot, Jacques, *Tales of the Yanomami Daily Life in the Venezuelan Forest*, Cambridge University Press, London, 1985.
Neel, J.V., *Man in the Tropics: The Yanomami Indians* from "Population Structure and Human Variation", Cambridge University Press, London, 1977.
O'Hanlon, Redmond, *In Trouble Again*, Hamish Hamilton, London, 1988.
Re, Giorgio & Fabrizio, with Laudado, Francisco & Luis, *Os últimos Yanomami? Um Mergulho na Pré-História*, Ediscóes Point Couleur, Turin, Italy, 1984.
Reichel-Dolmatoff, G., *Beyond the Milky Way*, Los Angeles, 1978.
Shapiro, Judith, *Sex Roles and Social Structure Among the Yanomami*, Colombia University, 1971.
Smole, William J., *Yanomami Indians: A Cultural Geography*, University of Texas Press, Austin, 1976.
Steinvorth-Goetz, Inga, *Uriji! Jami! Life & Belief of the Forest Waika in the Upper Orinoco*, Asociacion Cultural Humboldt, Caracas, 1969.
Taylor, Kenneth Iain, *Sanumá Fauna Prohibitions and Classifications*, Fundacion La Salle de Ciencias Naturalles, Caracas, 1974.
Wachtel, Nathan, *The Vision of the Vanquished*, Barnes & Noble, New York, 1977.

NEWSPAPERS, MAGAZINES AND REPORTS

A Crítica, Manaus, Brazil.
Correio Braziliense, Brasília, Brazil.
Diário Oficial, Brasília, Brazil.
O Estado de Roraima, Boa Vista, Brazil.

O Estado de São Paulo, São Paulo, Brazil.
Folho de Boa Vista, Boa Vista, Brazil.
Folho de São Paulo, São Paulo, Brazil.
O Globo, Rio de Janeiro, Brazil.
Jornal Do Brasil, Brazil.
Veja, Brazil.
The Guardian, London, England.
The Independent, London, England.
The Times, London, England.
Roraima: O Aviso da Morte, Comissao da Ação Pela Cidadania, São Paulo, 1989.
Urihi; serial reports of Comissão pela Criação do Parque Yanomami, São Paulo, October 1986 to June 1990.
Yanomami: A Todos Os Povos da Terra, Ação Pela Cidadania, São Paulo, 1990.
Albert, Bruce, *La Fumée du métal Histoire et représentations du contact chez les Yanomami Bresil,* L'Homme, April 1988.
Alcântara, Eurípedes, e Ribeiro, Antônio, *Ianomamis, A Morte de um Povo,* Veja, São Paulo, 19 setembro 1990.
Berwick, Dennison, & Steele-Perkins, Chris, *At Death's Door,* The Sunday Times Colour Magazine, London, 9th September 1990.
Chirone, Alberto, *O Crepúsculo do Povo Yanomami Sobrevivência ou Genocídio?*, Centro de Informação da Diocese de Roraima, Boa Vista, Brazil, 1988.
Lewis, Norman & McCullin, Donald, *Genocide – From Fire and Sword to Arsenic and Bullets Civilisation has sent Six Million Indians to Extinction,* The Sunday Times Colour Magazine, London, 23rd February 1969.
Santos, Adalberto Da Silva, *Garimpo: Morte e Destruição na Matas de Roraima, Diário de viagem de Adelberto Da Silva Santos,* Centro de Informação da Diocese de Roraima, Boa Vista, Brazil, 1989.
Yanomami, Survival International, London, 1990. (16 page illustrated report.)

GUIDEBOOKS, DICTIONARIES

Aliandro, Hygino, *Dicionário Português-Inglês, The Portuguese – English Dictionary*, Ao Livro Tecnico S/A, Rio de Janeiro, 1985. (excellent pocket-sized dictionary.)

Brooks, John, editor, *The South American Handbook*, Trade & Travel Publications Ltd., The Mendip Press, Bath, published annually.

New Michaelis Illustrated Dictionary, Volume 1 English-Portuguese, Melhoramentos, São Paulo, 1987.

New Michaelis Illustrated Dictionary, Volume 2 Português-Inglos, Melhoramentos, São Paulo, 1986.

South America on a Shoestring, Lonely Planets, Australia, published annually.

Werner, David, *Where There Is No Doctor: A Village Health Care Handbook*, The Hesperian Foundation, P.O. Box 1692, Palo Alto, California 94302, 1985. (Excellent reference book, available in numerous languages.)

MAPS

Healey, Kevin, *South America, North Section, no 151*, scale 1:5,000,000, Bradt Publications, Chalfont St. Peters, Bucks., England, 1982. Also ITM, Box 2290, Vancouver, Canada.

Operational Navigation Chart L-27, Defense Mapping Agency Aerospace Center, Missouri 631118, October 1982.

South America, North West, no 153, scale 1:4,000,000, International Travel Maps, Box 2290, Vancouver, Canada, 1986–87. Also Bradt Publications.

ADDRESSES & ORGANIZATIONS

Commission for the Creation of the Yanomami Park,
rua Manoel da Nóbrega 111 3, cj 32,
04001 São Paulo,
Brasil.

KWIA,
Lange Lozanastraat 14,
Antwerpen,
Belgium B-2018.

Survival International,
310 Edgware Road.
London W2 1DY,
England.

or 2121 Decatur Place NW,
Washington DC,
20008 USA.

President of Brazil,
Emxo. Fernando Collor de Mello,
Presidente da Republica,
Palácio do Planalto,
70,160 Brasília DF,
Brasil.

Index